The History of the Counts of Guines
and Lords of Ardres

THE MIDDLE AGES SERIES

Ruth Mazo Karras, General Editor
Edward Peters, Founding Editor

A complete list of books in the series
is available from the publisher.

Lambert of Ardres,
The History of the Counts of Guines and Lords of Ardres

Translated with an Introduction by
LEAH SHOPKOW

PENN

University of Pennsylvania Press
Philadelphia

10 9 8 7 6 5 4 3 2 1

Published by
University of Pennsylvania Press
Philadelphia, Pennsylvania 19104-4011

Library of Congress Cataloging-in-Publication Data
Lambert, of Ardres, b. ca. 1140.
  The history of the counts of Guines and lords of Ardres /
Lambert of Ardres ; translated with an introduction by Leah Shopkow.
      p.   cm. — (The Middle Ages series)
  Includes bibliographical references and index.
  ISBN 0-8122-3568-1 (alk. paper)
      1. Nobility—France—Ardres—History—To 1500.   2. Ardres (France)—
Genealogy.   3. Guines, Counts of.   4. Ardres family.   I. Shopkow, Leah.
II. Title.   III. Series.
DC801.A677 L36   2000
929.7′4—dc21   00-044311

Contents

Preface

I first picked up Lambert's history when I assigned it as reading for a graduate class in medieval historiography. Although my students grumbled about the difficulty of Lambert's Latin, some of his passages made us laugh out loud. As scholars, of course, we are expected to attend to what we can learn from reading medieval texts, and indeed, there is much to be learned from Lambert's history. However, there is also much sheer pleasure in his narrative. I hope that those who read this book will find that pleasure in this translation.

Every author should be as fortunate as I have been in readers. David Townsend and Theodore Evergates, who read the manuscript for the press, were generous far beyond the call of duty with their time and energy; their uncompromising and thorough comments were a further education and have contributed to a much improved text. Emily Albu (in the midst of her own manuscript) went over part of the text in a true act of friendship. Brigitte Bedos-Rezak read the manuscript at an earlier stage and also saved me from some painful errors. Errors no doubt remain (alas!), but they are (alas!) my own. Thanks also to Ann Carmichael, who read the text and offered her constant encouragement; without her intervention, Lambert's poetry would have been expressed in prose.

The wonderful maps were created by Suzanne Hull of Graphic Services, who patiently bore with my many changes of mind. Their production was underwritten by a Grant in Aid of Research from Indiana University.

THE COUNTS OF GUINES   THE LORDS OF ARDRES

Siegfried (928–c. 966) ~ *Elftrude*

Matilda of = Ardulf *(c. 966–c. 997)*
Boulogne

Ralph *(c. 997–c. 1036)* = *Rosella of Saint-Pol*

Susanna *of* = Eustace *(c. 1036–*before 1065)   *Herred* (1) = *Adele of* = (2) *Eilbold*
Grammene   *Selnesse*

　　Baldwin I = Adele of   Matilda of = Arnold I "the Advocate"
　　(before   Lorraine   Marquise (1) (d. 1094)
　　1065–1091)   Clemence of
　　 Saint-Pol (2)

Manasses = Emma of   Giselle = Winemar   Arnold II   = Gertrude
(1091–1137) Tancarville of   of Ghent   "The Old"   of Aalst
                        Guines   (1094–c. 1138)

Henry of = Sibyl / Rose   Petronilla = Arnold III   Baldwin = Beatrice
Bourbourg   of   "the Young"   (c.1139–47) of Guines
                               Bouchain   (c. 1138–c. 1139)

　　Beatrice = (1) Albert   Arnold I = Matilda of
(1137–c. 1142) "the Boar"   "of Ghent" Saint-Omer
　　 (2) Baldwin   (1142–69)
　　 of Ardes

                                              Adeline = Arnold IV
                                              of Ardres "of Merck"
                                                         (c. 1147–76)

        Baldwin II (1169–1206) = Christine of Ardres (d. 1177)

    Beatrice of Bourbourg = Arnold II of Guines and V of Ardres
              (1206–20)   (c. 1178–1220)

Genealogical chart of the Guines and Ardres families. Conjectural figures and dates
are given in italics.

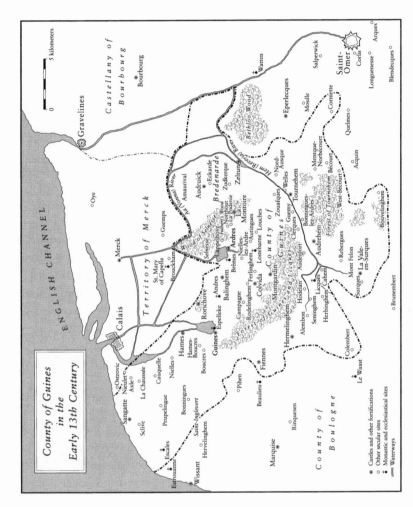

Map 1. The County of Guines in the early thirteenth century. Map designed by Suzanne Hull after Godefroy de Menilglaise.

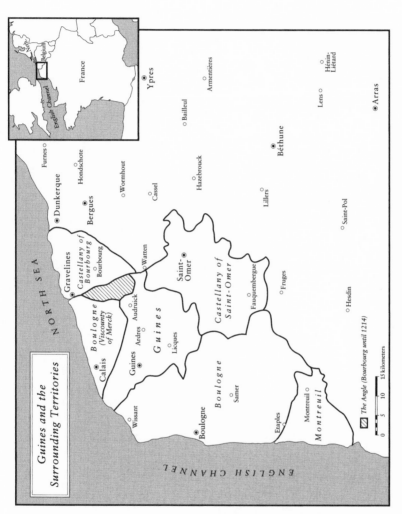

Map 2. Guines and the surrounding territories. Map designed by Suzanne Hull after Godefroy de Menilglaise.

Introduction

The *Chronicle of the Counts of Guines and Lords of Ardres* of Lambert of Ardres is a marvelous window into the Middle Ages, but a surprisingly little known and infrequently used text. It was hailed by E. A. Freeman, the great historian of the Conquest, as a superb historical source when the *MGH* edition was first published,[1] but Freeman also noted some reasons for the failure of modern scholars to take more note:

> It is a record which, if it ever brings us across the chief men, the chief events, even of its own age, does so only rarely and incidentally. It deals mainly with persons neither of the highest rank nor of the highest personal importance. Its scene is not laid in any of the great cities of the earth, or in any of the decisive spots of the world's history.[2]

I would add to Freeman's observations that the history chronicles a border region, that the history was also written in ornate and highly demanding Latin, that its author himself cheerfully admitted that he was reporting what people said and that he expected to be accused of lying, and that it is full of factual inaccuracies and tales that smell suspiciously like folklore. Because none of the manuscripts of the history date from before the fifteenth century, and because Lambert's attitudes in places seem suspiciously modern, there have also been some questions about the text's authenticity, although modern scholars accept it as genuine.[3]

Nevertheless, Lambert's history has not gone entirely unnoticed among scholars of the medieval nobility. Georges Duby returned to the text again and again toward the end of his career, using it as an illustration of noble behavior in the twelfth century; he has been Lambert's major modern interpreter.[4] E. A. Warlop has also made heavy use of Lambert for his study of the Flemish nobility.[5] Lambert's history has also been discussed with reference to the murder of lords, the history of fortification, linguistic boundaries, chivalric practices, and rhetoric.[6] However, most readers probably know about Lambert's text from the work of one of these scholars rather than from Lambert directly, for it would be safe to say that Lambert's history has not been widely read.

This light usage, however, has not exhausted all the ways in which Lambert's history is interesting, and particularly for modern readers. He was a first-rate storyteller with strong opinions, who made his characters live vividly, so his narrative is fun to read. Equally important, however, in the last two decades the scholarly approach to the Middle Ages has shifted from political history to an increasing interest in border and frontier regions, in rural society, in both noble and peasant mentalities, and in both monastic patronage and private religious conduct, in short, in "everyday life." For these aspects of medieval life, Lambert is a superb source. Therefore, it makes sense to make Lambert's work available in translation.

Lambert of Ardres and the *History of the Counts of Guines and Lords of Ardres*

Lambert of Ardres

Nothing is known about Lambert except what he tells us himself, much of this obliquely. He was the chaplain of Ardres and may have been a back-door relative of the ruling family. Arnold III of Ardres had an illegitimate son named Robert, whose son Arnold married a woman named Christine. She was the daughter of a Master Lambert of the church of Ardres.[7] Scholars such as Georges Duby and François Louis Ganshof have assumed that this Master Lambert is our author. If so, Lambert was probably born around 1140, give or take a decade either way. He does not say when he became the incumbent of Ardres, but he mentions writing Countess Christine's epitaph after her death in 1177, which suggests that he might already have been the chaplain.[8]

While Lambert's connection to the lords of Ardres may have opened the door for him to receive a living at Ardres, Lambert's own considerable talents certainly aided his advancement. He probably attended one of the important twelfth-century schools, for his text is the work of a highly educated man, a fact attested to by both his ornate and difficult Latin and the classical and literary works he refers to. His title of "master," however, may refer to his office at Ardres rather than his education, as a previous incumbent also had that title.[9] He would have needed to speak Flemish in that region,[10] and he is consequently able to offer etymologies of Flemish names, but as a denizen of the court, he would have spoken French as well.

Lambert began writing his history sometime in the 1190s. There are two pieces of evidence pointing to this date. First, he says his history was conceived as a sort of apology to his lord, Baldwin II of Guines, for offending him, and was intended to win back Baldwin's good will. The offending action occurred around 1194.[11] Second, he mentions that Siegfried, the first "count" of Guines, lived 233 years before Lambert began writing his history.[12] Lambert dates Siegfried's arrival to 928 and puts his death in 965 or 966, shortly after the death of Arnold I of Flanders.[13] The earlier date is probably not the one Lambert was thinking of; calculating from the later date suggests that Lambert began writing around 1198 or 1199.[14]

Determining when Lambert finished his history is much more difficult. The narrative as we have it ends around 1203. Among the last items mentioned is the first conflict between the Blauwvoets and Ingrekins, which was over by the end of 1201, and Reynold of Boulogne's participation in the conquest of Normandy (1202–4).[15] It does not mention the second uprising of the Blauwvoets in 1204. However, in the prologue, Lambert does not address Baldwin II of Guines, still alive in 1203, whose good grace this history ostensibly was to purchase. In addition, Lambert refers to Baldwin as being "of memorable memory," and "of worthy memory," which he would not have done of a living person. This would seem to put the date of completion after 1206, when Baldwin died.[16] On the other hand, Lambert is unlikely to have finished much later than that. He mentions only six of the nine children Arnold II of Guines (1206–20) and Beatrice of Bourbourg († 1224) eventually had; he would undoubtedly have mentioned them all had they been born.[17] Indeed, Baldwin's death in 1206 may well have been the event that encouraged Lambert to finish the history he had been working on and present it to his lord, Arnold II of Guines.

That Lambert presented the work to his lord is a conjecture, although it is difficult to tell what else he would have done with it. Because the book survived, it seems likely that it ended up in a monastic library, and Arnold may well have given the presentation copy (if there was one) to one of the local monasteries, perhaps Andres. Although William of Andres, a younger contemporary of Lambert, does not mention Lambert by name in his own chronicle, he read the history.[18] The manuscript was sufficiently accessible for John of Ypres, who was writing at Saint-Bertin in the late fourteenth century, to use it as well.[19]

The Structure of Lambert's History
Lambert's history consists of a single book of 154 surviving chapters. The table of contents shows that there were originally 156, but the last two chapters, as well as part of chapter 154, are missing in all the manuscripts.[20] Lambert's history begins with an elaborate prologue, in which he defends his history

from expected criticisms. The first part of the history (chapters 1–96) provides a history of the lineage of Guines through the youth of Lambert's patron, Arnold II of Guines. The second part of the text is contained in a framing narrative formed by chapters 97 and 147, within which Lambert hands the narrative over to Walter of Le Clud, an illegitimate son of Baldwin of Ardres.[21] Walter tells the history of the lords of Ardres from the mid-eleventh century through the lordship of Arnold IV of Ardres (1148–76). Lambert then retrieves the narrative from Walter and in the third part of the text continues with the history of the now combined holdings of Guines and Ardres.

This narrative strategy allows each lineage to stand in the light of glory independent of the other until they come together in the person of Arnold II of Guines (1206–20) and V of Ardres (c. 1177–1220). It also means that Lambert describes certain events twice, but generally does so from a different perspective each time, and thus each version is given a different emphasis. For example, when Lambert tells of the murder of Arnold III "the Young" of Ardres (c. 1138–c.1139) initially, he mentions it in the context of Arnold of Ghent's war to capture Guines. The important element of the story is that Arnold of Ghent, by supporting the succession of Arnold III's brother, Baldwin (c. 1139–47), to Ardres, won Baldwin's support in his own war. However, when Lambert returns to the story in the later part of the history, he describes the murder much more fully, stressing the evil qualities that permitted Arnold to be trapped by his murderers and which made his death (while an excommunicate) a form of just deserts.[22] On at least one occasion, Lambert takes radically different perspectives on the same individual. When he is telling the story of Count Eustace (c. 1036–before 1065), Lambert describes him as a man of justice and learning. Yet in the narrative about Ardres, it is Eustace who so bullies Adele of Selnesse to marry that she donates her property to the church of Thérouanne.[23] Although the narrative within a narrative may seem clumsy at first, it is actually a flexible tool in Lambert's hands.

Lambert's Ideas About History

Although Lambert's work is called a history, it raises some important questions about how he understood the purpose of history and the techniques and methods appropriate to it. Lambert's ideas and practices seem out of step with many historians of his day, who had been refining their genre and arriving at a consensus about how histories were to be written. Up to the eleventh century, Latin writers commonly used oral sources, which they did not consider inferior to written sources about the past. The historian's task was to report what people said, whether they said it aloud or in writing. The historian assessed the truth of what was said according to the reputation and character of the witness. The best witnesses were elderly people of holy character or writings produced by this kind of person.[24] This way of looking at history was entirely reasonable in a society in which most of the transactions for which we use writing—sales of land or commodities, marriage contracts, payment of taxes and fees, legal decisions—did not necessarily generate written records.[25]

However, during the course of the eleventh century, written documents became increasingly important in economic and legal transactions, and in the very long term the validity of these transactions came largely to depend on the survival of written documentation of them, although to this day oral contracts are theoretically binding. As documentation came to be more important in the legal and economic spheres, historians also came to prefer written records to oral traditions. An orally transmitted story which might have been uncritically accepted by an early eleventh-century historian might well be rejected by a twelfth-century historian, although this would not necessarily happen.

As historians came to depend increasingly on written documents, they also began to refine some of their notions of historical truth. To be truthful, a story had to have verisimilitude or had to be attested to either by a written source or by a trustworthy eyewitness. (The eyewitness was the sole exception to the rule that written testimony was generally preferable to oral testimony.) To ensure the truth of their assertions, historians might copy verbatim from the work of other writers, and they might also include documents.[26] These ways of ensuring truth were not philosophical, but conventional–a history was true when it adhered to the expected conventions.[27] Earlier historians had also sometimes written their histories in verse, as a way of ennobling their subject and adding interest to the text. However, by the middle of the eleventh century, historians writing in Latin had revived a classical commonplace that saw the poets as liars, and by the early thirteenth century historians writing in the vernacular were repeating this sentiment as well.[28]

Lambert swam against the tide on almost all these points. He defiantly preferred oral testimonies to the evidence provided by the written word, no doubt partly because there were few written sources available to him, but also, one senses, on principle.[29] He lists Virgil, Ovid, and Priscian among his authorities beside Moses—the first historian—Eusebius, Jerome, Sigebert of Gembloux, and Bede, thereby mixing up historians, grammarians, and poets.[30] Lambert does not comment on the commonplace that the poets told lies, but he tacitly breaks with it by writing portions of his narrative in poetry and by quoting poetry as well. Indeed, Lambert's history is exuberantly rhetorical in a way that was again out of step with the preferences of contemporary Latin historians, who were self-consciously, if disingenuously, claiming to eschew rhetoric.[31] As for his contemporaries' preference for written sources over oral ones, Lambert points out, quite rightly, that lies can be written down as well as truths.[32] In fact, Lambert makes a bit of a joke of the whole issue of authentication, when he, like Moses, implicitly lays claim to divine inspiration![33] Even his ostensible reason for writing, that he had offended his lord and wished to regain his favor, may be a literary topos rather than an historical fact. Lambert points out that Ovid had written the *Metamorphoses* for the same reason, and the *scholia* of the *Alexandreis* of the court writer Walter of Châtillon offer a similar explanation for the genesis of that work.[34] To Lambert, therefore, the writing of history was an opportunity for displaying the highest and most self-conscious rhetorical art, and his art was unconstrained by what most historians thought it should be.

Sources and Influences
Although Lambert vigorously defended the use of oral testimony in the writing of history, he clearly used written sources. Indeed, his comment that history was found in the form of notes in the margins or at the end of books or on loose sheets and charters accurately reflects the places where we do find sources for the history of Flanders.[35] He quotes the *Flandria generosa*, an important twelfth-century source for Flemish history, and mentions Sigebert of Gembloux, Bede, the life of Bertin, and the miracles of Sts. Rictrude and Rotrude.[36] No doubt he read other historical works as well. He had access to charters and other documents. All of this suggests that Lambert was able to use a library, not only the count's vernacular collection, but probably one or more monastic repositories, at least the libraries of Andres and/or Capella and perhaps even Marchiennes, one of the great centers for the writing of history in this period. However, he probably did not use these sources as historians would today, to check his facts or do research as we would understand it. There are numerous historical inaccuracies in the text and it seems likely that the "charters" Lambert "quotes" in the text were not copied directly from the originals. He is the only source for both and there are errors of dating in one that one would not expect in an official charter.[37] At best Lambert set down the gist of charters he had read; he may even have invented the charters.

Lambert had also read many classical Latin texts, as did his contemporaries, the court writers; he quotes some and mentions other authors, although he may not have read every author he mentions.[38] The *Pharsalia* of Lucan, in particular, lurks in the background, not only in the form of quotations from the text, but also in situations: the death of Beatrice of Guines

(1137–c. 1142) more or less on her marriage bed alludes to the lament in I.111–20 of the *Pharsalia* over the death of Julia, where symbols of marriage and death are also juxtaposed (although Julia's death begins, rather than ends, a civil war) and the description of the battle of Pharsalis in book seven of the *Pharsalia* similarly lies behind Lambert's account of the war between Henry of Bourbourg and Arnold of Ghent, as does the *Thebeiad* of Statius, which is actually quoted there.[39]

Although Lambert knew of and may well have read some of the most important histories of his day, he also seems to have been influenced not only by historians, but also by writers of court literature, many of whom were satirists and moralists. Indeed, his views on historical "truth" may owe more to these writers than to historians. For the court satirists "truth" was not evident, but problematic, and moral considerations were more important than a mere fidelity to fact.[40] They tended not to distinguish between "histories" and other kinds of writing, and were not averse to historical invention.[41] Like many of the court satirists, Lambert expected his work to be attacked and offers a defense against those who would accuse him of lying. He describes the motivation for these projected attacks as envy, the classic vice of court life.[42] Lambert had definitely read the *Art of Love* of Andrew the Chaplain.[43] The *Architrenius* of John of Hauville, the *Policraticus* of John of Salisbury, and the *Alexandreis* of Walter of Châtillon were all circulating toward the end of the twelfth century, and it is possible, perhaps even likely, that Lambert had read one or more of these.

However, Lambert clearly did not spend all his life in a library or know only Latin works, for his history is also influenced by the conventions of vernacular literature. Sometimes these conventions appear in a parodic version, as when Lambert relates the calculating campaign of Arnold II of Guines for the body and hand of Ida of Boulogne.[44] However, at times Lambert adapts them to his own serious purposes. When he describes the marriage of Christine of Ardres and Baldwin II of Guines (which he depicts as unabashedly dynastic), he borrows from romance conventions in describing Christine showing her pleasure in her face first, then responding, when asked for her consent. This is very like the response of Sordamors to Queen Guinevere, when she is asked if she wishes to marry Alexander (whom she has loved for a long time) in Chrétien de Troyes's *Cligès*.[45] Lambert's intent, I think, is to show that this was a good marriage.

Lambert may not have been a layman himself and he may have written his history in Latin, but he was deeply acquainted with the things that might have interested a contemporary lay audience. Indeed, the means by which

Lambert tells the story of the lords of Ardres is a literary version of a common court entertainment—the telling of stories in the evening or when the court was kept at home.[46] On a wet and windy day at Ardres, when hunting and outdoor amusements are out of the question, the older men tell stories to the younger men. They begin with histories of Rome and the Crusades, then Walter of Le Clud begins to tell the history of Ardres. Lambert goes so far as to record (in Latin!) Walter's references to his own vernacular and oral rendition of the past![47]

Language

However, Lambert wrote his history in Latin, not the vernacular. This requires some comment, as Lambert stresses that Baldwin II of Guines did not know Latin.[48] As the chaplain at Ardres, Lambert may have taught Arnold II of Guines some Latin, but he doesn't say he did, and Arnold may well have known no more Latin than his father. In that case, Lambert would have been producing a history his patrons could not read, when he could easily have written something that would have been accessible to them, for they could certainly have understood French read aloud. While the possibility certainly exists that by writing in Latin he intended to hide some of the contents of his history from his patrons, this seems a risky proposition; the *History of the Counts of Guines* lacks the kind of vituperative bitterness that tends to characterize "secret" histories.[49]

Instead, I would argue that the choice of language was bound up in the question of audience. Lambert may have been more concerned about reaching a broad audience than having Arnold read the history. After all, Arnold had heard the same tales about Ardres that Lambert had. To write in French (written Flemish was slower to emerge) was to choose an audience consisting of those who understood French. Moreover, in a region in which two vernaculars competed, to write in one was to snub those who spoke only the other. A work of Latin, on the other hand, might reach those who did not know about Guines and Ardres, so that if Lambert hoped his history would circulate widely, Latin was a better choice. But even if the work went no further than the nearby monastery of Andres, Latin was also the proven language of posterity. If Lambert intended his history to be a monument to his heroes, Latin was the language in which to create it. Finally, Latin was the language in which Lambert's own learning might be most appropriately demonstrated for those other clerical writers he no doubt hoped would form part of his audience. If Lambert had written at the end of the thirteenth century, when the quasi-official royal history of France was being translated into the vernacular (and becoming official), Lambert might have chosen differently. But at the beginning of the thirteenth century, the prestige of Latin still mattered.

Lambert's World

Lambert's use of romance elements in his history is one way in which his work reflects the world in which he lived, for the *History of the Counts of Guines and Lords of Ardres* is a window into the concerns of late twelfth-century northern Europe. Its protagonists were not the greatest nobles of that region. Rather they were men and women who were important enough to be relatively independent in their actions, but not important enough to do much as they liked. Because they did not have the freedom of the highest level of the nobility, Lambert's portrait of them gives us a better sense of what was normative in their society than a history of great nobles would have done. In addition, since the counts of Guines and lords of Ardres were not too exalted to have dealings with their peasants or to take a direct concern for the exploitation of their property, a narrative about them tells us something about this humbler stratum of life as well, although clearly not as much as it tells us about the nobility. Most important, the *History of the Counts of Guines* tells us about contemporary attitudes, primarily those of the historian himself, but also those he sometimes disapprovingly described as being enacted by his subjects. Among the arenas upon which Lambert sheds light are religious attitudes and practices, the development of the nobility as a self-conscious group, the experience of the peasantry, changing notions of ethical conduct, and the curtailment and growth of freedom.

Religious Life

The eleventh and twelfth centuries were marked by powerful currents of lay piety, whose influence can be seen in many ways in the *History of the Counts of Guines*. One form this piety took was the foundation of new religious institutions or donations to others. Another form was the gradual surrender by lay people of ecclesiastical revenues and offices into the hands of ecclesiastical persons. Finally, lay individuals took up the religious life, sometimes by entering religious establishments either in the prime of life or near death, and sometimes by making other sorts of associations with them.[50]

The counts of Guines and lords of Ardres participated in a relatively modest way in the founding of new monasteries and colleges. The first important foundation was Andres, the burial place of the comital family. It was

founded when Baldwin I (d. 1091), while on one of the great eleventh-century
pilgrimages, the pilgrimage to Santiago de Compostela in Galicia, stopped at
Charroux and there vowed to found a monastery that would be Charroux's
daughter-house.[51] This desire to associate one's new foundation with a rich
and successful one was quite common, although in this case it proved problematic.[52] Although the impetus to found Andres came from Baldwin, less
wealthy individuals also came forward with correspondingly lesser gifts to
the new establishment.[53]

Another eleventh-century form of establishment was the secular college
of canons; Arnold I of Ardres (†1094) established one of these at Ardres. One
of its advantages was that it permitted the founder considerable control over
the community. In the case of the college at Ardres, Arnold of Ardres created
livings for ten canons and established that these canons would be resident or
else forfeit a part of their living. Arnold also took the precaution of installing
one of his sons in one of the prebends and keeping the office of provost for
himself.[54] The properties Arnold donated to create his college at Ardres were
relatively modest: some pieces of land including a mill, but also tithes. This
granting of tithes accomplished a second purpose, which was to take ecclesiastical revenues from the hands of a secular individual (the lord of Ardres)
and place these in the hands of ecclesiastical persons. Arnold's foundation,
then, incorporates a response to various elements of religious renewal popular
in the eleventh century.

The twelfth-century counts of Guines continued to create new religious establishments. Count Robert/Manasses of Guines and Countess Emma
founded a convent at Guines, St. Leonard's, and placed at its head a comital
relative; she was followed as abbess by two of Manasses's great-nieces.[55] Later
in the century, Arnold I of Guines and his brother-in-law, Arnold of Colvida (Arnold IV of Ardres), each created leper hospitals, a new kind of pious
enterprise.[56] Old institutions in the region were also reformed in line with new
religious concerns. The house of secular canons founded by Robert of Licques
was first granted to the regular canons of Watten (regular canons combined
a monastic sort of life with service to a lay population), then became a house
of Premonstratensian canons, having thus evolved through changing ecclesiastical fashions.[57] A new foundation from around the same time, Beaulieu,
followed the rule of Arrouaise, another order of regular canons.[58]

Patronage (generally in the form of benefactions) was vital to the well-
being of all of these establishments. Oilard's small hospital at Saint-Ingelvert
was briefly a house of canons, but it was too poor to persist and eventually became again a simple hospice.[59] Competition was fierce between some of these

monastic houses for favors, and slighted monasteries were not happy. William of Andres reports meaningfully that when Arnold I of Guines chose to be buried at Saint-Ingelvert, rather than Andres, the traditional burial place of the counts of Guines, his body rotted quickly.[60]

The trend toward new forms of religious expression continued to the end of the twelfth century in Lambert's region. One of the figures he mentions from that period, Beatrice of Bourbourg, while deeply involved in the religious life, never took monastic vows and kept her own property; she looks suspiciously like a Beguine. The Beguine movement, which attracted both men (Beghards) and women (Beguines), but mostly women, developed in Flanders toward the end of the twelfth century, and many lived as Beatrice did. Another woman, Alice of Ardres, seems to have lived a similar life, never marrying and living on rents assigned to her by her brother-in-law, the lord of Ardres by marriage.[61] Beguinage may have become widely known in the early thirteenth century, but its practices seem already current by the end of the twelfth.

While Lambert describes the religious foundations of the nobility, he also offers us some insight into the relationship between the nobility and the church and the degree to which nobles internalized church teachings. Certainly some individuals were persuaded, sometimes but not always by close brushes with death, to resign into the hands of the church what clerics had decided belonged to the church. Baldwin, the lord of Ardres, for example, after being shot in the head with an arrow, handed over the office of provost of Ardres to the monastery of Capella and decided to replace the canons at Ardres with monks.[62] However, his great-nephew, Arnold II of Guines, was unhappy with the monks—one suspects because he had less control over the establishment than he would have if it had been composed of secular canons—and tried (unsuccessfully) to rescind the gift. The result was lengthy litigation.[63] Nor were all lay people happy to resign their ecclesiastical positions. Baldwin of Hondschote held the parsonage of the church of Hondschote, acquired from the house at Ardres, and refused to give it up.[64] While some foundations seem to have arisen entirely out of generalized piety—Baldwin I's foundation at Andres, for instance—others had a more specific purpose. Eustace of Fiennes founded Beaulieu in penance for having killed someone in a tournament.[65] Furthermore, concern for religious matters seems not to have forced the laity to subscribe to all of the behaviors prescribed by the clergy. More than one member of the house of Ardres was excommunicated; Arnold III the Young died excommunicate and it was only with some difficulty that he was posthumously redeemed.[66] The religious comportment of the laity Lambert describes bears a complex relationship to the "norms" officially posited by the church.

Family

The *History of the Counts of Guines* also contains an extraordinarily detailed account of the familial alliances and relations of the counts of Guines and lords of Ardres over nearly two centuries, and is thus an unparalleled source for what noble families "remembered" about their pasts. Lambert mentions not only the marriages of legitimate offspring, enumerating the resulting children, but also those of many illegitimate sons and daughters. The marriage patterns the families of the counts of Guines and lords of Ardres followed parallel the political history of the families, which is not surprising; kinship was frequently an instrument of politics, even in an age when theologians taught that consent alone created a marriage.

In the early history of the county of Guines and the lordship of Ardres, both families sought marital connections primarily in the southern region. Lambert places such a connection at the beginning of the lineage of Guines, when he reports that Siegfried the Viking impregnated the daughter of Arnulf I of Flanders, and that the counts of Guines descended from their son.[67] While this story is, in all likelihood, as legendary as Siegfried, the counts of Guines, once they emerge from legend into history, do bear names found in the family of the counts of Boulogne and Flanders, such as Baldwin and Eustace. Similarly, the marriages Lambert records for the first "historical" lord of Ardres, Arnold I (†1094), were within the jurisdiction of the count of Boulogne, the first to the heiress of Marquise in the Boulonnais, the second to the widowed countess of Saint-Pol (the counts of Saint-Pol did homage to the count of Boulogne).[68]

By the end of the eleventh century, however, both families branched out. Count Eustace of Guines (c. 1036–before 1065) married Susanna of *Gherminiis*, perhaps Grammene, not far from Ghent.[69] His son, Baldwin I (before 1065–1091), married Adele/Christine, who came from Lorraine or from Holland.[70] Baldwin's son Manasses (1091–1137) married Emma of Tancarville, whose family was Anglo-Norman; she was the widow of Odo of Folkestone in England and brought Manasses property connections in two regions. His sister Giselle married the castellan of Ghent, in the Flemish heartland. In Ardres, Manasses's contemporary Arnold II "the Old" of Ardres (1094–c. 1138) married Gertrude, a daughter of the house of Aalst in the north of Flanders.[71]

These marriages often had broad political implications. Giselle of Guines married the castellan of Ghent after Robert the Frisian's usurpation of the office of count of Flanders; her father had not supported Robert, but her husband, Winemar I, had.[72] This marriage, therefore, made a political statement, by allying Guines with a family in good odor with the new comital lineage. At the same time, of course, it was an expression of the status of the counts of Guines — equivalent in importance to these powerful regional officials, who had long been considered noble.[73] Another family marriage probably also reflects the new cordiality between Robert and Baldwin I of Guines. Baldwin's daughter Adelaide married Geoffrey of Semur-en-Brionnais in Burgundy. Although it is not clear why and how this marriage was arranged (it was much further afield than members of the family usually went to marry), Robert II of Flanders, the son of Robert the Frisian, married Clemence, the daughter of William II of Burgundy, around the same time.[74] Perhaps Clemence's marriage created an opportunity or perhaps Adelaide's was even arranged upon the count of Flanders's advice.

The competition between the families of Guines and Ardres was also acted out in the marriages they contracted for their children, as the families often married in the same regions at the same time. The lords of Aalst, like the castellans of Ghent, were advocates of St. Peter's in Ghent, so one way to see the marriage of Arnold II of Ardres and Gertrude of Aalst is as a parallel to the marriage of Winemar I of Ghent and Giselle of Guines. I suspect it is no coincidence that Count Manasses married a woman with property in England, as his rival, Arnold II of Ardres, had participated in the Norman conquest of England and held property there.

The most scrutinized marriage in Lambert's history, the marriage between Christine of Ardres (†1177) and Baldwin II of Guines (1169–1206), remedied the century-long rivalry between Guines and Ardres. Lambert offers more detail about this marriage than about almost any other. Christine's father, Arnold of Colvida, became the lord of Ardres sometime between 1146, when Baldwin died, and 1149, when Count Thierry returned to Flanders (Arnold did his homage to the countess, who was regent) and the marriage took place sometime thereafter. Warlop suggests it occurred around 1155, while Duby places it around 1150.[75] Lambert says that at the time the marriage was arranged Christine was an adolescent (*adulescentula*) or a "youth" (*iuvencula*) Thus, Christine seems to have been in her teens.[76] Baldwin was also fairly young, but he would have been at least thirteen in 1150, as Manasses of Guines († 1137) was his godfather.[77]

Marriage could, of course, play the role of expanding the family holdings, the most notable of these being the marriage of Arnold II of Guines (1206–20), Lambert's patron, and Beatrice, the châtelaine of Bourbourg. This marriage shows some of the characteristics Duby associated with "aristocratic marriage" in that political concerns seem to have outweighed issues of "suitability" and "compatibility."[78] Beatrice, although nubile, was quite young, perhaps roughly the same age as Christine at marriage.[79] Arnold, although not his father's oldest child, must have been born some time in the 1150s.[80] This would have made him around forty at the time of his marriage in 1194. The result, although Lambert's history ends too soon to show it, was not good. Beatrice of Bourbourg and Arnold of Guines seem to have been unusually unhappy together.[81]

The house of Guines seems to have had some ambivalence toward the noble strategy of giving most of the family property to the eldest male child and permitting only a few children to marry.[82] The oldest sons do seem to inherit the bulk of the family property; however, three of Arnold I of Guines's five sons and six of his eight daughters married, while four of Baldwin II's five legitimate sons who survived to adulthood and all four of his legitimate daughters married. This seems also to have been true generally in the house of Ardres and was probably still normal in Flanders at the end of the twelfth century.[83] The record from Guines suggests that in Guines, at least, there was in place no winner-take-all system by which only a few children married and only one inherited.

In sexual matters, the men of the family seem to have felt free to enter into numerous informal relationships, which produced many illegitimate children. Lambert's discussion of Baldwin II's insatiable sexual appetite is frank; his account is confirmed by William of Andres.[84] Nor is Baldwin the only individual in the family to have illegitimate offspring. What is interesting about Lambert's discussion of these connections is that it offers us a glimpse of how people may have actually behaved toward their illegitimate children and relatives. Although by the end of the twelfth century illegitimacy had become a legal impediment to full membership in a family, it is clear that in Lambert's world it was far less stigmatized than such enunciated standards would lead one to believe. While Walter of Le Clud's illegitimacy ensured that he would not succeed his father, Baldwin of Ardres, in the lordship of Ardres, it does not seem to have prevented him from being accepted in the family circle (or chosen as Lambert's mouthpiece). It is also interesting that not everyone in Guines agreed that illegitimacy was an impediment to some sort of inheritance. Philip, the son of Arnold II of Ardres, made war on his legitimate brothers to win what he saw as his share of the inheritance.[85]

Illegitimate children who did not inherit nonetheless had their uses. A number of illegitimate daughters of the house of Guines married into the lesser nobility of the region. This makes sense only if these daughters were viewed as part of the family, even if they were lesser citizens of it. Only in that event could ties of fidelity be strengthened by kinship.[86] Illegitimate sons were a different story. They seemingly enjoyed a peculiar sort of social mobility. Because of their paternity, membership of the fighting class was open to them if they were suitable; otherwise, they could become clerics and pray and work for the family's well-being.[87] Thus, illegitimate children provided a pool of talent that might be utilized by the counts, or not, depending on the child's abilities and attractions.

The Nobility

Patterns of behavior in marriage and other matters on the part of the houses of Guines and Ardres also shed light upon the increasingly self-conscious medieval nobility. This group was at the time coming to define its status by its descent, hence the popularity of genealogical history. However, it was also a class characterized by its military occupation, its leisure activities, and its manner of living, which became increasingly expensive as the twelfth century progressed.[88] High levels of consumption were to lead many families, including that of the counts of Guines, deeply into debt in the thirteenth century.[89] Part of the money went for increased costs of doing business, such as the construction of fortifications, or for the staggering costs of crusades, wars, or dowries for daughters, but some clearly could not be so easily accounted for. The nobility created more lavish dwellings, like Baldwin's "round house" at Guines or the socially segregated three-story house Lambert describes at Ardres.[90]

Male aristocrats, who were from the eleventh century defined as fighters, also participated in the new phenomenon of the tournament.[91] It was costly to go to tournaments, because of the travel expenses for the fighter and his entourage, as well as the cost of arms and horses, but it was particularly costly if one lost and had to pay a ransom. The house of Guines provided a number of enthusiastic participants in tournaments, according to Lambert, mostly successful, but tournament-going was still not cheap.[92] Furthermore, the nobleman had to give presents to show his generosity and his lack of avarice, another potentially cripplingly expensive proposition. Arnold II of Guines's spending was so profligate that even his father (not to mention Lambert) disapproved.[93]

To be noble also increasingly meant to be cultivated. The sociologist Norbert Elias suggested long ago that as the need for actual fighting on the part of the nobility began to decrease and as the most important lords, like the king of France and the count of Flanders, came gradually to monopolize violence, the nobility had to find means other than arms to compete, leading them to adopt good manners and other forms of cultivation.[94] Certainly in the twelfth century the church was beginning to espouse the code of noble behavior known to us as chivalry, as a way of curbing violence. And finally, to be noble was to love nobly, even if, like Arnold II of Guines, one merely went through the motions (and even if some observers, like Lambert, found the idea mostly ridiculous).

This ideology of cultivation, chivalry, and love was supported by an increase in the general level of education of the nobility. From the clerical point of view, to be educated was to be educated in Latin; anyone who could not read Latin was "illiterate," as was anyone whose proficiency in Latin was not very great, as was assumed to be the case with lay people.[95] Since not even every cleric was proficient in Latin, and since the church monopolized Latin education, most members of the nobility probably did not qualify as "literate."[96] However, some members of the nobility were educated in Latin, at least to the degree that they could participate in some places, most notably England, in governmental processes that required the keeping of Latin records.[97] In addition, from the mid-twelfth century on, the person who could read or understand French read aloud had access to saints' lives and legends, bestiaries and lapidaries, epics and romances, histories, and assorted other instructional types of literature as well.[98] This richness of vernacular literature is reflected in Baldwin II of Guines's sponsorship of vernacular translations. Lambert is a witness to a shift in the notion of literacy, for in his vocabulary "literate" and "clerical" are no longer quite synonymous; he mentions that a man named Hasard became "literate" in a "lay" manner, that is, in the vernacular.[99]

Lambert's view of these noble activities is mixed. He takes the military preoccupation of the nobility as a given, but is not equally accepting of all that comes with it. He has genuine admiration for the military activities of Arnold II "the Old" of Ardres, who fought in the Norman Conquest of England before he inherited and the First Crusade after.[100] He relates the successes of many of his heroes on the tournament field, but in referring to tournaments, he echoes the canon of the council of Clermont of 1130, *Detestabiles nundinas*, which banned them. Similarly, he praises Count Manasses for not wasting much time in tournaments and has Arnold II of Guines enter his foolish liaison with Ida of Boulogne because of his success at a tournament.[101] He has no use for courtly love—he disapproves of Arnold II's passion for Ida of Boulogne and is slightly mocking about the doomed love of Siegfried and Elftrude — but paints a sympathetic portrait of Baldwin II's grief at the death of his wife Christine.[102] He seems to prize some courtly manners, as when he praises Manasses of Guines and Arnold "the Old" of Ardres for behaving courteously toward each other, despite being at war.[103] However, he depicts Baldwin II's exuberant generosity to his guest, Archbishop William of Reims, as going over the top; Baldwin appears a bit foolish in the process.[104] Lambert is ambivalent about learning in the laity. Baldwin's apparently genuine interest in books is astonishing to Lambert, but it leads Baldwin to behave in a way not seemly for a layman, arguing with clerics. The whole question of living nobly, for Lambert, seems to revolve around the question of prodigality, which he condemns repeatedly, vociferously as it applies to more historically remote figures, and quietly in relation to more contemporary figures.

Lords and Subjects: New Economic Relations

This prodigality is, to Lambert, what lay behind the actions of bad lords. Lambert repeatedly presents the burden that lordship placed upon the subject peasant population, a subject that also concerned writers like John of Salisbury.[105] It is not that Lambert denies the right of the counts of Guines and lords of Ardres to rule, but he desires limitations on the power of lords over their subjects. He provides several edifying stories of lords who exercise their power in an arbitrary manner, and the penalty they pay for such behavior.[106]

Although Lambert describes a bad count of Guines, Ralph, he expends most of his venom on Rainier of Boulogne, who conveniently was not related to the counts of Guines, but whose much later successor in office, Reynold of Dammartin, was the enemy of the house of Guines.[107] First, Rainier favors new men, a practice that drew increasingly vociferous complaints in the twelfth century. Kings and members of the higher nobility replaced noble retainers with bailiffs, clerks, and administrators of common origins, some of whom became richer than members of the nobility. This trend accentuated the increasing status incongruity felt by the nobility in the course of the twelfth century.[108] Rainier is, on the other hand, submissive to the royal authority that the nobility saw as usurping their own prerogatives.[109] Rainier fails to reward his followers, although a good lord was expected to do so. Similarly, he does not curb his rapacious administrators. Finally, Rainier acts as though his own inheritance belongs to someone else and lays waste to it. (When Lambert wants to show how scrupulous Arnold I of Ardres was, when he became the husband of the countess of Saint-Pol, he stresses that Arnold treated Saint-

Pol as though it were part of his own inheritance.)[110] Rainier's failings set off a chain reaction of disorder through the social structure, so that people come to kill, rather than love, their neighbors. In the end, he is hunted down and killed. Lambert presents the actions of such men as subversions of a natural order that required them to be obedient to their overlords and clement toward their subjects.

Lambert's attitudes may arise from living after a period during which the nobility began to consolidate their holdings, acquire as many rights as they could in their domains, and extract more income from their property. Lambert is frank about the illegitimate means used to rationalize and increase noble holdings and to institute new taxes. Arnold II of Guines and Arnold III "the Young" of Ardres were both excommunicated for unjustly seizing peasant property.[111] Lambert also gives a rather fanciful story about the origins of the oven tax, in which Arnold II "the Old" of Ardres tricks his people into agreeing to pay the tax.[112] Whether the people of Ardres did unwittingly agree to pay an oven tax or not, these sorts of taxes were increasingly levied by those lords who could successfully demand them. Lambert is more pointed when he describes the efforts of Gertrude of Aalst, Arnold's wife, to create sheep farms and the severity with which her men demanded her due of the peasants.[113]

Lambert's sympathy with the peasants on these and other occasions is notable. Even when the nobility did not seemingly overstep their authority, he recognized that peasants were vulnerable. He includes in his description of the new fortifications built at Ardres by Arnold II of Guines the spectacle of dwellings, gardens, and orchards being destroyed, to the accompaniment of the groans of their former owners, and he makes sidelong reference to the fact that this was being carried out in the middle of a famine.[114]

Personal Freedom and Noble Autonomy

The vulnerability of the peasants also extended to their freedom, and one of Lambert's most indignant passages is that in which he describes the way Gertrude of Aalst enserfed formerly free people.[115] To Lambert, freedom was precious, and there are several anecdotes which relate to its defense, or to the implications of being unfree in Lambert's world. The most striking is his account of the "club churls" or *colvekerli*, a group of people forbidden to bear arms except clubs, who were also required to pay servile dues.[116] Lambert presents the attempt to force more people into this class as an attack on freedom that threatened the nobility as well as the peasantry. However, Lambert mostly addresses the freedom of peasants, such as the men of Hénin who settled at Ardres and came to be thought of as serfs; Lambert gives two separate accounts of how they came to be unfree.[117]

Lambert's anecdotes about peasant freedom parallel the shifting trends in Flanders generally and his region in particular. Between the mid-ninth century and the early twelfth century, freedom was on the decline in the peasant population generally in Flanders. However, by the mid-twelfth century, the loss of freedom on the part of peasants had begun to reverse itself. Although towns offered some avenues to freedom to peasants after 1163, the more important change, from the rural peasant's point of view, was simply a decline in the demands for labor.[118] This was made possible by the growth of a market economy. Nobles preferred to extract money rather than labor from their peasants. As this occurred, the difference between the unfree and free blurred, for it was difficult to distinguish between payments made because one was unfree and rents a free peasant might pay.[119] This process was not complete in Lambert's day, but it was certainly advancing. Furthermore, Lambert, living in maritime Flanders, was in a region freer than most others.[120] Lambert's stories about lost and regained freedom, then, reflect this shift toward a more free population and a sense on his part that this was proper, although his descriptions of the means by which peasants lost their freedom are probably unhistorical. His views were shared by contemporary writers, for one of the translators of the *Pseudo-Turpin Chronicle*, who was writing about the same time as Lambert, also mentions the loss of freedom due to "the evil customs of lords." [121]

Lambert was probably not seriously worried that the nobility would lose their freedom, despite the concern expressed in the story of the "club churls." However, he nevertheless does describe a decline of noble independence, albeit with equanimity. The characteristic that had originally defined the noble state was freedom from claims upon one's person or property, except for certain public responsibilities; this was in part made possible by the possession of allodial property. By the twelfth century, however, much allodial property in Flanders had been turned into dependent tenures, that is, into fiefs, and magnates, whose power depended on their independent wealth, found their political independence and power circumscribed as well.[122] The trend away from the ownership of allodial property to dependent forms of tenure continued into the thirteenth century, so the nobility experienced what amounted to a steady decrease in autonomy.[123] Lambert does describe this transformation of allodial property into fiefs, but without the discomfort he felt about peasant losses of freedom, suggesting that he saw nothing undesirable about the trend.[124]

Historical Writing in Flanders

Although the *History of the Counts of Guines and Lords of Ardres* reflects some
of the trends of its age and some of the concerns expressed by contemporary writers, its subject is primarily the history of a lineage of extremely local
character. The counts of Guines were not important enough to appear in very
many other histories. To give a sense of their status, it is useful to note that
Arnold II of Guines participated in the French invasion of England in 1216
with fifteen knights, more than those who came by themselves, but many
fewer than others brought.[125] Why then were secondary figures of this kind the
subject of a history of this length, detail, and quality? To answer that question,
we need to consider the question of historical writing in Flanders.

Flanders was unusually rich in historical writing of all kinds from the
tenth century through the beginning of the thirteenth century. There are a
number of reasons for this. The growth of historical writing in medieval regions tended to parallel the growth of an organized territorial power. Only a
strong prince could guarantee the peace necessary for monasteries to flour-
ish, and most historical writing was done in monasteries, at least before the
thirteenth century. Wealthy monasteries had property and prerogatives they
needed to defend, a project that was also a spur to some forms of historical writing, particularly cartulary histories, serial biographies, biographies
of individual abbots or local saints, and collections of miracles attesting to
the power of saints, and by extension, the abbeys that housed their relics.[126]
Monastic histories also contributed to institutional memory, and were sometimes composed for that purpose.[127] However, monasteries also identified
with the authority of territorial princes as the guarantee of the monastery's
own power, prestige, and prerogatives, so monks wrote histories to bolster
that authority, sometimes on commission, sometimes speculatively in the
hopes of a reward for this literary service.

However, not all historical writing, particularly from the twelfth century on, was monastic. Canons of cathedral chapters sometimes wrote histories, for reasons very similar to those that inspired monks, although some
of the histories coming from cathedral cities were written at urban monasteries. Finally, as the need for record keeping trickled down from monarchs
to members of the nobility, noble men and women came to employ educated
clerks or chaplains. A chaplain who looked after the family's religious needs
and the family's documents might also think of writing a family history.

All these conditions prevailed in Flanders. The counts of Flanders were generally strong enough to cope effectively with Viking attacks in the late ninth and tenth centuries, which meant that Flemish monasteries survived intact, contrary to what happened to many monasteries in coastal France. These monasteries preserved historical traditions that went back to the Carolingian period and maintained bodies of educated personnel, schools, and collections of books. Similarly, the dioceses survived intact, and although some of the cathedral schools declined after the ninth century, many rebounded toward the end of the tenth. From the twelfth century, Flemish nobles were increasingly literate (at least in French), and increasingly likely to commission works or have books copied for them. The result of this confluence of conditions was a treasure-trove of historical writing. What follows is an overview rather than a comprehensive account of this Flemish tradition of historical writing, one intended to indicate where Lambert's history fits into the larger picture of Flemish histories.[128]

Between the eleventh and the early thirteenth centuries, a number of extraordinary individual historians were active in Flanders. Probably the most widely known of these was Sigebert of Gembloux (active c. 1071–1112). He produced a large corpus of historical writing at the monastery of Gembloux, including a universal chronicle continuing the tradition of Eusebius of Caesarea and St. Jerome, a collection of biographies (*On Illustrious Men*), *The Deeds of the Abbots of Gembloux*, and assorted biographies and passions in both prose and poetry.[129] Sigebert's chronicle was widely known outside of Flanders and found many continuators. Andrew of Marchiennes, another prolific historian, wrote for the monasteries of Anchin and Marchiennes. Like Sigebert, his body of writing covered much ground; he produced an abbreviated history of the kings of France and counts of Flanders, the chronicle of Marchiennes, and a catalogue of the abbots of Anchin. He probably also wrote the genealogy of the counts of Flanders found at Anchin, the continuation of the chronicle of Sigebert of Gembloux housed there, and the history of Anchin.[130]

Other writers were less prolific, but equally important. Galbert of Bruges, a clerk and perhaps a canon of Saint-Donatien in Bruges, composed an account of the murder of Count Charles "the Good" of Flanders and its aftermath in the form of daily entries.[131] Walter of Thérouanne, the archdeacon of Thérouanne, and the author of a biography of Bishop John of Thérouanne (d. 1130), also wrote a biography of Charles.[132] Gislebert of Mons, a rough contemporary of Lambert of Ardres, was the chancellor of the court of Hainaut under Baldwin V, and a canon, then the provost of Saint-Pierre in Namur. He was also the author of the *Chronicon Hanoniense* (1050–1195), a history of Hainaut and the surrounding regions.[133] Finally, at the beginning of the thirteenth century, the monastery of Andres in Guines produced a remarkable historian in William of Andres.[134]

Numerous Flemish monasteries were sites of historical writing or places where important works of history were preserved. Saint-Vaast in Arras had a copy of the great annals known as the Saint-Bertin annals, the *Royal Frankish Annals* (eighth century) and its ninth-century continuations; upon this base, the monks built an entire history of Gaul to 900.[135] Some of the historical texts from Arras related to the bishops, for Arras became an episcopal see in 1095. Others, like the cartulary history of 1170, concern the monastery and its property.[136] Saint-Bertin also had an illustrious tradition of historical writing, which included a cartulary history begun in the tenth century and continued into the thirteenth, sacred biographies, and collections of miracles.[137] Herman of Tournai is associated with much of the historical writing at Saint-Martin of Tournai, which included various works about the monastery and a chronicle.[138] Production at Lobbes was similar: annals, a serial biography of the abbots, and miracles.[139] Saint-Amand near Valenciennes was also active; its histories include two chronicles, an account of an eleventh-century monastic fire, and the miracles performed by the saint during the rebuilding campaign.[140]

Historical writing was not confined to a few rich and important monasteries, however. Histories were written at Vicogne, Liessies, Hasnon, Hautmont, Maroilles, Saint-Pierre of Ghent, Watten, Floreffe near Namur, Anchin, and Affligem, among others.[141] Vast numbers of collections of miracles, saints' lives, or individual biographies were composed at, among other places, Brogne, Hammes, Blangy, Bergues, Waulsort, Saint-Bavon in Ghent, and Maroilles.[142]

In addition to these monastic compositions were works created for bishops or about episcopal sees. At Cambrai there was a serial biography of the bishops of Cambrai, with continuations.[143] Lambert of Wattrelos, a canon at Cambrai, wrote a universal history beginning about 1152, while another chronicle was composed in the episcopal circle around 1133.[144] A serial biography of the bishops of Liège was composed toward the end of the tenth century, as was a chronicle.[145] Finally, the circle around the bishops of Thérouanne produced a short catalogue of the bishops of Thérouanne.[146]

While many of the monastic and even the episcopal histories were produced for the consumption of the clergy, Flanders is particularly interesting in that it produced a surprising number of genealogies and genealogical histories of lay figures. Many genealogies of the counts of Flanders have survived. The earliest of these, a brief genealogy of the counts of Flanders composed by Witger between 951 and 959, was preserved and possibly composed at Saint-Bertin.[147] A monk at Saint-Pierre of Ghent wrote a note concerning Arnulf I, Baldwin II, and Arnulf II on the back of a charter sometime in the eleventh century; it is this kind of historical notation that Lambert seems to be referring to in his prologue.[148] Another genealogy was also kept at Saint-Bertin around the turn of the twelfth century with copies at Saint-Vaast, Marchiennes, and Vormezeele. This genealogy was the first to introduce the legendary progenitor of the counts of Flanders, Lideric of Harlebec.[149] Someone, again probably at Saint-Bertin, turned the genealogical catalogue into a poem around 1120.[150] Finally, Lambert, a canon of Saint-Omer, who had access to the Saint-Bertin historical materials, composed a genealogy of the counts a little after 1164, using as one of his materials an anonymous catalogue composed around 1120.[151] The most notable genealogical history of the counts, however, was known as *Flandria generosa* or *Noble Flanders*. It was based on the genealogy composed by Lambert of Saint-Omer, with notes from other sources, and was composed around 1164 or shortly thereafter. In the early thirteenth century the work was continued and expanded and it exists in a number of different versions.[152]

However, not only the counts of Flanders were celebrated in genealogy. The counts of Boulogne were also the subjects of a genealogy dating from the late eleventh century and continued in the twelfth.[153] Another set of genealogies concerned both the counts of Boulogne and the counts of Namur.[154] More humble individuals were also interested in genealogy. Lambert of Wattrelos, the author of the annals of Cambrai, in the year of his own birth inserted his own genealogy, that of a man descended from knights rather than great nobles.[155] Where the great led, lesser individuals followed.

Lambert's history, then, arises from an environment in which historical writing was actively pursued and often took genealogical forms. Lambert was familiar with both types of history. However, this does not explain why Lambert thought a genealogical history would please (or placate) his patrons. The explanation for this lies in an increasing interest in and taste for history (as well as other sorts of literature) among members of the nobility, and particularly in the circles in which the counts of Guines traveled. Most of this writing was in the vernacular. While churchmen lamented the inability of the laity to read Latin, laymen and women were commissioning the translation and/or composition of works in the vernacular for their use, and some built extensive libraries, as did Baldwin II of Guines.[156] Most twelfth-century vernacular histories, such as accounts of the crusades (which Lambert mentions were delivered orally at Ardres), were composed in poetry.[157] Early in the thirteenth century, the first vernacular prose histories were composed, the *History of the Fourth Crusade* of Villehardouin, the marshal of Champagne, and the *Conquest of Constantinople* of Robert de Clari, a nobleman from the region around Corbie in northern France.[158]

These were followed by an explosion of vernacular prose histories composed for the Franco-Flemish nobility. The relatives, friends, and enemies of the house of Guines were important patrons of vernacular literature, particularly histories, among them the count and countess of Saint-Pol (Baldwin II's brother William married into that family); Robert of Béthune (Matilda of Béthune was the mother of Beatrice of Bourbourg, the wife of Arnold II of Guines); and Roger IV of Lille (his grandmother was Adelaide of Guines). William of Cayeux, who was probably the nephew or other relative of the Arnold of Cayeux whom Arnold II of Guines took as his companion, was another great literary patron.[159] The great enemy of the counts of Guines, Reynold of Dammartin, the count of Boulogne, was also an important patron of historical writing.[160] Lambert's history needs to be placed, therefore, in the context both of a vigorous Latin tradition and of increasing lay interest in historical writing.

The County of Guines

Sources for the History of Guines

Lambert's *History* is one of the few sources for the history of Guines, which lay on the border between France and Flanders. Not only was it therefore disputed by these powers, but from 1352 until 1588 the fortress of Guines was held by the English, while Ardres remained in French hands. French, English, and Burgundian armies repeatedly ravaged the region and many monasteries, including Capella and Andres, expired. Records that previously existed undoubtedly disappeared.[161] But the rural character and relative poverty of the region must also have played a role in limiting the surviving historical sources for Guines. The episcopal center was at Thérouanne and later at Boulogne, both lying outside of Guines; there were only minor market towns; the religious houses were mostly of only local importance. Whereas customs (collections of local civil law) survive for other French regions from the thirteenth century, the *Customs* of Guines are extant only in a sixteenth-century manuscript of what seems to be a fifteenth-century redaction.[162] Only two histories that treat Guines directly are extant: Lambert's *History of the Counts of Guines* and the *Chronicle of Andres* written by William of Andres some twenty to thirty years after Lambert's history. The works of the Anonymous of Béthune, the *Chronique des rois de France* and the *Histoire des ducs de Normandie et des rois d'Angleterre*, composed in all likelihood for Robert VII of Béthune, a neighbor and relative of the ruling family at Guines, treat the battle over the Artois generally, and make mention of Guines and its lords from time to time, but the lords of Guines are generally peripheral to the author's main concerns.[163]

Perhaps because of this paucity of sources for the history of Guines, or for reasons of nationalism, there have been few recent works that consider the region of which Guines was a part.[164] Antiquarians from the seventeenth through the nineteenth centuries have provided most of the secondary litera-ture on Guines; their work has generally been reprinted in the absence of new scholarship, although many depended on Lambert more than modern his-torians would be comfortable doing.[165] I offer the following overview of the history of Guines and Ardres to show where Lambert's text intersects with the fragmentary historical record, so that readers may have some context for the events that Lambert describes. I follow Lambert's lead in starting with the history of Guines, which begins at the end of the tenth century, and bringing in the history of Ardres when it becomes relevant to the main narrative.

The History of Guines and Ardres

There may have been a fortress at Guines for some time, but what is possibly the first mention of it appears in Flodoard's annals under the year 938.[166] Flo-doard reports that Louis the Pious attempted to restore a maritime fortress that was somewhere near or in Flanders, for Louis proceeded from that site to the court of Arnulf I of Flanders. Flodoard calls the fortress "Guisen," which could be Guines. Guines only emerges for certain into the historical record toward the end of the tenth century.[167]

By that time, however, the county of Flanders, of which Guines was but a small part, had been in existence for about a century. Baldwin I (d. 879), traditionally seen as the first count of "Flanders," held one of the small Caro-lingian counties, probably the region around Ghent, when he eloped with Judith, Charles the Bald's daughter, in 861.[168] When the dust settled, Charles granted Baldwin the territory around Bruges, then known as Flanders (the name came only later to describe all the possessions of Baldwin's descen-dants). Baldwin later acquired some other territories, including the Ternois (the region lying around the cities of Thérouanne, Saint-Omer, and Aire) and the land of Waas (to the north and east of Ghent).[169] His son Baldwin II (879–

918) brought Courtrai under his control, part of the Boulonnais (the region around Boulogne), and part of the region around Tournai; in other words, he ruled the bulk of the later county of Flanders and some other areas besides.[170]

Baldwin II gave the northern part of his territory to his older son Arnulf I (918–65) and the southern part, including the Boulonnais and what would become Guines, to his younger son Adalulf (918–33). After Adalulf's death, Arnulf murdered one of Adalulf's sons, dispossessed the other, and took over the southern region himself.[171] Toward the end of Arnulf's life or early in the reign of his grandson, Arnulf II (965–88), who was four when he succeeded in 965, part of this southern region — including Guines — slipped from Flemish comital control.[172] Adalulf's surviving legitimate son, Arnulf, successfully claimed the Boulonnais and the southern part of the Ternois, which became the county of Saint-Pol, while Arnulf II's son and successor, Baldwin IV (988–1035) was able to hold on to the northern part of the Ternois (which included the town of Saint-Omer, the site of the rich and powerful abbey of Saint-Bertin) and the episcopal see of Thérouanne.[173]

The county of Guines formed about this time as a break-away from Boulogne.[174] What came before its sudden appearance in 988 has been the subject of considerable conjecture. Lambert reports that a Viking named Siegfried, descended from St. Walbert, a seventh-century count of Guines, came to claim his inheritance around the middle of the reign of Arnulf I of Flanders.[175] While this story may well have been received tradition in the region, it is clearly fictive. Among other things, the name Siegfried raises suspicion — the surviving version of the *Nibelungenlied* was just being written down around the time that Lambert was writing — as does the fact that no county of Guines existed in the seventh century, and Walbert, who also appears in Folcuin's cartulary, is not St. Walbert.[176] However, Vikings were active in the region in the tenth century, and it is possible that the leader of such a band would be granted a holding, as happened elsewhere.[177] Some scholars have accepted, therefore, the Viking origins of the counts of Guines, if not their descent from someone named Siegfried.[178]

There are other possibilities. The counts of Guines may have been descended from a local family that made good during the Viking invasions. Many families fled from Flanders during the period of greatest Viking activity in the area (between 879 and 883), when Baldwin II was a minor and when the west Frankish kings put few of their resources into defending the northern part of their holdings.[179] In this period, some families who stayed and fought were able to increase their possessions and power significantly. Count Baldwin II's success as a Viking fighter, similarly, explains why he owned outright such extensive property in the northern part of his domain.[180] According to this scenario, the counts of Guines would have been local potentates, perhaps the castellans of the fortress so briefly mentioned by Flodoard, who benefited from this situation.[181] Another possibility is that the counts of Guines established their power based on a relationship with some monastery. The castellans of Ghent began as the advocates of St. Peter's in Ghent, while the lords of Béthune started as the advocates of Saint-Vaast in Arras.[182] Lambert clearly knew, but rejected, a tradition that said that the counts of Guines had originally been the provosts of Saint-Bertin.[183]

While Baldwin IV (988–1035) actively created the system of castellanies, and he and his successors had real control over the castellans, the counts of Flanders, who did not have much domain land or power in this southern region, did not create the office of count of Guines; they simply accepted its creation.[184] As a result, the counts of Guines were often politically independent. For example, when much of Flanders supported the usurpation of Robert the Frisian (1071–93), Baldwin I of Guines (before 1065–91) supported Richilde, the mother of the hereditary count, Arnulf III (1070–71).[185] However, although the count of Flanders's power was not great in Guines, Guines was so small that the count of Guines could not afford to stand out as a target for the count of Flanders's wrath. Thus when Robert the Frisian triumphed, Baldwin immediately moved to effect a reconciliation. Shortly after the usurpation, Count Robert became Baldwin's son's godfather and gave the boy his own name.[186]

Because of its peripheral location, some events that shook Flanders seem to have affected Guines only indirectly. Count Manasses of Guines (1091–1137) seems not to have been involved in the civil war following the murder of Count Charles the Good of Flanders (1119–27), although Lambert wanted to depict the family as allied to Charles.[187] The castellans of Bourbourg and Ghent, both allied to Guines by marriage, however, did become involved and in each case opposed the eventually successful claimant of the comital office, Thierry of Alsace (1128–68).[188]

While Manasses might choose not to be involved, however, Guines felt the effects of broader political changes. Count Thierry's opponents came to blows with each other in the succession crisis in Guines following Manasses's death in 1137. The legal claimant was Manasses's granddaughter Beatrice (1137–41), whose father was Henry, castellan of Bourbourg. Her rival was Manasses's nephew, Arnold "of Ghent." Thierry became involved because of the danger that whoever succeeded would enhance the power of his family, which might make them more successfully able to resist the count's authority;

at the same time, the crisis offered Thierry a chance to punish some of his enemies. Thierry seems to have concluded that Beatrice's father, Henry of Bourbourg, was the greater threat; for that reason Thierry supported the claim of
Arnold of Ghent, but without enough assistance to let Arnold win outright,
for the crisis was resolved only by Beatrice's death in 1141. Perhaps Thierry
was uncertain of where his best interests truly lay, and his caution would have
been wise, for after Arnold of Ghent became count (as Arnold I of Guines
[1141–69]) his brothers died without male heirs, leaving Arnold in line for the
castellany of Ghent. With some maneuvering, Thierry prevented Arnold from
holding the castellany of Ghent, thus keeping all the lines of power roughly
as they had been.[189]

Despite the difficult succession in Guines, Count Arnold was able to
establish his authority firmly in Guines after 1141, and another event added
to Arnold I's strength. Sometime around 1150, Arnold married his son Baldwin II of Guines (1169–1206) to the heiress of Ardres and combined the two
holdings.

Ardres was a lordship within Guines, controlled from a fortification and
town of the same name. The lordship of Ardres developed from the advocacy of the wealthy monastery of Saint-Bertin in the town of Saint-Omer. The
first individual to be called the "lord" of Ardres was Arnold I "the advocate"
(† 1094), so the lordship of Ardres seems to date from about the middle of
the eleventh century. The lords of Ardres may not originally have been subordinate to the counts of Guines; Lambert suggests they were not. However,
they were not powerful enough to resist the claims of the counts of Guines
without help. Arnold I of Ardres seems to have sought that help by attach-
ing himself to other lords. He became the seneschal of Count Eustace II of
Boulogne (†1093), who was much more important than Baldwin I of Guines.
Arnold I's sons were among Eustace's soldiers during the Norman Conquest
of England, and as a result they held estates there.

However, Arnold I also used other strategies to ensure his independence
of the counts of Guines. Late in his life, Arnold became a peer in the court of
Flanders. The institution of the peers seems to have appeared in the second
half of the eleventh century. The function of the peers may have been the defense of the Flemish border, where the count was weak; the peerages lay in
a ring surrounding the Flemish heartland.[190] The appointment of the lord of
Ardres as a peer solved the problem for Robert the Frisian of the disloyalty
of the southern lords; the lords of Ardres could be expected to be loyal to the
counts of Flanders against their enemies the counts of Guines. At the same
time, the peerage in the court of Flanders offered the lords of Ardres an addi-

tional measure of independence from the claims of the counts of Guines. This independence, despite periodic eruptions of warfare aimed at ending it, was maintained through the reign of Arnold II "the Old" of Ardres (1094–1138).[191]

Naturally the lords of Ardres were interested in the succession crisis in Guines, as it might have a direct effect on their independence. There was a new lord of Ardres at the time, Arnold III "the Young" of Ardres (1138–39), who had inherited the holding of Ardres, leaving Baldwin, his brother and eventual successor, without property. This may have been a source of bitterness, for in the previous generation, the inheritance had been shared out.[192] Arnold of Ghent (Arnold I of Guines) saw an opportunity to divide and conquer, and, as soon as he laid claim to Guines, he struck up an alliance with Baldwin of Ardres. When Arnold III of Ardres was murdered shortly thereafter, Baldwin became the lord of Ardres (1139–46) with Arnold of Ghent's active assistance.[193] Thus a temporary alliance was effected. A return to the normal rivalry came about quickly, however. When Baldwin was wounded during the war between Guines and Bourbourg, he ceased his active participation in the war. Indeed, he saw an opportunity to supplant Arnold of Ghent by marrying Countess Beatrice of Guines, who was estranged from her husband. Henry of Bourbourg, delighted at acquiring an ally against Arnold of Ghent, arranged an annulment and Baldwin immediately married Beatrice. Nevertheless, Baldwin's plans went awry, for Beatrice died almost immediately.[194]

The end of the succession crisis in Guines seems to have brought peace between Arnold and Baldwin, a peace secured for good in the next generation. When Baldwin died on the second Crusade, leaving no legitimate offspring, the lordship of Ardres passed through Baldwin's sister, Adeline, to her husband, Arnold, viscount of Merck, also known as Arnold of Colvida (Arnold IV of Ardres [c. 1147–c. 1176]), making their daughter, Christine, the heiress of Ardres. Arnold I of Guines seized the opportunity to swallow Ardres and married his son Baldwin (Baldwin II of Guines [1169–1206]) to Christine.[195] The first son of this marriage, Arnold, became Arnold II of Guines (1206–20) and Arnold V of Ardres (c. 1178–1220).

Arnold II of Guines, like his predecessors, was highly desirous of increasing his family's power and in the late twelfth century achieved the kind of expansionary match that had eluded his predecessors, after several abortive attempts. He tried at first to marry Ida of Boulogne, who with her sister was one of the heiresses to the county of Boulogne, but according to Lambert he was outmaneuvered by Reynold of Dammartin, who became the next count.[196] He then became betrothed to Eustacia, the second daughter of the count of Saint-Pol. This seems to have been a stop-gap, for Eustacia's older sister inherited the title; she would have had to die childless for the title to pass to Eustacia, which did not happen.[197] Finally, Arnold united two regions already bound by ties of kinship since the days of Count Manasses when he married Beatrice, the heiress of Bourbourg, shortly after her brother's death; she was technically also the heiress of Aalst, although Aalst had been taken over by the counts of Flanders in 1166.[198]

Although the counts of Guines seemed to be in a position to make themselves truly important men toward the end of the twelfth century, they were about to get caught up in the larger patterns of Flemish history to their detriment. The county of Guines was the battleground in a series of wars between the counts of Flanders and Philip II of France, and Baldwin II and Arnold II of Guines were blown hither and thither in the interests of more powerful men. These wars were set in motion in 1180, when Guines, Ardres, Arras, and Saint-Omer — the heartland of the later county of Artois — were passed to the French crown as part of the dowry of Isabel of Hainaut (†1189) when she married Philip II "Augustus" of France (1180–1223). The count of Flanders, Philip of Alsace (1168–91), who was her uncle, was supposed to be allowed to use these territories for his lifetime.

However, in 1182 Count Philip got into an altercation with Philip Augustus over the county of Vermandois. Count Philip's wife Elizabeth was the elder daughter and heiress to the county of Vermandois, making Philip the count of Vermandois as well as Flanders. Elizabeth had signed the properties over to Philip, and this conveyance had been ratified by both Louis VII (1137–80) and Philip Augustus.[199] When Elizabeth died in 1182 without heirs, Philip Augustus repudiated this confirmation and supported the claims of Elizabeth's sister to the land and title. Naturally, Count Philip did not want to relinquish his acquisitions. He remarried and in retaliation assigned his second wife, Matilda/Theresia of Portugal, dower lands that were part of Isabel's dowry. The resulting altercation produced a short war, which Count Philip lost. Although Count Philip was permitted by the treaty of Boves (1185) to keep the title of count of Vermandois, he lost most of the land.[200]

This was not, however, the end of the story. After Count Philip's death, his brother-in-law, Isabel's father, became Count Baldwin VIII of Flanders (1191–94). There was quiet between France and Flanders during his reign, but when Baldwin VIII was succeeded by his son, Baldwin IX (1194–1206), the battle over the southern part of Flanders was reactivated. In 1198, Baldwin IX reconquered the lands ceded as part of Isabel's dowry. In the treaty of Péronne (1200), Philip Augustus was forced to recognize Baldwin's right to some of them, including Guines.[201] Counts Baldwin II and Arnold II of Guines fought on the Flemish side in this conflict, and their service was recognized by grants of money and formal recognition of Arnold's rights, through his marriage to Beatrice of Bourbourg, to part of the Aalst inheritance.[202] There matters rested for the next few years, for Philip Augustus was too busy to spend much energy on Flanders; instead, he was conquering Normandy, Maine, Anjou, and Brittany from King John of England (1199–1216).

The premature death of Baldwin IX, however, offered Philip Augustus a new opportunity to exert his authority over Flanders. Baldwin and his wife both died while on the fourth Crusade.[203] Their two daughters, both under the age of five, were left behind in Flanders. When their parents left, Joan and Margaret were placed under a council of regents composed of relatives and other important Flemish dignitaries.[204] However, when word of Baldwin's death came, Philip Augustus claimed his right as the girls' overlord to wardship, and he also demanded and got physical custody of them. As their guardian, Philip was able to choose their spouses, and the dowager countess of Flanders, Matilda, successfully offered the king a financial inducement to marry Joan to Matilda's nephew Ferrand of Portugal. After they married in 1212, Joan and Ferrand were forced to surrender part of the land Baldwin IX had reconquered (Saint-Omer and Aire, but not Guines) to Philip's son, the future Louis VIII of France (1223–26). This drove Count Ferrand into the enemy camp: in 1213 Ferrand joined King John of England, Reynold of Boulogne, and the German emperor Otto IV in an alliance against Philip Augustus.[205]

As Guines was a disputed territory between 1200 and 1214, it was, naturally, a war zone. In 1201, the dowager countess Matilda/Theresia attempted to assert her rights over her dower lands and brought an army south toward Furnes. Arnold II of Guines, in his capacity as castellan of Bourbourg, mobilized his troops, probably with the intention of protecting Guines and Bourbourg, for Matilda laid claim to Bourbourg as part of her dower. Arnold's precautions proved unnecessary, as Matilda lost badly to an army raised against her at Furnes, and Arnold was in the fortunate position of being able to offer her escort to safety, without having to take further action against any claims on his own lands that she might have had.[206]

Matilda proved to be far less threatening than Arnold's neighbor, the count of Boulogne. Reynold of Boulogne (1190–1217) was an opportunist with shifting allegiances. He initially supported Baldwin IX against Philip Augustus, but defected to Philip in 1198. Reynold returned to the Flemish party by 1199, but was again in Philip's entourage between 1202 and 1213.[207] Thus, for

most of the first decade of the thirteenth century, Reynold of Boulogne and
Arnold of Guines were on opposing sides, while Guines lay, temptingly, in
the middle of Boulogne.[208] In 1205, Reynold attacked Guines and took Baldwin II of Guines captive. Although Baldwin was released, he never recovered
from the experience and died early in 1206.[209] Arnold II of Guines, according to William of Andres, negotiated a peace with Reynold, and things seem
to have been quiet for the next three years.[210] However, in 1209, Reynold attacked Guines again, this time in coordination with Philip Augustus. Philip
destroyed Bonham and captured Colvida, Sangatte, and Rodelinghem, leaving royal garrisons there, while Reynold destroyed the fortifications at Rorichove, which bordered on the viscounty of Merck and was held by Count
Arnold's brother Manasses.[211] To complicate matters, Countess Beatrice seems
to have begun to act independently of her husband at this time, for William
of Andres says that she connived in the destruction of Rorichove because she
did not like Manasses.[212]

Once Philip Augustus became seriously decided upon a Flemish campaign, Arnold was caught between the king and Count Ferrand. In 1213, Philip
Augustus again led an army through Guines, taking hostages, while his son
Louis destroyed some hamlets. In 1214, Count Ferrand invaded from the other
direction with the assistance of Reynold of Dammartin, who had now joined
the Flemish side. The Anonymous of Béthune tells how the host rode through
Guines, burning Colvida, and later returning to burn Bonham and scorch the
earth of Guines.[213] Arnold was forced to choose sides, and he chose the king;
thus, unlike many of the borderland nobility, but like some of his relatives,
he fought at the battle of Bouvines (1214) on the victorious French side.[214]
Countess Beatrice was also forced to choose, and she seems to have chosen
the other side. Caught at Guines by Reynold's and Ferrand's invasion, she was
extracted from it through the intervention of Robert of Béthune, her relative.
She retreated to Andres, which had purchased its safety. From there, she and
her children were taken to Flanders, where she stayed for the next four years,
although the elder daughter Beatrice and the future Baldwin III of Guines
were probably reconciled to their father before 1216.[215]

Because of his support of the French king in 1214, Arnold II of Guines was
more fortunate than many of the other nobles of the region; he did not face
the financial penalties for disloyalty exacted from other nobles.[216] Guines was
rather effortlessly incorporated into the county of Artois, created in 1237.[217]
However, the history of Guines in the thirteenth century was hardly smooth.
The counts became impoverished, as did most of the other nobles of the region, and toward the end of the century Arnold III of Guines sold his county

to pay his debts, although Arnold's granddaughter, Jeanne, successfully re-covered Guines in 1295.[218] Jeanne's grandson was the constable of France dur-ing the first phase of the Hundred Years' War and the lords of Coucy were also descended from the counts of Guines The peerage of Ardres passed through the female line of the family to Arnold III's daughter Alice and her husband, Walter Bertout of Mechlin, who held lands in Flanders.[219] Thus, despite its thirteenth-century difficulties, the family survived through the fourteenth century.

Culture, Institutions, Economy

Guines lay along a linguistic and economic border; it was part of "la Flandre flamingante" in the twelfth century. The name Guines itself derives from the Flemish name for the county, Wijnen.[220] While there were probably pockets of French speakers, and the nobility seems to have spoken French, read French books, and gone to French tournaments, scholars have concluded that they used Flemish for their everyday business.[221] The abbot of the monastery of Andres, the traditional burial site of the counts of Guines, argued that the abbots of his monastery needed to know Flemish to carry out their judicial duties; otherwise the nobility would balk at judgments they could not under-stand.[222] Flemish was spoken in the cities of the region until the eighteenth century, and perhaps in the countryside until shortly before the First World War.[223]

While parts of southern Flanders were rich, Guines probably was not. It did not belong to the great Flanders of the towns. The important Flemish towns developed at transition points between farmland and the coastal ter-rain and downriver from grain sources.[224] Saint-Omer, probably the earliest important economic center of southern Flanders, lay to the east. Guines lay on the Aa, which emerged into the Channel at Calais, in other words, out-side the territory of Guines. The waterways of Guines, some of them already canalized by Lambert's time, connected the region to ports outside the ter-ritory, such as Calais and Gravelinges.[225] The lords of Ardres made the town of Ardres a free town,[226] but there is no suggestion that it ever became more than a local trading center. Nor were the counts able to take advantage of the coastline so that the county might benefit from trade in that way. As Lam-bert's discussion of Sangatte suggests, the coastline of Guines was too unstable to maintain a great port.[227] The great ports of Calais and Wissant lay to the northeast and southwest respectively and both were controlled by the counts of Boulogne.

The economy of Guines seems then to have been based on what could be locally produced, although here again the terrain was not particularly encouraging. The landscape was composed of undulating hills, with marshy land in between, lightly wooded with scrub. Not surprisingly, it was sparsely populated until the end of the tenth century. In contrast, neighboring Picardy was already densely populated by the early eleventh century, while to the south and east of Guines, the sand gave way to loam, more agriculturally productive.[228]

This meant that the land was not particularly well suited to cereal agriculture. However, the grasses and scrub the land could support were suitable for sheep-raising, as Lambert noted.[229] In addition, through draining and damming, the counts of Guines and lords of Ardres (and probably other nobles as well) created fish ponds, which were generally accompanied by mills.[230] So Guines did have some resources, which its lords exploited as best they could. However, while the rulers of Ardres and Guines may have been locally magnificent, they could not escape the second rank by relying solely on the resources available to them at Guines. Consequently, the only avenue open to the lords of Guines to rise above their secondary status was a rich marriage, which they attempted, but were never able to bring about.

The Text and the Translation

Manuscripts

Eleven manuscripts of Lambert's work survive; however, none date from his own day. The earliest of these, Vatican, Reg. lat. 696, was copied in the fifteenth century, by which time, Lambert's text had probably already lost its final two chapters. According to Marie-Françoise Bourdat, this manuscript was probably copied for Louis of Bruges. All the other manuscripts were copied from the Vatican manuscript, either directly or through intermediaries; they date from the sixteenth through the eighteenth centuries.[231] When the text was rediscovered at the end of the Middle Ages, it was translated into French; two manuscripts of the translation have survived.[232]

Editions

Lambert's text was first printed in its entirety in the eighteenth century in Johann Peter von Ludewig, based on a single manuscript.[233] Extracts were also printed by Duchesne in the *Recueil des historiens des Gaules et de la France*.[234] Godefroy de Menilglaise published his edition of the Latin with the Renaissance French translation facing in 1855, based on eight Latin manuscripts and one French one. Although Godefroy de Menilglaise reported that the *Monumenta Germaniae historica* had left no space for an edition of Lambert's text, Johann Heller undertook an edition not long afterward, which is dependent on Godefroy de Menilglaise in ways that are not always acknowledged.[235] It should be regarded as a revised version of Godefroy de Menilglaise's edition. Finally, Marie-Françoise Bordat completed a critical edition, based on the Vatican manuscript, in 1970 as a thesis for the Ecole des Chartes. Her edition has never been published, and I have been unable to consult it.

This translation is based on Heller's edition, but in the notes I have greatly depended on Godefroy de Menilglaise's work, as did Heller. The two editions are cited separately in the notes to the translation as "Godefroy" and "Heller."

Comments on the Translation

Do not be surprised, fathers and lords, and particularly you chaplains and clerics, if in the recollection of this privilege I shape my words less aptly. For when words are translated word for word from one language to another, even by a learned or eloquent man, they are presented less properly and less elegantly. Most of all this happens when they are laid out in the vernacular, no matter how well they have been understood or grasped by the clergy.[236]

Lambert's words acknowledge what all translators feel at one time or another as they work: that thoughts expressed in one language can be rendered only approximately, and perhaps unsatisfactorily, in another. On the humble level of the individual word translation is complex, since the semantic fields of supposedly synonymous words almost never coincide completely. Moreover, the structure of a language and the context in which it was (or is) written make possible effects of style and narrative strategies that defy translation. This is particularly true, as Lambert noted, for translations from Latin into the vernacular, and never more so than when the translation is created for a modern audience used to "sound bites" and impatient with syntactic complexity and slow narrative.

The issue extends beyond language, of course, because medieval writers of Latin were part of a very restricted educational elite. They represent only a small percentage of those who knew and used Latin and an even tinier portion of the population at large.[237] Facility in writing Latin was the end of a lengthy process of educational indoctrination, which included wide reading in classical and Christian texts. A written text, therefore, was frequently intended to signal this profound cultivation to its readers; Lambert's text is no exception.

In addition, Lambert wrote for his contemporaries, assuming that they knew roughly what he knew about the world he was describing. Consequently, Lambert says little about the most important political events of his day, except when he wishes to highlight the role of his heroes in them. For the most part, his narrative can be followed without any special knowledge of Franco-Flemish politics; however, when one knows the background, the stories gain in significance. To translate Lambert's work, therefore, is to attempt to translate both the cultural and political presuppositions of its author and the language in which he told his story.

Both of these enterprises present difficulties. Previous editors have identified many of Lambert's quotations and allusions, and I have reproduced their findings in this translation; quotations and allusions are written in italics in the text. I have also explained the significance of some of the mythical and biblical figures he refers to, given regnal years or obits for political and ecclesiastical figures (when available), and explained contemporary phenomena. However, the modern reader obviously cannot enjoy the pleasure of recognition of a classical allusion or the easy understanding of both the explicit and the tacit description of society that an educated contemporary of Lambert's would have felt.

The stylistic features of Lambert's writing present a different problem. Whereas many Latin historians renounced "rhetoric" (however disingenuously), and thus wrote in a relatively plain style,[238] Lambert's style is possible only in Latin, for his sentence structure takes full advantage of the properties of a synthetic language. The sentences are long—much too long in the eyes of many modern English stylists—and full of parenthetic passages and complex subordination. They often contain five or more participial phrases or strings of phrases modifying a single noun. When he mentions an individual, Lambert may follow the mention (generally by rank or by pronoun) with a description of the person's father or mother, siblings, children, and/or earlier or later deeds and then only after that the name, before continuing with the individual's actions in the situation at hand. Lambert's characters move in a wash of participial and predicative activity that defines their place in his world and their relationship to others. Furthermore, Lambert may have had some legal education, for his frequent use of two coordinated verbs to express a single action makes his prose read like legal boiler-plate. (It is worth remembering that Lambert was writing in a language honed by a millennium of use as a legal language and in a period in which Roman law was being enthusiastically studied.) To complicate matters, Lambert often separates the two verbs, placing the second of the two verbs at the end of his sentence. He often uses several words where one would do, e.g., "the poor of wretched condition" rather than "the wretched poor," which conveys the same idea. Finally, Lambert occasionally inserts poetry in the midst of his prose narrative, sometimes a single line, but sometimes more extended verses. Some of these are quotations from classical writers, while others are apparently his own compositions. He employs many elaborate figures of speech and metaphors involving figures from classical myth. He loves plays on words and alliterations.

The result is a very rich brew for someone attuned to the pleasures of highly stylish and artificial writing. Lambert's style continually calls attention to itself, to its artfulness, to his role as its author. It is "writerly." This kind of writing, however, is bound not to satisfy the tastes of the ordinary modern reader, who prefers a more "readerly" text. This is a shame, because Lambert knows how to tell a good story.

Translating Lambert's prose presents many of the problems also to be found in the works of the great court writers of his era. No literal translation of Lambert's prose into English would be comprehensible, much less readable, to a modern reader. And so, although some readers may murmur against me, I have committed a large number of translator's sins. I have tried to keep some of the characteristics of the language (no doubt, too many for some readers!), but I have taken many liberties with Lambert's prose, in the process doing serious violence to many aspects of Lambert's style. I have broken up Lambert's very long sentences and have often sacrificed Lambert's complicated syntax. Many of the participial phrases have been rendered using conjugated verbs. I have rearranged many of the phrases, which inevitably changes Lambert's emphases; in the process many of his better effects have been lost. The relationship between individuals in Lambert's sentences is often made clear by the cases of the words; since English has only a limited case system, I have often supplied a proper or common noun where Lambert uses only a pronoun or the pronoun implicit in a verb to clarify who is doing what to whom. I have sometimes translated participial phrases into full clauses. Where Lambert uses two verbs, I have occasionally used only one, particularly if the verbs seem almost identical. I have explained puns and wordplay in the notes, but have not attempted to replicate them. I have sometimes changed passive constructions into active ones, shifting the emphasis to the agent from the object, and turned negative statements into their corresponding positive ones. The historic present is entirely gone—although it quickens the pace in Latin, it sounds affected to modern readers. I must, however, echo the despairing words of a much superior translator, M. R. James, about his translation of the *Courtier's Trifles* of Walter Map: "These obvious expedients have not completely succeeded, even in my own opinion, let alone that of critics, in freeing my author from cumbrousness and obscurity."[239] However, I have retained, I think, Lambert's dryly ironic tone.

In other ways I have adapted Lambert's text to English usage. I have generally translated the authorial "we" as "I," since the former sounds stilted to modern ears. However, this obscures one feature of the text, for in putting words in the mouth of Walter of Le Clud (chapters 97–146) Lambert often uses the first person singular, rather than the plural, whereas for his own narrative, he invariably uses the plural, even when talking of events in which he was personally involved. As far as finer points are concerned, I have chosen to give an English equivalent for most personal names; that is, Guifridus becomes Geoffrey, Matildis becomes Matilda and so forth. A few, like Ingelramnus, have been put in a French form (Enguerrand), where there is no English equivalent. Some have been left in the Latin, as in the case of Rosella, and a few have been "Englished," that is, deprived of their Latin ending but otherwise left unchanged (for example, Oilard for Oilardus). In other words, I have not followed a consistent rule, but have instead chosen what seems right to my ear.

The name Arnold/Arnulf requires a particular comment. The two names were different versions of the same name, one generally used in Flemish or German-speaking regions, the other generally used in French-speaking regions. Lambert, as we might expect of a man on a linguistic border, uses both. Although in the introduction above and in the index, counts of Flanders who bore that name are called "Arnulf," while counts of Guines and lords of Ardres are called "Arnold," in the translation itself I have followed Lambert's usage, translating "Arnulfus" as "Arnulf," and "Arnoldus" as "Arnold" where these names occur. The reader should be aware that someone referred to as "Arnulf" in one place may be called "Arnold" in another.

I have given the modern form of the place name, where the place still exists, although the modern sources differ in their spellings of the modern place-names and I have, of necessity, had to choose one. When places have both a French and Flemish name, I have generally chosen the French version, at the risk of offending Flemish speakers. Thus I have preferred "Furnes" over "Veurne" and "Courtrai" over "Kortrijk," although I have preferred "Aalst" to the French "Alost." However, I have used the English "Ghent" rather than the French "Gand" or the Flemish "Gent." I have, for the most part, followed Godefroy de Menilglaise's place-name identifications.

To describe the ruling family of an area, Lambert often simply uses a geographic adjective; for example, he uses *Alembonenses* (the people of Alembon) to describe the grandchildren of Adele of Selnesse by her first marriage.[240] I have translated this variously as "the family of Alembon" or sometimes in other cases, the "lineage of Alembon." However, in some contexts, where such a term refers to the followers of a lord, I have translated this phrase as "the people of Alembon," or "the men of Alembon" (the latter where there is a military connection). The various ways these kinds of terms can be translated reflect a truth Marc Bloch noted long ago, the parallelism of ties of kinship and of dependence.[241]

I have tried to be true to terms that Lambert uses to describe dependent relationships. I have translated *fidelis* as "faithful man," and *homo* as "man." Where the term "fief" appears, it is always a translation of the word *feodum*. Where the expression "as a fief" appears, it is always a translation of the term *feodaliter*. I have translated the terms *pertinenciis* and *appendenciis* as "dependent properties" and "associated rights" rather than "appurtenances" or "appendages." I hope the less technical terms will give the nonspecialist reader a sense of the complexity of property rights in the Middle Ages.

I have sometimes translated Lambert's biblical quotations directly from his Latin, rather than using a standard translation, because the modern translations do not entirely conform to the text of the Vulgate, and Lambert's quotations are frequently engineered to mesh with his own text. However, I have given modern psalm numbers where these differ from the Vulgate numeration. The translations of classical passages are my own.

Lambert does not give many hard and fast dates, but when he does, he invariably specifies that he is dating from the Incarnation, which I have translated as "anno domini" or "a. d." dating.

Finally, I hope the reader will indulge me, for I have translated Lambert's quantitative poetry into English rhymed meter. When Lambert's contemporaries turned away from writing in poetry to writing in prose, denouncing poetry as the language of lies, they had in mind among other things the way the poet is forced to change meaning to accommodate a rhyme or metrical scheme. They were assuredly right. While my verse renderings approximate the meaning of Lambert's verse, they do not fully capture it, and they add to Lambert's words things he has not said, although not, I hope, in a way that violates his meaning. The reader should therefore be forewarned that my translation of the poetry is considerably freer than my translation of the prose. Nonetheless, I find it appropriate to celebrate Lambert's defiant resistence to the taxonomic thinking of his contemporaries with similar abandon. Perhaps in reading my amateur verses the reader will find some of the pleasure that this amateur poet took in composing them.

THE HISTORY OF THE
COUNTS OF GUINES AND
LORDS OF ARDRES

Here begins the prologue of Lambert, priest of the church of Ardres, concerning the history of Guines and Arnold of Guines.

Although I am entangled and fettered by the affairs of my household duty and so ought to forego the responsibility of writing, nevertheless, I bow to your frequent requests, most vigorous of knights, Arnold of Guines, who are our patrician and lord,[1] and undertake this arduous work, the matter of your most outstanding lineage.[2] I am not unaware of my presumption in taking this matter on, particularly since I see that my small wit is insufficient to execute such a work. I also predict that I will be slashed by the *pale teeth of baying rivals* [cf. Horace, *Epistles*, 5.47], particularly since in the past the most well-known clerics of the land of Guines left this material untouched and pristine, and since I have chosen to treat the report of old people more than what I have seen myself, at least until the end of the work. Indeed, I intend to commemorate not only what I have seen, but what I have heard and know and what our fathers have told me.[3]

For since I am illuminated and made certain by the more lucid ray of the truth, I neither dread nor worry about opposing the writings of certain fabulists, which have been discovered written down in detail or briefly and corruptly here and there in the margins or at the ends of books, or on loose little sheets, or in charters (albeit among authentic and divine writings).[4] I also take care to explain and elucidate the less clear, keeping silent concerning the clear and obvious. Therefore, because I cannot confront all who whet their malevolent tongues on me, nor clarify the chronicles of the regions, notes from the provinces, and statements from the localities for every individual nor respond on every point, I do not doubt that I will be rebuked and reviled by envious and pedantic people, who argue that I sometimes pursue excessive brevity and sometimes lapse into profligate prolixity and thus often depart from the truth.

Perhaps they will challenge me, because I am about to treat the history of Guines, as to why I have begun my narrative with Arnold the Great or the Old, the count of Flanders,[5] or rather with a certain Walbert, formerly the count of the people of Ponthieu and Thérouanne (or Saint-Pol) and Guines, who lived almost two hundred years before Arnold the Great—even though this same Walbert, according to the careful calculation of the chronicles of Flanders, ruled the dominion of Guines two hundred years and more before Siegfried (who is, after Walbert, opined and said to be the progenitor of the nobility of Guines).[6] For Siegfried undoubtedly sprang from the kin of this same Walbert, and at last, after many years, having been promised by a long anticipation, he was received with joy into his paternal inheritance at Guines, without the knowledge of Arnold the Great (or the Old). I do not judge this event to be worthy of astonishment, since the Danes also still wait with similar anticipation and after the span of many years hope and expect to be restored and returned to the kingdom of the English, which they captured before whenever and by whatever means they could.[7]

They will also bring forth against me the many years lying between Walbert and Siegfried. They will also challenge me, as though I dared to make a determination concerning uncertainties, about what authors I have leaned upon, that I should dare to commemorate such a noble genealogy hidden and unknown for so long to more prudent authors — or rather, to more simpleminded ones! — since Siegfried was the count of Guines almost 233 years before I turned my writer's pen to this work, but Count Walbert lived two hundred years and more before Siegfried, as I have just said above.

I bear it *with patience* [Eph. 4:2] in accordance with the apostle and respond, even though I am caught between the hammer and the anvil, to those who oppose me (albeit wickedly) and grow indignant and demand where or whence I have gotten this, and who, when the clamor has died down, murmur against me: Who does not know that Moses, the lawgiver, teacher, and leader of the Israelite people, and the narrator of the creation of the world, was born in the time of Pharaoh many years after the flood and then prospered throughout all Egypt by his wit and through divine grace? Nevertheless, this man, undertaking to treat divine genesis beginning with Adam, who was created in the image and likeness of God 2242 years before the time of the flood (according to the careful and infallible calculation and truth of the Hebrews), began and spoke, "*In the beginning God created heaven and earth.*" [Gen. 1:1] And thus after the creation of the first man and the multiplication of the many men of his posterity, he continued his treatise to this same Pharaoh, and from there he sprang forth and mounted higher. Nor can there be discovered a single man numbered among the wise who in reading asks where Moses received speech of such divinity or its secret, since the Holy Spirit breathed it into him, and Moses made it known and asserted to others that it was written by the finger of God for him.[8]

Again, Ovid studied and wrote books in the time of Germanicus Caesar. Nevertheless, as he strove to recover the grace of this same Caesar (from which he had fallen by sinning a trifle), intending to praise Caesar through the nobility of his family, he began in a more lofty fashion. Shortly to treat cosmography from the origin of the world, he began, continuing his narrative below after his theme and invocation (as authors customarily do), and said:

Before there was the sea or land or sky
That all things else embraces from on high,
In all the world the face of nature was one,
That they called chaos.⁹

Moreover, calling upon the help of divine spirits, he said,

Gods, inspire these things I have begun,
And lead my song to my times ere it's done,
From the beginning.¹⁰

And then he moved forward in an appropriate way to that Germanicus whom he intended to praise and for whose grace he began this work.

But no one speaks condemning Ovid's writ;
Instead he reads, rereads, and prizes it.
The spirit bears changed forms in bodies new.¹¹

So also that most marvelous and learned of poets (who was imitated to perfection in the divine *Aeneid*), Homer, was born many years after the destruction of Troy, as Cornelius Africanus witnesses — or rather Pindar, and Dares Phrygius.¹² Nevertheless, he described and expounded the story of the destruction of Troy fully and elegantly. Nor did Virgil ask anyone where Homer found or received this so very truthful fable.¹³ So also our Priscian, the rhetorician, glories that he is the imitator of Appolonius and Herodian;¹⁴ however, they flourished in the grammatical art among their people in Greece a long time before Priscian. And there are innumerable others like this. Indeed, the ancient authors did not trouble themselves about this; for them, *a thousand years were the same as the day that ended yesterday.* [Ps. 90:4] Thus, they boldly and confidently wrote about and expounded the long-ago deeds of the ancients in the same way as contemporary ones, with *one and the same Spirit working and dictating in them, who apportions to each one as he wishes, where he wishes, and when he wishes.* [1 Cor. 12:11]

However, I believe in a most true prophecy: Malicious envy will hamper me to no small degree and earnestly wrinkle its nose in derision at the innocence of my name,¹⁵ because I have undertaken to measure out a course of almost 233 years. But these people do not know that our more ancient authors in their own times treated a course of 2395 years and perhaps more in writing. Of these, Eusebius is the first and most important; then after him, his imitator Jerome; after these, Prosper, the monk Sigebert, and the venerable priest Bede[16] (Not, however,

> That I am so demented as to claim
> That I could equal men of such great name!)

For they thoroughly taught the chronology of many realms, namely of the Hebrews, of the Gentiles, and of the Latins. However, I will briefly and succinctly compile only the deeds of the illustrious counts and also the nobles of our most august county, unless incidentally, because of certain occurrences in the narrative I have undertaken, I need to extend my quill far from our nest in writing.

If they persist in the zeal of their malice and argue that I write things no one has ever heard of, or even that I make events up or write fiction, I say that if they should hear old matters that they haven't heard or known about that they accuse me of excerpting furtively from books of commentaries, I will cry out and say, "I have won! I have won!" For it is an act of great prowess in some way to tear Hercules's club from him in order to shorten — or rather to broaden — the path of a new work and a labor one has undertaken.[17] Thus they have judged, whether they want to or not, that I am supported by the authority of certain writers. If, however, they again complain that I compose novelties (which I cannot completely deny) and they conjecture that the sequence of the chronology (which frequently touches on many matters) has been changed or distorted by a reversed order of narration or that suitable names for the princes or for other matters have been drawn, as it were, from elsewhere or even invented, I would say this. If there is something here that sets their teeth on edge,[18] these people whom no one can satisfy except someone who is totally habituated to writing or composing, let them diligently seek the truth from those same people from whom we have never at any time imbibed anything but the truth. Or if something I have heard from someone or other displeases them, let them read no further.[19]

Nevertheless,

> *Good Homer sometimes nods,*[20]

and we have scarcely been able to find a poet who speaks so very eloquently in any time, as Jerome says. Therefore, in this case, I piously implore the reader and strenuously insist that he examine this work before he judges it and go through it for a second time before condemning it. Indeed, an ill-advised rush to judgment, as they say, deprives the verdict of its honor and impugns the judge.

To you, therefore, most loving prince and lord, who are the beginning, end, and reward of the work I have undertaken, to *you who are my glory; to you who raise my head* above my enemies [Ps. 3:4]; to you who are my shield and my protector; to you, lord, I say, I entrust and devote this work taken up by me in the sweat of my brow, so that, if there is any glory to be found in reading it, *not to us, lord, do not grant the glory to us, but to your name.* [Ps. 115] Indeed, I do not seek my own glory, but yours, and that of your no less glorious father and his most noble progeny, and that of your progeny, so that the Father and Son and Holy Spirit may be glorified by all people and in all things, *one God and the Lord of all* [Eph. 4:6], *who magnifies* and glorifies *the well-being of kings* [Ps. 17:51] in magnificence and glory forever. Amen.

Here ends the Prologue

Here begins the preface of that same Lambert, priest of the church of Ardres, addressed to that same Arnold, concerning the history of Guines.

In these circumstance, I have pondered the fact that

The years, like flowing streams, go rolling on,
Time cannot be called back when it is gone,[21]

and I remember that all things under heaven are fleeting and transitory in time, unless they are set down in letters,[22] and that those things that the attention of mortals now seizes upon, when the hand is turned from them, are forgotten in the blink of an eye. And I remember that the memorable names and deeds of noteworthy and illustrious men, namely of the counts of Guines and no less the lords of Ardres, are almost completely entirely effaced — for shame! — from common memory, because of the feeble envy (or perhaps the negligence) of writers. And so I have undertaken, to the degree that I am able and am made knowledgeable by truthful narrative testimony, to commemorate and write what is glorious, honorable, and necessary to the praise and glory of these noble men and their memorable successors, and no less our contemporaries, and above all else of you, most loving prince and lord, Arnold of Guines, for whom I labor. I will insert in the proper place and time

material concerning the foundations of the churches, both those of Guines
and those of the surrounding region.

Here ends the Preface

Here begin the chapters in the history of Guines

1. Of Baldwin the Bald and of the division of Flanders and Boulogne.
2. Of Arnold the Great, the son of that same Baldwin the Bald.
3. Of Count Walbert.
4. That the monks of Saint-Bertin allege that all Guines is theirs in alms.
5. Of the building of the cell and the construction of the church at Escales.
6. That the land of Guines, which was deserted and deprived of closely related heirs, was drawn back into the hands of the Flemish.
7. How Siegfried came from Denmark to Guines.
8. How Siegfried built a keep at Guines and surrounded and protected it
   with an earthwork.[23]
9. How Arnold the Great took it badly when he knew that Siegfried was
   ruling at Guines.
10. That Arnold the Great and Siegfried became friends.
11. How Siegfried impregnated Elftrude and died at Guines.
12. How Baldwin's son Arnold took charge of his paternal aunt Elftrude and
    Ardulf, her son and Siegfried's, and how Arnold gave him all of Brede-
    narde as a godfather's present.
13. A description of Bredenarde.
14. How Ardulf married Matilda, the daughter of Count Erniculus of Bou-
    logne.
15. A refutation of those who say that Erniculus divided his lands among his
    three sons.
16. How Ralph was born and became count of Guines.
17. How Ralph married Rosella, the daughter of the count of Saint-Pol, and
    had Eustace by this same Rosella.
18. How Ralph, who lived too prodigally, was unjust and hateful to his
    people, and died not a timely but a miserable death through their curses.
19. How Eustace, when he became the count, both appeared to be and was
    most gentle toward the people.
20. Of Count Rainier of Boulogne.
21. How Rainier killed Humphrey of Ordres.

Therefore, to the praise and glory and honor of the counts of Guines and the magnates of Ardres, beginning my narrative with one Arnold, I have decided to end the labor of the work I have undertaken with that other Arnold, namely the man for whom I write, to whom I have attributed the glory of this work, who is, as I have already said and will say as long as I am able to speak, our patrician and lord. But so that I may more properly get to the business of this project, let me turn my pen to certain other things, which are by no means alien to my project, although they are more lofty.

1. Of Baldwin the Bald, the division of Flanders and Boulogne, and other matters.

Therefore, just as one may learn and find out from the most commended chronicles of Flanders, *when Baldwin the Bald, who was simultaneously count of Flanders, Boulogne, and Thérouanne, died, his sons Arnold* (who I mentioned before was called the Great or the Old) *and Ardulf divided their father's land, which was called by these three names.*[27] *Arnold, who was older, took Flanders, but Ardulf took Boulogne and Thérouanne together. But when Ardulf died without children or bodily heirs and was buried at Saint-Bertin, Arnold took his county in hand.*[28] (These items, none other than what I found out by reading from time to time in the annal books of the chronicles, or learned from authentic, aged, and truthful fathers, or, toward the end, saw with my own eyes, I note down in my work, mixing fictions with authentic writings and thus heaping labor on labor.)

2. Of Arnold the Great, the son of that same Baldwin the Bald.

And because as we have said, *this Arnold the Great or the Old was the third count after Baldwin Fierebras,*[29] *he is reckoned to be the sixth count* and palatine *in the lineage after Lideric of Harlebeke, who was appointed the first count of Flanders in 792 a. d.*[30] Spreading his hand over all parts of Flanders, Lideric attached the estates of Guines to the empire under his sway. And thus indeed Lideric's successors did the same.

3. Of Count Walbert.

As one may find in the oldest records, Count Walbert held by hereditary right the counties of Ponthieu and Saint-Pol, as well as all the land from Arques to the boundary of Escales and from both sides to the western sea.[31] This included the farm of Sythiu,[32] which a certain very rich man named Adroald granted to blessed Omer, who was then the bishop of Thérouanne. Walbert gave the village of Arques with its associated rights, Sythiu, Longuenesse, Quelmes, Acquin, Coyecques, Audenfort, Escales, and many other properties in free alms to the holy man Bertin of blessed memory.[33] St. Bertin raised Walbert's son from the baptismal font and received him as a son by adoption; he named and called the boy Bertin. And Walbert, along with his son Bertin, made an offering pleasing to God at Sythiu in the monastery recently built under the administration of blessed Bertin in honor of the apostles Peter and Paul and made himself a monk.

4. That the monks of Saint-Bertin allege that all Guines is theirs in alms.

After this action had been carried out, the monks of the aforementioned place spoke under their breaths among themselves and showed their agreement with their eyes, for they did not dare to speak aloud, primarily saying that they ought to possess the lands, scrub, woods, tithes, rents, and other little possessions that are now in Guines, as though Walbert had conferred upon this place and their foundation all of his estates—which are now called Guines. But for all that, they said this particularly because the mother church of the fortress of Guines was founded and built in memory and veneration of their father and patron St. Bertin. However, more particularly and as though putting forward a stronger case, they said that the count of Guines should hold the fortress of Guines of them by hereditary right for an annual rent of a quarter mark or five shillings, inasmuch as it was the capital and lynchpin of the county of Guines.[34]

Nevertheless, so that this foolishly erroneous viewpoint shall not spread and extend like a sucker from a plant, I say this to those seeking and wisely believing the truth. From the long-ago time of Count Walbert, the monks had a steward or provost in Guines, whom their more ancient writings call their vassal. He reported to them as a steward concerning all the tithes and little possessions which they held there. For a long time, he held land liable for rent payments[35] near the keep of the fortress of Guines. But later on, when Siegfried, the founder of the noble family of Guines, wanted to surround the keep or the fortress of the stronghold of Guines with a double earthwork and there was not enough space on his own property to complete it, he exchanged other land with the steward of that time for the land near the keep, and thus at length he finished the earthwork. And so he gave the aforementioned monks one quarter mark or five shillings each year as payment for that land, which contained almost eighty yokes or square perches.[36] When Siegfried became the count of Guines, he left the overseer's or provost's job to the steward and his heirs, from whom the stewardship or the provost's office once again passed down to the lords of Ardres, who hold it to this day.[37] For that reason, the founder of the church of Ardres, the outstanding Arnold, was called the advocate or provost in the monks' charters and ours, namely in Guines.[38] Because of the grace of this business, toward the end of his life, Arnold became a monk at Saint-Bertin, and at length died and was buried there.

5. Of the building of the cell and the construction of the church at Escales.

Hence it was that the monks built themselves a little dwelling, a cell, and a church almost at the edge of their holding, not far from the seashore, either to commemorate this transaction or to create a stronghold in honor and under the patronage of their father and patron, St. Bertin, almost as though they were supposed to hold the land lying in between from Arques on all sides as far as Escales as a gift under the same condition. (The much mentioned Count Walbert [who is nevertheless about to be mentioned again] gave them that village, along with Audenfort, in a similar fashion.) But since it is characteristic of *the stupid, of whom there is always an infinite number* [Ec. 1:15],[39] to give a definitive opinion in doubtful matters, I now bow concerning these declarations and poorly defined matters to those inquiring most carefully, those who have at some time truly studied and read the confessions of the venerable father, abbot, and count Walbert at Luxueil, which Walbert himself named Luxueil "the light of the sheep," because of the sanctity of the inhabitants.[40] I, however, shall return to the chronology as God has granted it and as I know it from a true narrative.

6. That the land of Guines, which was deserted and deprived of closely related heirs, was drawn back into the hands of the Flemish.

After Count Walbert of beloved and worthy memory had become a monk in the monastery of Sythiu and was raised to the honor of the priesthood, he was chosen by God and appointed the abbot of Luxueil in Burgundy, succeeding St. Austasius. At the same time, his immediate heirs stayed for a while with Walbert's son Bertin, and then, as seems clear to those who investigate carefully, scattered all over the place. It does not pertain to my project to speak concerning them about each one of them in detail, but I have no doubt that many of their names are written in heaven. Afterward St. Faro, this same Walbert's brother, became bishop of Meaux, and the remains of the land left to him by his brother came to him by right of kinship.[41] He built a monastery of monks at Estrouanne, just as the history of Meaux attests, near the port across from Great Britain that in the vernacular is called Wissant because of its white sand.[42] (It was later burned and torn to the ground for its sins by the army of warriors attacking Gormond and Isembard.)[43] Then he rendered his spirit to God and bones to the earth, along with his sister, the blessed virgin Fara,[44] but they left no progeny behind.

When the course of a great many years had passed, the land of Guines, which was almost deserted and destitute of a ruler and proper lord, was then in great part drawn back into Flemish hands. For that reason both the estates of Saint-Omer that were divinely donated to and conferred upon St. Omer by Adroald, and no less the estates of Arques with their associated rights that were piously donated and granted in the Lord to St. Bertin by Count Walbert, which are almost cut off from the body of Flanders by the entirety of the land of Guines, are indivisibly attached and conjoined to the regions of Flanders to this day. The estates of Eperlecques were given as a fief to the count of Boulogne by the counts of Flanders and the estates of Nord-Ausque were given to the castellan of Saint-Omer.[45] The estates of Mentque and Cahem were resigned into the hands of the count of Warenne and were taken as a fief by him, without anyone gainsaying it to the present time and many other estates were similarly taken as fiefs by the barons and knights of this land. Also many that had been given to churches in alms and that had been purchased with money by churches were chartered in perpetual possession. Count Arnold, surnamed the Great or the Old, usurped for himself and won for Flanders all the other estates in the orbit of Guines, as though they were deserted and were held to be of no account by their legitimate heir. Thus indeed, as I have already said, his predecessors had done from the time of Lideric, the first count of Flanders. After Count Walbert bade farewell to the world and to his property along with the world, Lideric joined Guines to Flanders and usurped it for himself and placed his own steward in Guines. However, in that time when the aforementioned count of Flanders, Arnold the Great, was ruling the princes and people of Flanders, God had mercy on the people of Guines who were devoutly calling out to him. In the end he procured an heir, who issued forth by proper and hereditary succession, for the people of Guines.

7. How Siegfried came from Denmark to Guines.

In 928 a. d., while the aforesaid Arnold the Great ruled the Flemish and Bishop Stephen of pious memory held the pastoral staff at Thérouanne,[46] there was a certain man named Siegfried.[47] He was noble in spirit and notable in family, for he came from the blood of the aforementioned Walbert, count of the people of Ponthieu, Thérouanne — or Saint-Pol — and Guines. (Although to those who denigrate and envy me the lineage may seem to go far back, it is known and held as certain by those who record the true genealogy in writing and who to this time keep the verisimilar and memorable truth in memory.) Because he served the king of the Danes for many years, he was surnamed "the Dane." He was a man quite active in preparedness for war and he was very famous and well-known throughout Denmark, because he was the nephew and brother-in-law of the king and the king's advisor; he was second in status after the king.[48] He had for a long time and long since heard in his ears and received here and there from fame's shining pen and the truest testimony of genealogical writing the outcome of the business concerning his long-ago predecessor, Count Walbert, and also Walbert's son Bertin and Walbert's brother Faro and sister Fara. He knew that the count of Flanders, Arnold the Great had unjustly usurped the county of the land of Guines, just as his predecessors had done, and that he held it in his power to that time, Guines, which Siegfried had learned pertained and belonged to him by hereditary succession. So Siegfried gathered knights and retainers, both from his family and unrelated men, left Denmark and the honor of the royal court, and went hastily to the land of Guines, as it was his own property, left to him by his ancestors by hereditary right, owed to him, most justly belonging to him, and awaiting him for these reasons, although Guines was wooded and uncultivated and inhabited by few residents up to this time. He occupied it; he had no eyes for the counties of Ponthieu or Thérouanne (Saint-Pol).

8. How Siegfried built a keep at Guines and surrounded and protected it with an earthwork.

And when he saw that through the negligence of his predecessors the land was unprotected and that it was exposed on every side to the assaults of whatever enemies there might be, and that the citadel of Guines was not fortified by a rampart or fortress, he first raised a very sturdy defensive motte and encircled and enclosed it with a double earthwork. Without consulting the count of Flanders, Arnold the Great (of whom I made mention earlier), he laid claim, as was truly proper, to the whole land of Guines by his own authority, and subjugated it to his dominion's jurisdiction.

9. How Arnold the Great took it badly when he knew that Siegfried was ruling at Guines.

When Arnold the Great (or the Old), the count of Flanders, heard that Siegfried possessed the lordship of Guines, he was so angry and so swollen with the force of his intense bitterness and indignation, that he could scarcely bear for Siegfried to go unpunished. But first, Arnold hastily sent messengers and had Siegfried summoned to him. Accordingly, when Siegfried had received the messengers of the lord of Flanders with celebration and congeniality, he listened attentively with ears by no means deaf to the envoys' message, and he understood fairly clearly the indignation of the great prince. Then as a wise man does, he spoke with the more discerning people in his land, consulting thoroughly with them about what ought to be done about this situation. Whether he was confident in himself or fearful, he put his faith always in the Lord God and in the power of His virtue, and so following the advice of the wiser and more authoritative elders, Siegfried gathered his kin and close friends and went unafraid to the prince of the Flemish dominion. He found Arnold in the village of Sythiu, where this prince frequently stayed, amusing himself and joking in the midst of the most important magnates of the province.

When Siegfried saw and recognized him, he remembered that *fortune favors the bold.*[49] (Oh, how worthy of memory was the audacity of that spirited man!) Leaping boldly into the midst of the group, he greeted the prince and his people very elegantly and urbanely, with his head bowed in respect toward Arnold. The knights together with the nobles of the Flemish court and no less the entourage of the aforementioned heroic prince — Siegfried, like a prudent and foresighted man had enlisted and prepared them to aid him — received the man with benign favor, showing him respectful attention, and with carefully marked enthusiasm strove to commend him to their prince. The king of Denmark's brother, a certain man named Cnut, who was also Siegfried's nephew, his close kinsman, and dearest friend, toward whom Siegfried had often shown the most enthusiastic respect when he was in Denmark,[50] stood before the prince with the other knights and along with them poured forth such support for Siegfried, that Arnold's rage was calmed and his furious indignation put to flight. He then showed a kindly and peaceful face to Siegfried, who was properly a man worthy of respect. Having grasped Siegfried's right hand, Arnold greeted Siegfried and his men in return.[51]

10. That Arnold the Great and Siegfried became friends.

Thus they became friends on that day, and Siegfried at once did homage with appropriate reverence to the prince of Flanders for the lordship of Guines. And he was so fully received into Arnold's grace that he was kept by Arnold as a companion of honor and was made his familiar and courtier. And since he was discreet in his advice, illustrious in his prudence, munificent in his generosity, and exceptional in the complete integrity of his character, he was the second in both name and fact after the prince in the court of Flanders.[52] At length, when the most reverend count of Flanders, Arnold the Great, was taken from their midst, Siegfried remained with his son Baldwin.[53] And because his father had loved Siegfried with a fervent love and honored him in many ways above many others, Baldwin loved Siegfried with all the greater love and the more ardent affection.

11. How Siegfried impregnated Elftrude and died at Guines.

Now then, the aforementioned Count Baldwin had a sister of wonderful beauty named Elftrude, for whom Siegfried pined with great love.[54] She was named after the Elftrude who was once the wife of Baldwin Fierebras.[55] After many of the colloquies of love and furtive pleasures of desire, at last, disporting without force, he took her by force and secretly impregnated her. (She did not want to want him, or rather, she wanted not to want him.) When the matter became public knowledge and was manifest, Siegfried feared for himself and, not daring to await his lord and count, returned to his territory and got as far as Guines. After he wasted away there for a short time with a disease caused by his intemperate and secret love, he showed himself to be another Andrew of Paris and died a miserable death.[56] When a few days had passed, his lord Count Baldwin of Flanders, who had caught smallpox, also died and was buried at Saint-Bertin. Consequently, Baldwin left behind as the heir to Flanders his son, Arnold, who had been conceived and borne by Matilda, the daughter of Duke Herman of Saxony. Arnold was the father of Baldwin the Bearded.[57]

12. How Baldwin's son Arnold took care of his paternal aunt Elftrude and Ardulf, her son and Siegfried's, and how Arnold gave him all of Bredenarde as a godfather's present.

Then, when this Arnold, who was already an adolescent, found out that his aunt Elftrude was pregnant and that Siegfried of Guines had died a miserable death, he occupied Guines,[58] and pitying his aunt Elftrude, he took her under his care. Now, Elftrude bore a son, whom Count Arnold of Flanders raised from the baptismal font and upon whom he imposed and laid the name Ardulf. Arnold took care of Ardulf and his mother in every way.[59] So the boy grew up and was called Ardulf of Guines, as a token of the future. Then, when Ardulf became an adolescent and was growing in manly strength — his mother was now dead — he so rose in the love of Count Arnold of Flanders, who was his first cousin and godfather, that Arnold, swearing him in with military oaths, made him a knight, and appointed him as count of Guines. Over and above that, Arnold increased Ardulf's lands and made his territory larger.[60]

13. A description of Bredenarde.

Now, there was in those days a fairly broad and wide pasture between the river called the Vonna [the Aa] on the east, and the springs of the Nielles on the west, and between the river called the Reveria [the Hem] to the south, to the other side of a marsh that spread and extended far and wide on the north. (The Reveria was called this, meaning "the possession for true men," because of the river's pleasant effect, or "in truth.")[61] Because of the fertility of the grass, the pasture was very useful for feeding the herds and flocks from the surrounding areas, although these were few as yet. So this land was called Bredenarde in the vernacular, because of the breadth of the pasture.[62] It was inhabited only by the odd inhabitant and up to this time few peasants cultivated it, or almost none. So the memorable count Arnold of Flanders (the father of Baldwin the Bearded, as I just said) gave this land to Ardulf, his first cousin and godson, to possess freely and to hold forever by hereditary right, so that Arnold might increase his own honor and that of his kinsman,[63] make Guines larger, and also increase Ardulf's fief.

14. *How Ardulf married Matilda, the daughter of Count Erniculus of Boulogne.*

And so, a few days later, Ardulf, burning with desire for his paternal inheritance, received permission from his lord, kinsman, and godfather, Count Arnold of Flanders, and took himself off into his country to Guines. When he had freely ruled there for a time and was glorified by a secure peace, he married Matilda, the daughter of Erniculus, the widely renowned count of Boulogne.[64]

15. *A refutation of those who say that Erniculus divided his lands among his three sons.*

One should pay no attention to those people who say, as if they were dreaming, that the man whom I just called Count Erniculus of Boulogne (said to be buried under the name of Arnulf at Saint-Vulmar in Samer-en-Bois,[65] with his two sons, namely Arnulf and Eustace, in that same place), ever held the lands of Boulogne, Saint-Pol, and Guines together at the same time and that he distributed his land proportionally to his three sons, according to how well they loved him, what their pursuits were, and how suitable their love and pursuits were.[66] When one has examined, read, and reread all the chronicles of both Flanders and Boulogne — to the extent that they are authentic — and one has heard and understood the tales and fables of many elders, one does not discover at any time or anywhere that Guines was part of or attached to Boulogne, but instead that after Count Walbert's day, it was completely subject to Flemish dominion.[67] If one asks, however, whence this barren offshoot of a notion sprang and emanated — a notion long quiescent before it came to be bruited about among the people — I answer that this view, which seems so reasonable to the simple and easy to the credulous, was born of the truth, but became a fable by degrees.[68] The people of Boulogne transformed it from the true fact of the matter into a fable for their consolation and delight — or rather they elaborated it.

For as I have read in the annals of the ancients and heard from time to time from aged fathers, when many years had passed after Count Walbert of pious recollection and worthy memory (of whom I have already spoken), who ruled and governed the land of Ponthieu and Saint-Pol and Guines, had paid the debt of the flesh, and when a dispensation had been made according to the will of God in his lands, there was a powerful count named William, born in Ponthieu of the noblest family of the Franks.[69] As he was no less famous for his bodily strength than for his noble family, he prospered and his fame spread far and wide. Since his own possessions were not enough for him, he stretched out his hand into neighboring areas with great force and fortitude. And so he subjugated all of Boulogne to his men and joined it to what lay between. Besides, he knew from old men's tales that his ancient predecessor, Count Walbert, was once so strong that justly or unjustly he exercised dominion as far as the western sea. So William got the same idea and carried out and satisfied his desire as well as he could.

Now since this William had four sons, he gave the land that is now called Ponthieu, as the most worthy and excellent part of his dominion, to the most worthy, the firstborn, because with glorious eagerness he took pleasure, as regards knighthood, in weapons and horses. To the second, because he devoted his spirit to the pursuit of the hunting occupation and said that nothing was any fun or pleasure without dogs, he gave arboreal woodlands—now called the land of Boulogne—as a fief and domain. To the third, because he was devoted to agriculture and the gathering and preserving of crops, William gave Thérouanne, which is to this day called the county of Saint-Pol, as a perpetual fief.[70]

And then, not least, William had decided to give the fourth the land called Guines, because he gave his whole attention to raising cattle and sheep and the land, partly hilly, is covered with little woods and thickets, and also has pasturelands and watery expanses of marshland. But when William heard that Siegfried, a man of the noble blood of Count Walbert, had recently come from Denmark, and that by feigning ignorance, he had rightly and manfully gotten Guines in his power, William feared for himself and wisely changed his mind. William left Siegfried in peace under the protection of Count Arnold the Great of Flanders and married his fourth son to the daughter of Reynold of Saint-Valéry-sur-Somme. These things, which come from the annals of the ancients and not from popular opinion, should be sufficient to contradict what the people of Boulogne say.

16. How Ralph was born and became count of Guines.

Then, after Matilda, the daughter of Count Erniculus of Boulogne, had married Count Ardulf of Guines, she conceived and bore him sons named Ralph and Roger. The firstborn of these, Ralph, became count of Guines when Ardulf died. The second died young, before he entered puberty. Thus, Ralph became the count of Guines. Bearing the proud stamp of the nobility of both Flanders and Boulogne, he was haughty, fierce, and warlike.[71] He belonged to a lineage of both human and divine stock, namely the Flemish — who were descended and took their origin from blood of imperial nobility, and from kings and dukes — and the lords of Boulogne — whose forebear, led to Boulogne in a heavenly manner by a real, divine swan (not by some phantasmagorical one),[72] established the beginning of a noble lineage and divine nobility. So because of the outstanding fame of the origin of his birth and of the fighting prowess of his grandiose name, this heir acted with arrogant pride, seasonably and unseasonably, zealously, diligently (or rather ardently), far and wide in the lands and territories of noble kings and princes.[73]

17. How Ralph married Rosella, the daughter of the count of Saint-Pol, and had Eustace by this same Rosella.

Now this Ralph married the daughter of the vigorous knight, Count Hugh of Saint-Pol. She was called Rosella either because of her dewy smell or her rosy coloration. By her he had the noble Eustace and other sons, who were inferior to their father in neither warlike arms nor splendor, and daughters with beautiful faces and praiseworthy bodies. In order to avoid boredom and expense, I do not plan to speak about them, nor is there space to talk specifically about the attributes of each individual. Indeed, since I propose to say nothing of them, let me turn my pen from them so that I may with my author's quill delineate Eustace, the firstborn, at greater length.

18. How Ralph, who lived too prodigally, was unjust and hateful to his people, and died not a timely but a miserable death through their rebukes.

I add this about Ralph, that he was said to be so pervaded by the trait of prodigious prodigality, that what he possessed could not suffice him. When for that reason, he did not have enough of his own property to apportion to his retinue, he rampaged among his subjects, making much more unjust exactions than was proper, slandering them unjustly, oppressing them with force, and plundering them frequently. But it happened one day that he was rushing toward France to those execrable festivals they call tournaments.[74] And coming to the traitor's mount or the fuller's mount or Philo's mount —

its vernacular name is Montfelon — near Surques,[75] he discovered a great multitude of shepherds who were gathered there because of the generous size of the pasture.[76] Then when he disguised his followers and transformed himself, using a false sort of speech and turning his head away, lest he be recognized by them, he said without greeting them first, "Alas, shepherds, what is said of the count of Guines? Is he well? Where is he? Where is he going?"

But the shepherds, as they were men of great simplicity, and meager in reason and speech, didn't look for any trap. Blurting out what they thought in their response because of their state of mind, they answered, "Alas, that man so deadly to his own land! While he strives to equal Hercules, Hector, and Achilles, he rampages among his followers, scourging and torturing and beating them. And although he is not ignorant of how *to wage war against the proud*, he little *knows to spare* his wretched subjects.[77] How can this little piece of land satisfy a man whom the whole world could not sate? Lo! now he has gone away, they say, from his own place and prepares to go to France, so that he may make his reputation more widely known and so that his name shall be known and magnified among the people. But would that he would drown in the depths of the Seine or the Loire before he returns, or that his eyes would be struck out by an ambush or arrow, so that he cannot come back to punish us further. Or may his guts be run through by the spear of some Romulus,[78] so that his noxious blood will be shed and flow into the depths of Hell!" All said this same thing:

> With one voice the companions all cry out;
> And say, "Heed, Nemesis! Bring this about!"

When the count heard this, he left much angered by the murmuring.

And so when he came to the tournament and battle grounds, it happened by a just judgment of God that in the first foray of the battle, the count received a wound in his navel and was in peril of his life. Then, when he was borne off almost dead to a place among the archers, an arrow coming from the other team pierced his right eye, and the archers from the other team prevailed. They seized the count, who was only half alive, and despoiled him. Then having given him mortal wounds, they were moved by no mercy and threw him unmercifully into the Seine, whereupon he was never to be seen again.[79] Thus, thus, it often happens, that unjust and evil men, who earn the wrath of God and the curses of their people as payment for their just deserts, against their wills lose their lives through untimely death, as God's just judgment demands. Then Eustace, hearing that his father Ralph had died a wretched and unexpected death, trembled in his spirit. But accepting a temperate moderation with respect to his abundant grief, he hastened into France without delay and looked for his father everywhere. But since he could by no means find him, he went home. And when he had received consolation for the death of his father and prudently eased his sorrow a little, he hurried to Flanders. After he had done homage with proper reverence to Prince Baldwin of Flanders (that is, Baldwin the Bearded) he returned home.

19. How Eustace, when he became count, both appeared to be and was most gentle toward his people.

Therefore, when he became the count of Guines,

He was called a not unworthy limb
Of that most noble man who sired him

except that Eustace appeared very gentle toward his people in every respect. Because he was very generous and righteous to the degree that the rigor and rectitude of justice permitted, he strove,

To show his mercy to the conquered foe;
Also to fight to lay the haughty low.[80]

Indeed, this Eustace was said to be so kindly, so peaceable, and so benevolent among his people that he was believed to have been given that name Eustace as an omen of the future, because he was said always and everywhere to persevere in goodness.[81] And for this reason, his people were wont to say, frequently praising him:

"You take your name from the reality.[82]
Live here, oh Count, and in eternity,
And to your people be forever kind.[83]

"Lest, like your father, at some time

"Accursed ills should follow close behind,

"and you should suffer bodily harm and spiritual peril because of the curses of your subjects."

Consequently, once when people were dining at Guines during the natal solemnities of the holy incarnation of the Lord Christ, they warned him to contemplate the death of Count Rainier of Boulogne with careful attention.[84] But as Eustace was benign and in every way behaved in a pious manner toward his people, he was not moved to anger, but asked them carefully, as though he were ignorant and wisely unaware of the matter, who the Rainier was of whom they spoke and how he died.

Then a certain old man, getting up their midst and motioning for silence, spoke when it had gotten quiet:

"Gentle count, I speak now with your peace,
May what I say not make your wrath increase,

"and, on the contrary, let it warn you, if you should at some time recognize your father in that man, Rainier, of whom I begin to speak.

20. Of Count Rainier of Boulogne.

"Now then, Rainier was the count of Boulogne, who rampaged among his people beyond what lords customarily do. He despised the noble men of the land, oppressing them as much as he dared or could, as though he would trample them underfoot, but by a perverse reversal of praiseworthy custom, he respected, raised, and promoted the ignoble to honors. (For shame!) He once heard, 'Depose the powerful from their seat and exalt the humble,' [Lk. 1:52] but he took the meaning literally, like the Jews.[85] He was completely submissive to royal power, and he appeared generous and openhanded when he was giving gifts with his superiors outside his land, but when he was dealing in his country with his subjects and lesser men, he grew pale and withered from floods of avarice. In one place, he stole; in another, he carried things off as spoils. He accused one man of hateful slander; he ordered another to be exiled without hope of returning. He sent one man to a squalid prison, and he tortured and hanged another one from the gallows. He was savage and bitter to his knights. To city-dwellers he was harsh and contentious. To his retinue he was truculent and tyrannical. Toward his servants he was cunning, as though he suspected them of robbery.

"And for this reason, his judges — who both feared him beyond measure, as though they were serving Satan at the time when he plummeted down and fell away from heavenly justice, and themselves raged against the people — preferred to obey tyrannical orders rather than law. One man was beaten at Boulogne. Another was punched at Devres. Another one was torn bodily from a church at Calais and cut limb from limb and castrated, and his genitals were kicked around by girls and women, as though they were playing a game of ball. Another was killed by his neighbors' swords at Merck, since the people of Oye did not come to help him. In some other place, those who complained were sent to their deaths, like pigs to the market. Thus the maddened Rainier set every sort of rage ablaze.

"He loathed the people of Boulogne and persecuted them with evil enmity. He placed a weighty burden on the people of Calais, so that either they were exiled forever or purchased from him for immeasurable sums of money whatever peace they could. He beat the people of Merck, weighed them down with iron collars, and imprisoned them in Hardrei castle. He devastated and destroyed the houses of the people of Guemps with a great fire. He insulted the people of Cayeux as rebels and wretches and tore at them with loathing and vexation. More than all the rest, he vexed, afflicted, and tortured the people of Ordres in all things. And although he was most vigorous in his knighthood, this most evil of counts inflicted these things and other similar intolerable damages and injuries upon his subjects and people, while his neighbors and the people who lived nearby trembled. It was as though he did not possess this land by right, namely, as though there was an omen that some future count would hasten and arrive from somewhere else.

21. How Rainier killed Humphrey of Ordres.

"And so made drunk by a certain barbaric passion of his embittered soul, he conspired in the murder of Humphrey of Ordres, the leader of all the people of Ordres.[86] He did this in order to satisfy the savagery of his rage in all things and to set his own life's limit by engineering the undeserved death of his own man. When he had trumped up and discovered a reason for Humphrey's death, he seized the time and place and unexpectedly shortened Humphrey by a head; he slew him with an unexpected death.

"However, when the horrible deed became manifest and word of it became openly known, Humphrey's wife planted within her female sex a manly spirit and manfully stripped the bloody and scarlet undershirt or singlet from her murdered husband. Not without tumult in her heart, she put it aside for the time being. (Oh, virtuous woman!) She showed it often to her sons, not without sobs from her embittered throat, as an instigation to avenge their father; thus, she urged and inspired them to take revenge for their father.

"But since no power long endures, it happened one day as divine vengeance urged and the day of his death approached, that Rainier, who was devoted to hunting with his huntsmen and dogs, incautiously entered the forest of Boulogne near Macquinghem. The mother of the family of Ordres, crossing upon the same road by chance, saw the count and looked upon him with malice. (Oh, the inexpressible ordering and disposition of the fates!) And urging her horses on with her spurs, she came home faster than you would have thought possible in order to accomplish what she desired. And having found her sons and also the people of Cayeux of one accord, she stirred her whole family and home into motion with ululation and tearful lamentation. And suffering no delay, she showed her sons and household her husband's shirt and told them the facts of the matter concerning the count and the place where he was hunting with a few men, and urged them, by any incitement she could, to avenge their father.

22. How the men of Ordres killed Rainier.

"The men of Ordres, therefore, rising up with the men of Cayeux, who were associated with them because they had a common and personal cause with them, crossed the forest grove here and there. When the count had been looked for everywhere and at length discovered, they pursued him up to a quarry or stone-cutting site of the margravate.[87] Following him and seizing him, they overcame him by force, and fulfilling their vow, they slew him with swords and left him cut limb from limb like a slaughtered stag for his bellowing huntsmen and baying dogs."

These things now said, they watch the count and fear,
They say to one another, "Our tale is clear."
With signs and nods they bid the old man cease,
"Your finger to your lips," he hears. "Now, peace!"

After the old man had prudently and sufficiently taught the count and his nobles the moral meaning of Count Rainier's story, the count, who was no deaf auditor of this tale, praised the old man with a few words, and said in response,

"Live long, old man; your prudent words to me,
Shall reap a harvest of morality!
May Rainier and my sire live on for ay,
And may both also reign with Christ on high.

"But I, to whom you show Rainier and to whom you intimate that he ought to be recognized in my father, will remember in future, with God's help and favor, that I will have deserved a similar death for thus ever rampaging among my people or among others." When he had said these things, the count fell silent, although his speech was noted.

As Eustace thus was proceeding from strength to strength with giant steps, as I have said, he acquired a good and notable name for himself, both in faraway places and in those nearby.

23. How Eustace married Susanna, the daughter of the chamberlain of Flanders.

Then he married the daughter of the most noble chamberlain of Flanders, Siger of Grammene,[88] who was named Susanna. She conceived and bore him Baldwin, William, Reinhelm, Adele, and Beatrice. Their father Eustace first infused them all with the liberal pursuits of letters. However, he educated his sons and arranged for them to be thoroughly schooled in military matters among the most important youths of Flanders. Since he was by no means a *man of blood or treachery*, God did not *cut short his days* [Ps. 55:23], and because he always *had the years of eternity in mind* [Ps. 77:5], he proceeded in his days and, paying the debt of the flesh when he was full of days, he ended his life with a seasonable death.[89]

24. How when Eustace died, Baldwin succeeded him.

Then, when Eustace died, his son Baldwin of pious memory, a vigorous knight indeed, and illustrious for the complete goodness of his character, succeeded him in the county of the land of Guines.[90] Although he esteemed knights with marvelous affection, he was, however, prudent and modest concerning knighthood. Indeed, a knight himself, he did not, through pride in his rulership, become savage toward his knights and people by exalting himself, but he considered himself a peer and companion in his ministration. He was a consoler of orphans and a pious helper of *widows in their tribulations* [Jas. 1:27]. He did not demand or violently extort anything from his subjects, knights, or people, except what was owed to him by custom. He offered ecclesiastical and religious men the respect of complete veneration with total eagerness, and he supported them with painstaking protection and defense. Inasmuch as he was a man learned in letters, just as devoutly and fervently as he gave punctilious veneration to God, just so frequently did he understand and grasp the proof in a learned way, through the reading of sacred scriptures performed by his naturally good and most pious and Christian father. He wisely kept in the little chamber of his heart what he sucked from the innards of his pious father through education.[91]

25. How Baldwin married Adele, who was called Christine, the daughter of Florentin of Lorraine and had sons and daughters by her.

Then he married the daughter of florid Florentin, an exalted and incomparable man from Lorraine and the leader of the army.[92] She was formally named Adele; however, because of the tokens of her fine qualities and the marvelous feats of her virtues (and not without a mystery of an exalted sort), her given name fell into disuse and she was called by the more fitting name of Christine.[93] This was truly appropriate, and I believe it happened through the generosity of a heavenly gift that Adele, born with most Christian natal rites and in name and deed a Christian woman, as has been said, might be bound to a most Christian husband through the transaction of an ecclesiastical bond. The notable and praiseworthy Baldwin had a child of the greatest nobility by her, namely Robert, later the count of Guines. He had two names as was the custom then and is still often done, but as the proper signification of his naming was suppressed and the customary use grew, he was called Manasses.[94] She also had Fulk, the count of Beirut in the Promised Land, who in the end was buried there, and Guy, the count of Forez; Guy, however, was buried at Andres.[95] There was also Hugh, an archdeacon of the church of Thérouanne, but he was afterward a knight and was similarly buried at Andres; there were also Adelaide of Semur and Giselle of Ghent.

As to the first of the girls, namely Adelaide, she was legitimately married to Lord Geoffrey of Semur-en-Brionnais,[96] with the aid of Godfrey, the bishop of Paris,[97] the brother of count Eustace of Boulogne, whose kinswoman and relative she was. Because of the outstanding praise of his wisdom, Geoffrey shone like the sun far and wide in all of Burgundy—long-sleeved, long-haired, and broad-garmented Burgundy.[98] Through Adelaide, Geoffrey engendered Geoffrey, the most powerful knight of all Burgundy—he was no degenerate son of his father—and other sons and daughters. Since I have proposed to say nothing else concerning these people, I pass my pen to the writers of Semur to write, if it is worthwhile, lest through disparagement born of malice the people of Semur, envious of us, should murmur something about someone.

Then afterwards a man named Winemar,[99] the castellan of the fortress of Ghent and a man notable for his power, followers, and family, married Giselle.[100] Upon her he sired a firstborn son named Arnold, to whom I will come and about whom there will be abundant speech.[101] There were also Winemar, and Siger,[102] and Baldwin, who was first a monk of St. Peter in Ghent, then a knight, and at length was killed by a wretched and unexpected death at the hands of the people of Licques, while he was protecting a certain knight and trying to save him from death.[103] There was also one daughter named Margaret,[104] who afterward married the knight Steppo of Ghent.[105]

26. That Baldwin planned to build a monastery.

Then Count Baldwin of Guines, a man with his eyes and hands always intent upon heaven, fixed his whole spirit upon churches or monasteries of monks, so as to omit no part of our duty. He persisted devoutly and whole-heartedly through the night in prayers, vigils, and fasts, in *no false charity* [2 Cor. 6:6], and in distributions of alms. And so, when he had flourished in God's law, he began to perceive the harvest time of the fruit of justice in his own time. Thus outstanding as he was in the reputation for virtue and worthily filled with the Holy Spirit, this man was from day to day more devoted to celestial desires than earthly ones. Still, he judged and considered that he would be more happy[106] and nearer to God, if in his lifetime, among his other works of piety, he were able to erect a church of God in his land and to construct and build a habitation for men of God. The Lord God, who is never unmindful of His servants, granted an opportunity to arouse and satisfy this dear vow and desire devoted to Him, and He sharpened the goad of pious devotion and kindled an increase in Baldwin's love.

27. That Richilde wished to return Flanders to servitude.

So then Baldwin heard (and it did not fall on deaf ears) that Richilde, the daughter of the count of Mons and the countess of Flanders, presumed to exact an unaccustomed, unheard of, and unwonted tribute from the Flemish.[107] In all parts of Flanders, she boldly and evilly and irreverently demanded four pennies for every door and no less for every bed or pallet. And when she entered Guines with the same intention, the pious and prudent Baldwin wisely put up with this until the remarkable Robert the Frisian came at last to Flanders (he had been summoned over and over again) and Richilde went back to Flanders leaving the people of Guines in peace and free security.[108] Count Robert, coming toward her with his whole army, attacked her near Wouhe mountain, which is called the Wombergh in the vernacular and is situated near Mount Cassel. There, when she threw magic dust over Count Robert and his army with her sacrilegious hand, the wind changed at God's command and the dust turned back on Richilde herself and her men.

28. That when Richilde had been conquered, Count Robert founded the churches of Watten and Cassel.

And so Richilde, understanding and aware that she had lost her case and was now conquered in war by the will of God, made way for the count. And after she was thus conquered and her son Arnold killed[109] (he is buried before the great altar in the church of St. Omer at Sythiu), she returned in shame to Hainaut from Flanders, not without a great slaughter of her followers, and she never again appeared in Flanders. When Count Robert had gotten the rule of all Flanders, as a memorial and monument of this deed he built a church in honor of the blessed and ever virgin Mary at Watten and placed thirty canons regular there to celebrate the office. He was not content with this, for he had enjoyed victory over Richilde on the day of the solemnity of the throne of St. Peter, the prince of the apostles,[110] through the intercession and merits of this same prince of apostles, to whom he and his men had commended themselves on the day of strife and battle, divine grace leading the way. So he built and founded a church in honor of St. Peter, the prince of the apostles, on the high peak of a tall mountain inside the walls of the castle and fortress of that place, in the parish of the holy Virgin Mary at Cassel.[111] And he arranged for the church to be inhabited by twenty clerics or secular canons for worship.

29. How Count Baldwin and Enguerrand of Lillers went abroad to Santiago de Compostela.

And so, Count Baldwin of Guines, the devout servant of God, understanding the divine ruling concerning the divine and properly memorable works of Count Robert of Flanders (namely the acquisition of Flanders's liberty and the restoration of its churches—Robert was raised up on account of this more lofty desire), began to consider how and where he might more properly and appropriately establish a monastic church. Meanwhile, he chose Enguerrand, the lord of Lillers castle, as his companion and associate, who was burning with a very similar desire, born out of pious devotion, for a holy pilgrimage. And when the man of God was going abroad to Santiago, he came, not by a chance event, but led by divine prophecy, to the monastery of the Holy Savior at Charroux.[112] Making a brief stop there, he confessed his sins with a contrite and humble heart to the abbot of the same monastery, Peter, namely the second of that name,[113] and he also spoke about taking up his pilgrimage and about the fervor of his pious devotion to the church of God. And when the chapter met, Baldwin told them all that he had for a long time conceived a vow and was long since determined to build a monastery in his land. Assenting completely, therefore, to the very wholesome advice of the most holy father abbot and of the monks, he gave them the chapel of the blessed Virgin Mary in his castle at Guines in free alms, which he owned free and clear, along with its associated rights, tithes, and land; the wood at Autingues; also the tithe of Espelleke; and whatever he possessed in Zouafques at that time, with this stipulation: that as soon as he returned to his country and the time and place might be found and prepared to construct a monastery, they would undertake to send him a convent of monks with an abbot to celebrate the divine office and mystery. Upon making this agreement, when he had completed his pilgrimage, he returned by a fortunate voyage to his country. In order to carry out his vow as quickly as possible, he spoke to the venerable Gerald, the bishop of Thérouanne.[114] Discreetly and reverently following the wholesome advice and will of the venerable bishop in every detail and in all things, he acquired the free church of St. Medard at Andres.[115] When this had been done, he recognized that

It costs one dear to put off what's arranged.[116]

So when he had quickly sent messengers to Charroux, as had been decreed in the foundation charter,[117] in joy and exultation, he solemnly introduced

Abbot Gilbert[118] (who is said to be the first abbot of Andres) into Andres together with a convent of monks. Among these, the venerable monks Everard and Humphrey of Betberga were first in vocation and sanctity.

30. How Count Baldwin established the monastery of Andres.

And thus with the agreement, help, and advice of a certain rich inhabitant, Baldwin Bochard, to whom this land, which was preordained to be a place for the dwelling of God's monks, partly belonged,[119] Count Baldwin of Guines of pious memory, the kinsman and loyal friend of Count Charles of Flanders,[120] and a man loved by the Flemish, fulfilled his vow and proposal and built the monastery of Andres and placed monks in it in 1084 a. d. At this time the venerable Pope Calixtus, second of that name, who granted the monks free burial,[121] was governing the world's monarchy under the protection of the apostles Peter and Paul; Philip was governing the kingdom of France; Count Robert was ruling Flanders; and Bishop Gerard was holding the throne and staff of Thérouanne.[122] (Gerard was deposed later on by Pope Urban and is buried at Patras.)[123]

In their church he placed the body of the blessed virgin Rotrud in magnificence, with joy and glory, not without the greatest honor and reverence on the part of the nobles and people. The body was brought to them divinely, accompanied by the clear evidence of miracles. Indeed, the venerable bishop Milo II of the church of Thérouanne showed the most reverend little body of this most holy virgin to the people and carried it around in the time of Peter, the abbot of the church of Andres, when Count Arnold was ruling and governing Guines.[124] But if the little book or treatise of the memorable father and abbot Peter (whose book was placed in the church of Andres and read every year on the virgin's feast day to those eating meals in the refectory) does not satisfy those who are asking about where the most glorious body of the sacrosanct virgin was gotten and whence it was brought, let them carefully ask the people of Marchiennes, if this is expedient. However, these people, hiding the truth or the likely story with a certain mockery, are accustomed to insult the people of Andres derisively.[125]

Thus, when the monastery of Andres had been built, Count Baldwin of Guines, a man of honest and most holy life, who was illustrious and dear to God, gave many others an example of church building and the construction of hospital buildings for holy and pious imitation — though not in his lands, but in other adjacent lands — and he inspired devout love and pious fervor toward the church of God.

31. How Countess Ida of Boulogne founded the monastery of blessed Mary of Capella.

Hence, Countess Ida of Boulogne,[126] who was venerable both in her name and in the holiness of her life, in imitation of this so pious operation founded a church and established a monastery of outstanding religiosity in honor of the blessed, glorious, and ever virgin Mary in the territory of Merck, in the village once called Brouckham.[127] She was the daughter of the former Duke Godfrey of Lorraine[128] and the widow of the late count Eustace of Boulogne,[129] and the mother of Eustace of Boulogne[130] and of Godfrey[131] and Baldwin[132] — they were the kings of Jerusalem after the holy city of Jerusalem in the kingdom of Judea was completely freed *with a strong hand and outstretched arm* [Dt. 5:15; Ezek. 20:33, 34], for Jerusalem had previously been conquered by Arabs and Muslims and other foreign and infidel folk. And in that same church, she placed eleven hairs of the blessed Virgin Mary, more precious than gold or a precious stone. These she had begged, with much labor and zealous diligence, from Ansculf, the king of Ireland, and offered (along with other innumerable relics of the saints) to be honored beyond all others in the holy place. She also established and introduced into the dwelling that had been prepared a holy convent of monks, composed of the venerable man Abbot Ravenger, who came from the monastery of Hammes,[133] which had been recently built by Lord Enguerrand of Lillers, and also other brothers of honest and religious life to serve in memory of the holy Mother of God, the ever virgin Mary, and continually to worship forever before God eternal.

Indeed, this most famous place of St. Mary, while the still new and tender infancy of holy religion was still sprouting there, outshone all other places and surpassed those nearby, inasmuch as God illuminated it unceasingly with his presence, and the blessed Virgin visited it with that grace by which she was once imbued, and she offered innumerable gifts to those who piously requested them there. It was a place most well-known through fame's publication and noted for its virtues, glorious in the frequency of its miracles, most holy in its charity and religion, very rich in the abundance of its possessions, and highly endowed with people worthy of promotion and preferment to every honor because of their moral characters and their knowledge no less of the liberal arts than of theological writing—may all malicious envy be absent!

That place was therefore believed to have been of such a name and of such reverence that when certain nobles (and other faithful people of God) in the adjacent land had little churches or some other ecclesiastical benefices, or even little estates, they either gave them whole and intact to this place or were content to subordinate or link them to the monastery's jurisdiction through some title of subjection. They judged (or rather knew for certain) that their little churches would survive and fight with greater success if they were subordinated to such a holy and venerable place by some bond of subjection than if these churches persisted and remained in the liberty—whatever that might be—in which they had been founded. Thus, indeed, it seemed to these nobles and others who considered the matter that the churches would fight under a better name and they would shine with fuller title of authority.[134]

That place, indeed, is known to be completely free from every flaw of shame and taxation and unusual custom. For that reason it is called Capella, a chapel, I say, of the highest bishop, namely of the Lord Pope, built in honor of the blessed Virgin Mary. In memory of its liberty and in warrant for it, the church of that free place owes twelve pennies to the church of Rome every year. The abbot of that most holy place gathers them together and sends them to Rome every five or ten years in recognition of his liberty, as I said. Indeed, the abbot of this place has such dignity in the Roman church that if this same abbot were to be present in the Roman church at the Lord Pope's mass, he would hold the book of the subdeacon while that subdeacon intoned the epistle. But lest I should draw out my words too long at the expense of the knights, who will murmur against me, let this little I have said about this holy place and the monks living there suffice until in a greater and more fervent study, time, and place, I may turn my authorial pen to them in order to insert other things.

32. Of the construction of the church of Ardres.

For the most manifest and pressing reasons of the affairs of Guines, I have placed the monastery of Andres (constructed by Count Baldwin of Guines) and the monastery of blessed Mary of Capella (built by Countess Ida of Boulogne) first after the memorable deed of the venerable consul of Flanders, Robert the Frisian, who founded the churches of Watten and Cassel, as I have already said. These monasteries were founded in imitation of the count of Flanders, Robert the Frisian, but I have made it appear that these two monasteries were the earliest founded (although my pen was shaking and almost protesting). So, truthfully to tell the true story, the hero Arnold, the lord of and first heir to the citadel of Ardres, from the beginning a hero among the first heroes of the nobles of Guines, through the nobility of his soul obtained both a reputation for knighthood and the county of Saint-Pol. He founded a church in honor of blessed Omer in the castle of Ardres, where there is now a cemetery and a cell of monks, in imitation of the very pious work of the memorable count of Flanders, Robert the Frisian, and he procured ten secular canons to serve God in this same church in perpetuity. This church was given afterward by Baldwin, the lord of that same citadel, to Abbot Thierry and the monks of the Chapel of the blessed Virgin Mary [Capella], in the village once called Brouckham, as I have said. But I will speak more fully and satisfactorily about the foundation of this church and of the transformation or conversion of its clergy or secular canons into monks in the time and place when I shall, in closing, say something concerning the deeds of the nobles of Ardres, according to what I have planned.[135] Indeed, as one can judge from the privileges of these churches which I have discussed and spoken of, the church of Ardres was founded in 1069 a. d., that of Andres afterward, in 1084, and the church of St. Mary of Capella after that, in the year 1091.[136]

33. How Manasses succeeded Baldwin, when Baldwin died.

When he had completed the dispensation allotted to the flesh, Count Baldwin of Guines, venerable in life and name, underwent temporal death. He was buried in hope of eternal life in the church of Andres which he founded with his most Christian wife Adele (who, as I have said, was nicknamed Christine) alongside his two sons Guy and Hugh, not without the lamentation of noble men, monks, and the people of the whole world.[137] Thus his son Robert, who, as I said, was also called Manasses by growing usage, succeeded him and undertook to rule the people of Guines. To the degree that he shone brightly with his rightly memorable father's virtues, just so frequently did his magnanimous ears receive tributes, for his fame sparkled everywhere. And although he is remembered to have been sometimes immersed in worldly matters, still he was not unmindful of spiritual mysteries; laying aside worldly cares in an appropriate time and place, he heard with open ears all the more readily the mysteries of the sweet-singing church. And he also strove with not dissimilar zeal and affection to honor those people he knew that his pious father had honored in his life. He was well prepared and competent in tournaments[138] and warlike illusions. But although the world sometimes deceives with vainglory, as he was undeceived, he did not often permit himself to be among the knights seeking vainglory.

34. How Count Manasses sired Adelaide, the mother of the lords of Balinghem.

Meanwhile, he had an affair with a certain outstandingly beautiful girl from Guines, by whom he had a daughter named Adelaide; he gave her as a wife to Eustace, the son of Heremar of Balinghem.[139] Eustace had five sons by her: Eustace, the firstborn, died as a youth after he had been knighted. Hugh married Matilda (who was called by the childish nickname of Matha), a daughter of Laurette of Hames, and had by her Adelaide, who was first married to Arnulf of Cayeux, then to Daniel, the brother of Siger, the castellan of Ghent.[140] There was also Gregory, a monk and the abbot elect of the church of Andres, but he was deposed voluntarily before his benediction.[141] There were also Frumold and Simon and one daughter, named Avice, who married Baldwin the Old of Hermelinghem, the constable of Boulogne. I know the great and notable deeds of this family of Balinghem and I have narrated some of them. In order to maintain moderation in every way and in all things in these matters, now that the inkwell has been emptied, I draw my dry pen out, to write something else, having prevented the narrative I have planned from accidentally turning into a treatise on them.

35. How Count Manasses married Countess Emma.

Count Manasses, a most notable and celebrated man, was not unworthily very famous far and wide in the whole world for his magnificence and glory. Thus he was famous in France, famous in Normandy, and most famous in England. For this reason, as he often stayed in England and visited King William of England, he married Emma, the daughter of the chamberlain, Robert of Tancarville, Normandy,[142] the widow of Odo of Folkestone, England.

36. Of the "club churls."[143]

In those days there were certain men armed with clubs or club-bearers living in Guines, whom I have heard called "club churls" in the vernacular. They were called the men with the clubs or the club-bearers after their clubs, for they were not permitted to carry any sort of arms, just clubs alone. They were held by the lords of Hames by a sort of injustice as though bound by the yoke of servile status. So they were each forced to pay a penny each year to the lords of Hames and also four for weddings and no less at death.[144] The lords of Hames had long since received this right as a perpetual fief from Ralph, the former count of Guines, who imposed these and other similar evil and shameful things upon his subjects. Ralph granted it to them and confirmed it as their fief that any new arrival who should come to Guines from elsewhere and remain on their land for one year and one day (or should live there longer or for a more protracted period) would incur both shame and the shameful tax and should pay it as if this were legal.

Now it happened that a certain free old soldier or rear-vassal named William of Boucres married Avice, a similarly free female rear-vassal from Fiennes.[145] She had scarcely lain down on the boards of her marriage bed at Boucres, when men came from the lord of Hames and demanded the club-churl tax from her. But she blushed for a little while, coloring out of shame and fear, and protested that she was completely ignorant of what the club-churl tax was, that she was entirely free, and that she came from a free family. Then with difficulty procuring a grant of liberty for a scant fifteen days from the retainers, at length she presented herself, along with her relatives and friends, to the lords of Hames at Hames on the day appointed for her. She asserted that she was born of free people, both living and dead, present and absent, and was completely free herself and that she was prepared to prove it with a loud, constant, and free voice against any shameless men and reprobates [who might claim otherwise]. But as the voices and arguments of the men of Hames grew stronger, not only did she soon leave the court just as she had come, but she also went home completely undone by notorious dishonor, infamy, and scandal.

However, when she had taken private and better advice, she spoke with Emma, the lady and countess of Guines of venerable name, telling her about her shame. She said that the shame and infamy of the land of Guines was spoken of far and wide, and that, unless Emma promptly and carefully intervened and gave her assistance, nobles, just like commoners, would be reduced to and enmeshed in servitude by a not dissimilar decree of this contract; they would be insolently and irreverently forced to pay the club-churl tax by the same reasoning and a not dissimilar arrogance. The noble heroine, therefore, not so much motivated by compassion for this woman's dishonor (or rather the dishonor of this matron of worthy memory), as she was by the shame of the whole land, spoke with the count; she embraced her husband, showing to him and lamenting the miseries and shame of Guines. Thus softened, the count therefore acceded justly and piously to the prayers of his pleading wife and of the other woman, and he had the lords of Hames brought to him as quickly as possible. And with their agreement, he completely abolished and eliminated the club-churl tax and the shame and dishonor of the land. To increase their fief to five carrucates and to compensate for the club-churl tax, he gave the men of Hames the land lying piecemeal around Alembon, Pihen, and Saint-Ingelvert. Thus the woman from Fiennes was returned a free bride to her home in Boucres (as I have mentioned), and at the same time all the club churls were manumitted and made free in perpetuity and emancipated. Indeed, since I have strayed somewhat from the path of my plan because of the details of this event, lest I dwell any longer on the club churls, I shall go on to what I have planned.

Count Manasses, who was most praiseworthy in the appearance of his elegant body, looked like a giant in the height of his person and a greybeard in his personal authority. He was handsome in face and appearance (or rather vigorous in virtue), and lovable to all, except that to the people of Ardres alone, who were often rebellious and contumacious to him, he was hateful and odious. But I will put off talking of their stubbornness and rebelliousness for a time.

37. That Count Manasses proposed to build a monastic church.

Then Count Manasses of Guines lived with all modesty in tranquility and peace and *in no false charity*. [2 Cor. 6:6] But although he took care of all of the churches in his land and showed reverence toward them, by a special preference he was most ardently devoted to and more vehement about the promotion of the church his father Baldwin of pious memory had founded at Andres.[146] And now he took it in mind (or rather he told and disclosed to his venerable wife Emma and others of his counselors) to build some monastic church in his land in imitation of his pious father. However, since other matters interfered, his pious wife Emma afterward carried out with the highest

devotion what he had piously planned and was not able to bring to completion.[147]

38. That Robert the Bearded established four canons at Licques.

And so the barons and faithful people of this land, seeing the most pious
devotion of their pious count toward the church of God, themselves also
began, because divine grace was growing in them, to become drunk with the
same ardor toward the church of God and toward religious men, to the degree that their means allowed. Hence also a certain Robert of Licques (called
"with a beard" or "the bearded," because anyone in that time who did not have
an abundant beard was called effeminate and was held in derision and disrespect),[148] a contemporary and sometime schoolmate of Arnulf or Arnold,
founder of the church of Ardres, established four secular canons at Licques in
honor of the blessed Virgin Mary, giving them the same number of prebends
to be held in perpetuity, and he made himself the fifth canon and the provost. His successor Baldwin, similarly called "the Bearded" or "with a beard,"
gave and subjected the prebends, along with the clerics and canons of that
place, to the regular canons of Watten, when he was going on pilgrimage to
Jerusalem with his four sons to venerate the Lord's tomb.

39. That Bishop Milo I of Thérouanne established Premonstratensian canons at Licques.

But afterwards, the most religious bishop Milo of Thérouanne, the first
abbot to wear the Premonstratensian hood,[149] before the full synod of Thérouanne granted that same church of Licques (with its associated rights) to
the regular canons wearing the white pelt of Prémonté[150] so that they could
construct and establish a monastic church to be held in perpetuity.[151] The
canons of the church of Watten were present, but they did not, as some people
gossip, protest or interrupt with remonstration, but rather offered their good-
willed assent. And in 1132 a. d., the venerable father Henry was taken, along
with a white congregation of regular canons, from the church of St. Martin
of Laon. Milo solemnly introduced and enthroned him in the church, which
was to be inhabited forever.[152]

*40. How Eustace the Old of Fiennes founded the church of Beaulieu and
established canons of the order of Arrouaise in it.*

There was then in those days a certain great-hearted well-tried fighter
or rear-vassal named Eustace, surnamed "the Old," who took his origin on
one side from Ardres and who at that time ruled and governed the people
of Fiennes,[153] and who had sons. Namely there was Eustace, who although he
married Margaret, the daughter of Count Arnold of Guines, slept in the Lord
without leaving behind any offspring by her. There was also Enguerrand, who
although he married Sybil, the noble sister of William Faramus of Tingry[154]
and had William, Thomas, and Eustace and daughters by her, sought Jerusalem with Count Philip of Flanders.[155] And when this righteous hero met with
the unrighteous Saracens, he assailed them, but since he did not return from
the assault, he was never again seen by his men. There were also Gilbert of
Blequin and Ralph, the pious servant of God, who married Adelaide (she had
been married before to Eustace of Cauquelle),[156] the worshipful daughter of
Henry of Campagne[157] and that most gifted woman, Adelaide of Conteville.[158]
And there were also daughters, of whom Baldwin of Hames,[159] who shone in
the glory of knighthood throughout the whole world, married one, namely
Adelaide, by whom he conceived offspring, namely Eustace, Enguerrand, and
Baldwin; they were not inferior to their father in nobility and knighthood.

Now this Eustace the Old of Fiennes piously heard that the neighboring
nobles who lived all around were stirred in spirit by the fear of God and assisted by grace and had founded new churches and established new monastic
dwellings in their lands to the degree their means permitted. He built a conventual church in honor of the blessed Virgin Mary in Beaulieu, as penance
for his soul and those of his predecessors and successors, and especially for the
salvation and redemption of the soul of a certain knight, the lord of Ponche-
Estruval in Ponthieu, whom Eustace had killed in a tournament. (He had
been expressly ordered to do this on this man's account.) In the time of Count
William of Boulogne and Manasses of Guines,[160] Eustace solemnly gathered
and installed in this church canons of the order of Arrouaise, who came from
the church of Blessed Mary in the Wood [Ruisseauville][161] with their venerable father and abbot William, to serve God in perpetuity.

41. How Oilard founded the "Field of the Saints," which is also called Saint-Ingelvert.

Oilard, also inspired manifestly by the same divine desire, restored the poorhouse at Saint-Ingelvert, a place of refuge and a shelter where people might recuperate. Concerning the establishment of this house of holy hospitality, the truthful tradition of the inhabitants and the brothers of the holy place asserts that a certain knight of Wimille,[162] born of illustrious parents, Oilard by name, seeing and observing in his soul that the decline of this untrustworthy world had rewarded him very well with prosperity, abandoned himself and his possessions and also exhorted or rather reprimanded himself for his scurvy secular sins, and of his own free will became a poor man on earth but a rich man in heaven. This man, who earlier was crushed by the weight of his sins but was now converted to God, decided to labor in holy works and to struggle for God as long as he lived, or rather to fight to serve Him.

And so he heard and knew, because the place was not far away, that there was a woody and dangerous place between Guines and Wissant that lay in the brush and not on the road, called not inappropriately the Criminals' Field, because of the evil acts of wrong-doers in that place (that is, of criminals), and it was called Sontingevelt in the vernacular.[163] Indeed, if one can credit the truth, robbers (because of whom taxation was first established and paid at Guines, as they say) hid at one time in holes in the ground and warrens there and plotted against passersby. They grabbed the loads from some, seized packs from others, and threatened others with death; like murderers (rather they truly were murderers) they even killed some of them with javelins, hidden swords, or daggers, once they had stolen the goods of these passersby.

And so the servant of God, coming to help the faithful of Christ, procured a place in the breadth of the field with money and purchased it with prayer from the inhabitants in order to make a poorhouse (or rather a hostelry) for those who passed by and asked piously for shelter in the Lord. Then as the inhabitants saw that the man of God daily showed an assiduous obedience toward God by laboring in the works of piety and charity, and that he approached God more nearly from day to day in the sanctity of his life, they liberally gave him their small holdings in alms and gave him many other benefices from their temporal possessions. To celebrate the divine mystery as properly as he could, he built a church of God in that same place.

Thus, in this way, the discernment of divine dispensation ordained that where the blood of the innocent had been frequently shed by malefactors, a daily sacrifice of the blood and body of Christ should be offered in perpetuity by Christian priests for the mystery of our salvation; that where there had been criminal conspiracies, the vigils of God's servants should be celebrated; that where death's destruction had daily threatened those passing by, an unlocked shelter should welcome the poor to a safe asylum and a comfortable place to recuperate; that where once there had been a field of the dying, there should be a habitation for those resting in Christ. Hence, the field both lost the name of the sinners and won the name of the saints. Thus, the place was named Santingheveld, through conversion by the saints.[164]

Consequently, the hospital was commended to the abbot and canons of Arrouaise at one time, but because the number of lay brothers among the canons was growing, the canons returned to Arrouaise and the hospital was restored to its earlier state.

42. How Count Manasses had Rose and Rose had Beatrice.

Then Count Manasses of Guines knew his wife Emma and by her he had a single daughter, officially named Sybil, but called by the nickname of Rose. Afterward, when her nubile years required it, she was given to the glorious castellan Henry of Bourbourg.[165] She similarly conceived and bore a single daughter named Beatrice. When Beatrice was newborn, her mother Rose (or rather Sybil) died (alas!) and was buried in the monastery of blessed Mary of Capella before the altar of St. Benedict, not without the tearful lamentation of her people.

43. How Count Manasses married his granddaughter Beatrice to Albert the Boar.

Then Count Manasses of Guines grew old, and as his hair was whitening in old age, he eked out his years in vexation and weariness, no less worn out by the sorrow he felt at the death of his daughter than by his age, and most of all because he despaired of the life of his granddaughter Beatrice, for she was afflicted with the stone and was sickly. Consequently, he feared for himself and took as much care for the future with cautious foresight as he could on his own behalf, or rather on behalf of all of Guines, lest Guines beg for one of his sisters' offspring as an heir, that is, a person almost from an alien seed because he had left no seed of his own body (for his brothers had all died and were buried without any bodily heirs, as I have related above).[166] He therefore married his granddaughter Beatrice to the noble Albert the Boar in England[167] (even though she was afflicted with the stone and sickly, as I said above) upon the advice of his wife Emma, because she had a greater acquaintance when she lived in England than anywhere else; Henry, the glorious castellan of Bourbourg, gave his assistance.

Now then, so that I may complete my project in every way, disclose the genealogy of the counts of Guines as a whole, and more swiftly pursue the execution of my work, I have produced one necessary item to sum up some necessary things concerning Giselle, the most noble daughter of the most glorious count Baldwin of Guines, the wife of Castellan Winemar of Ghent. Therefore, leaving aside the three sons and the daughter of Giselle and Castellan Winemar of Ghent, since they do not enter into my project, I shall proceed concerning Arnold alone.[168]

44. Of Arnold of Ghent.

Arnold, then, was a knight of Ghent, who was very energetic in war. I judge it unnecessary to write or to confect anything concerning his reputation for knighthood, in this way delaying the labor of my obedience, since the whole world resonates with his praises and the glory of his integrity. Seeing, therefore, that his maternal uncle, Count Manasses of Guines, was burdened with old age, that he was whiling away and eking out a life troubled by age and sadness, almost without offspring, Arnold conceived an idea in the depths of his heart that he afterward carried out when the time came, concerning the county of the land of Guines. Adapting the idea conceived in his mind to the circumstances without delay, when he had gathered together some soldiers from his kin in whom he had as much confidence as in himself, Arnold went to Guines and spoke peaceably and humbly with the count of Guines, his uncle. Arnold, in fact, did not disclose to Manasses his whole heart's intention. However, mentioning on the surface of his conversation things he did not doubt everyone knew, he hid the things he had deliberately told to no one except those aware of his secret.

To tell the truth, deep in the hidden chamber of his heart he thought that if he could approach the confines of the land of Guines in some way and he could put his foot there in some way by some promotion to a fief, he could attain the rulership of the whole land as easily as he might think of it. When certain people aware of this hidden secret told the venerable old man — *noth-*

ing is hidden that may not be known [Mt. 10:26] — he took it bitterly, but bore it in silence. Indeed, he did not show his nephew the rough side of his tongue, speak with a bitter voice, nor inveigh against Arnold with obscenity or ugly accusations, but for the time being he *endured everything; he tolerated everything.* [1 Cor. 13:7] [169] Completely unaware that his uncle knew anything of his intention, or that his uncle, forewarned or forearmed about his secret, was considering any advice, Arnold came to him in manly fashion, and like a prudent man, and not an arrogant one, he asked Manasses with humble gentleness if he would be so good as to grant him some benefice within Guines to sustain him and advance his honor.

45. How Count Manasses gave Tornehem with its associated rights to his nephew Arnold of Ghent.

And so, when the venerable old man had weighed the desire and the intention of his nephew upon the dish of the scale, he considered more fully than the ear may grasp on one hand his great-spirited nephew's strength in war (he had no doubt of the nefarious expectations of the people of Semur),[170] on the other hand, that the illness of his granddaughter Beatrice, who suffered from the stone, daily grew worse and more serious; on one hand, that Arnold was preparing to occupy the land while he himself was still alive; on the other, that Albert, whose wife was languishing, was despairing of his wife's life and also of getting the land; on this hand, the contumacy of the rebellious family of Ardres; who roared against him; on the other, the strength of the family of Semur, if they were to ally themselves with the family of Ardres, and the failure of his own strength (for this reason he was seized by the greater pain). As a result of all these things, concealing these blows, he prudently chose to lead his life in peaceful tranquility as long as he lived, rather than to drive his nephew away from him (or rather away from the land) through an increase of cruelty. For Arnold was distrustful of him and prepared to insist upon the land with hatred and anger. Manasses, therefore, granted Tornehem, along with its associated rights, as a fief to Arnold, as his nephew and as a most well-known and powerful knight among knights, both to augment the peace and perpetual love and to support his bodily needs.

When Arnold had thus received the benefice of a little lordship in Guines, and was approaching the county on another footing than he had had in mind, he placed his hope both in the Lord God and in the power of his own strength that he might seek out and gain better things. Consequently, when he had offered and given his thanks for the benefit of this fief and this reward with reverence proportionate to the size of the gift he had accepted, seeing that his uncle was right now approaching death and the granddaughter was no less ill and slipping away into death,

> The fierce and savage Arnold on rampage,
> Spurs on his horses, stirring them to rage;

he went as fast as he could to Castellan William of Saint-Omer,[171] and received him before any others, made peace with him, and allied William to himself as a friend, principally because being at Saint-Omer, William was nearer to that land to which Arnold aspired with all his heart's inclination and also because William was quite rich in worthy relatives and friends and was quite prepared to turn Arnold's hopeful proposition into a fact.

46. That Castellan William of Saint-Omer married Millicent, the daughter of the vidâme of Piquigny.

Now, this William (in telling you this I am not digressing from my plan) long ago married a woman named Millicent, who was descended from the most noble lineage and family of Charlemagne, the king of the Franks;[172] she was the daughter of Arnulf, the vidâme of Piquigny. William had noble sons by her, namely William, afterward the castellan of Saint-Omer;[173] Hosto;[174] Gerard, the provost of the church of Saint-Omer; Hugh of Fauquembergue; and Walter, the prince of Tiberias;[175] and he also had daughters born to propagate the offspring of a great lineage. The first and most important of these was named Matilda, who is the one who matters most to my plan. Euphemia, the second, was married to Baldwin of Bailleul,[176] who had sons by her — Gerard and Hosto — and daughters — Adelaide of Commynes, Matilda the abbess of Wherwell in England,[177] Ylessenda, and Margaret. The third daughter was Giselle of Montreuil. The fourth and fifth were Leutgard and Beatrice, nuns in the monastery of Estrun.[178]

47. That Arnold of Ghent married Matilda, the daughter of the castellan of Saint-Omer.

Therefore, when Arnold of Ghent had discussed many matters with the aforesaid castellan William of Saint-Omer, at length he married Matilda, the daughter of this ever so noble man, and he conferred Tornehem with all its associated rights upon her as her dower.[179] Although I now proceed speaking directly of her procreation of children, still many things happened in the interim, which, as shall be very clear, followed these things I have put first.

48. Of Arnold of Ghent's procreation of children.

Matilda, then, advanced in her days and conceived by her husband, Arnold of Ghent; she bore him Baldwin, whom Count Manasses of Guines, Arnold's maternal uncle, received as a godson from the baptismal font; William, called of Guines, who married Flandrine, the granddaughter of Count Hugh of Saint-Pol;[180] Manasses; Siger; and Arnold, who died as an adolescent. When Arnold was being carried to be buried with his brothers Manasses and Siger at the monastery of Andres, he rested in the brush near a crossroad or fork in the road on the hill above Brêmes. To commemorate this event, a wooden cross was carried and raised there, and a poplar and a linden were planted near the cross for the rest and refreshment of pilgrims or any sort of travelers. But later on, a great force of wind blowing from the other direction tore the cross from its place and, as one can see today, it was hung on the poplar so it would not be completely destroyed.

Now, Arnold had these five sons by her and eight daughters: namely Margaret,[181] first married to Eustace of Fiennes,[182] then to Roger, the castellan of Courtrai;[183] Beatrice, first given to be the wife of William Faramus of Tingry, afterward the wife of Hugh, the castellan of Beaumetz-les-Laires; Adelaide, first married to Castellan Hugh of Lille (who had earlier been the provost of St. Piatus of Seclin),[184] afterward married at her dower lands at Sainghain-en-Weppe to Robert of Wavrin, the brother of Hellouin, the seneschal or steward of Flanders;[185] Euphemia and Leutgard, first nuns in the monastery of St. Leonard at Guines, then abbesses in that same place (Leutgard succeeded Euphemia); also Matilda, given as a wife to Baldwin, the son of William Morannus of Hondschote;[186] also Giselle, wed by the law of matrimony to Walter of Pollaer of Aa or Aqua;[187] also Agnes, married in the Promised Land upon the advice of her nephews, namely the sons of the above-mentioned Walter, the prince of Tiberias.[188] In accordance with her father's desire to send his famous lineage to the far and remote reaches of the earth, having left the sweet soil and place of her native fatherland for the sake of honor, she went into exile so that she might, as I have just said, bring forth an outstanding and proud race for her father. (Oh, how great a love for such a glorious father! Oh, how praiseworthy the complete submission of a daughter!) But having taken poison in her food, as they say, or being medicated with potions, she died at once and was buried there. Therefore, now that these necessary matters have been rehearsed with a certain anticipation of the narrative, I turn my dutiful pen to linking the matters above to those placed below, so that I may faithfully follow my plan.

49. How Count Manasses died.

Thus Count Manasses of Guines of venerable memory, once exceedingly handsome in face and body, when he had become an old and decrepit man and ailing and afflicted, suffered with patience many things due to old age that a youth could scarcely manage to tolerate. Since he could by no means further resist or survive by bodily or spiritual strength the circumstances that assailed him and conspired against him on all sides, he began to lose his bodily strength completely. Seized by the harsh illness of fevers and laid on his death bed, he lamented, cautioning his followers on many things concerning his granddaughter Beatrice, many more concerning his nephew Arnold, and still more about the destruction of the whole land. He finally slept with his fathers[189] and was honorably buried in hope of a blessed resurrection with these same fathers at the monastery of Andres,[190] where all the counts of Guines and their sons ought to be buried (as the authentic writings of those monks who are bound to serve in that place attest).[191]

50. How Castellan Henry of Bourbourg announced the death of Count Manasses to Albert the Boar.

And so Castellan Henry of Bourbourg, hearing that Count Manasses of Guines had recently gone the way of all flesh, announced the death of the count to his son-in-law Albert, along with the outcome of the whole business; he predicted as a fact what he feared might happen. He announced a sort of clairvoyant prophecy of a future event, namely that Arnold of Ghent, a man who was tricky and desirous of the land of Guines, would immediately occupy the fortresses of the land and the land itself (not without some de-population of the land), unless Albert speedily helped both himself and the territory. Thus, the aim of Henry's message was contained in these words, namely that Albert should come from England to Guines as quickly as he could and be established in due order and by hereditary right and succeed Count Manasses of Guines, who was now dead and buried.

Although Albert labored honorably near King William of England doing the king's business,[192] he acceded, therefore, to his father-in-law's demands and came to the land of Guines as quickly as he could and when he had also performed the rite of homage to Prince Thierry of Flanders,[193] he became the count of Guines. But staying only a short time in the land of Guines, he hastened to England to the king to receive the land which came to him on his wife's account, leaving his wife Beatrice with his father-in-law, Castellan Henry of Bourbourg.[194] There the king demanded from Albert what he had a right to ask, so Albert remained with the king for a long time, weighing a certain force of necessity against his own desires. He knew that his wife was sick and suffered from stone and was afraid to pay the marital debt to him.[195] But when his wife Beatrice became more ill than usual, even though he was many times sent for by his father-in-law, he put off his arrival and refused to come to Guines.

51. How Countess Emma built the convent of nuns at Guines and how at length she died and was buried there.

Meanwhile, the venerable widow, Countess Emma, through a pious understanding of heart, fully rekindled and revived outside herself the fire of divine love that she had earlier lit inside herself for her husband, namely Count Manasses of Guines, and she decided that as soon as she could, she would carry out the vow to God that her pious husband, the companion of her bed and devotion, had earlier made. She truly heard and well understood the words in the psalm: "*Make your vows to the Lord your God and carry them out; let all who are around him offer gifts to God, who is to be feared, who makes an offering of the spirits of princes.*" [Ps. 76:11–12][196] Thus, just as I outlined at one time in what I said above, the friend of God, Count Manasses of Guines, decided to build a house on earth created by human hands and to establish somewhere a conventual church while he still lived in prosperity and glory, so that he might dwell in heaven in a house not built by human hands and possess it with the angels. But since many matters impeded the holy vows of the count and these vows did not lead to the completion of the work according to the desire of his soul, his venerable widow, who was also praiseworthy in all things to God, discharged and fulfilled these vows to the Lord God for herself and for her husband.[197]

And so from the revenues earmarked for her table, she built the church of St. Leonard, confessor and bishop, and the cloister of a monastery at Guines to aid her soul and that of her husband, Count Manasses of Guines, and their predecessors and successors. To it she summoned nuns from the monastery of Estrun to serve God in perpetuity. And she appointed over them the most religious abbess Sybil or Sybilla, a woman who came from the family of the former countess Adele of Guines (who, as I said earlier, was called by the nickname Christine) in the region of Lorraine.[198] And in 1102 a. d. she enthroned Sybil to rule over the nuns recently introduced into the church of St. Leonard at Guines.[199] Matilda of Campagne was the first to succeed her. Then Adele of Mardick succeeded her.[200] After her came women (or rather matrons) venerable in their noble family and in the sanctity of their name, the daughters of Count Arnold of Guines, who were nuns of that place: Euphemia, who because of the meaning of her name did not cause one to forget that she was a good woman,[201] and after her in succession, as I have said, Leutgard, who was her full sister in body and blood, her daughter in Christ in the name of holiness and religion. Then when no great space of time had passed after the establishment of the monastery of Guines, the venerable matron and lady, Countess Emma of Guines, put on and dressed herself in the nuns' habit and clothing and paid the debt of the flesh at Guines, and there she was sung for, piously lamented in the Lord, and honorably buried like a nun (or rather truly as a nun) by the nuns.

52. How Arnold of Ghent took counsel with his counselors and supporters at Tornehem.

But Arnold of Ghent heard and understood through his careful inquiries that Albert despaired no less for the life of his wife than for the county of the land of Guines, and that because of this situation, although Albert had been ordered to come to Guines often and over and over again by Castellan Henry of Bourbourg, he put off coming from day to day because of a certain negligence or sloth of spirit. Therefore, Arnold of Ghent, who was completely and totally solicitous and ambitious concerning his own advancement, entered his castle at Tornehem, upon the advice of his father-in-law, Castellan William of Saint-Omer, of his brothers-in-law, and of some individuals who were in on his secret, disguising his intention with as much skill as he could. And remaining there for a little while with his followers, he commanded and ordered his men, under a threat to their life, to keep secret and hidden among themselves whatever he thought and whatever he said to them in council, and it should be completely hidden from Arnold the Eater of Hames. (For when Count Albert was going back to England, he appointed Arnold of Hames, called the Eater, the son of Robert, as his bailiff in the territory of Guines, and he commended the whole territory to his safekeeping.) [202]

Though the barons of the whole territory awaited Count Albert's coming for a long time — they had often (and more and more frequently) sent messengers to England who were authorized men and full of good advice, who had forceful and authoritative written messages that urged him to come quickly to help the land, because all around they saw a fearful and frightened people — he utterly refused to come to Guines. Therefore, Arnold of Ghent, who was aware of this matter while he was staying and tarrying at Tornehem, for he had sent spies and officials throughout Guines, asked assiduously and unceasingly if he had any supporters to carry out his will. And so when he had received letters from certain barons of the land, he heard something that raised his spirits somewhat. He spoke secretly, therefore, with some barons, to whom he communicated his intention and made it public. And when he knew the strength of their forces, the officials who kept Guines were corrupted with pleas, money, and promises; they were seduced and enticed into submitting to him and satisfying him and forced without difficulty to do what they did not want, assailed and conquered by threats no less than by words and blows. Then he energetically fell upon Guines and manfully occupied its fortresses unafraid.

When Viscount Arnold of Merck learned of this,[203] he began to fear more and more for himself, although he had his brothers, Simon of Merck and Jordan (a man most able and audacious in arms), who were energetic knights, and other innumerable followers of great name and strength. And calling his brothers and intimates and friends together, he asked them what ought to be done. Following their advice willy nilly, he promised Arnold of Ghent through messengers that if Count Albert did not come to the aid of the territory of Guines within forty days, he would voluntarily do Arnold of Ghent homage as the count of the territory, as long as the peers and other barons of the land did likewise.

53. *How Baldwin, the son of the lord of Ardres, went over to Arnold of Ghent.*

Now when Baldwin, the son of the lord of Ardres, heard that Arnold of Ghent was plotting at Guines, he flew to Arnold of his own free will, even though Baldwin held little or almost no land in the territory and had always hated and mistrusted the counts of Guines as his predecessors had formerly done — for the lords of Ardres deigned to show the counts of Guines no reverence or submission. And others had neither confidence nor assurance in their strength and now despaired of Count Albert's coming and of help for the territory, and so similarly allied themselves with Arnold of Ghent. Of their own will they offered and promised him their hand in aid, proffering their faith, although they did so disloyally.[204] What more? Arnold of Ghent allied and linked and confederated almost all of the barons of Guines with himself, except Arnold of Hames, who had accepted all of the land of Guines from Count Albert in safekeeping, as has been said.

And so Arnold called "the Eater" learned that Arnold of Ghent held Guines with the support of his followers, that he was conspiring with the people of Guines, and that the barons of the land consented to him and did not propose to expel him, but at that moment instead fairly openly lent and mobilized men and forces for him as a favorable sort of assistance in war (if this were necessary). When messengers had been sent as quickly as possible from the castle of Audruick (which was so named long ago, meaning "the Elders' place"),[205] to which Arnold the Eater had pressed on with his men and forces, he told Castellan Henry of Bourbourg of the situation: that Arnold of Ghent, who held Guines, had won the favor of all the barons of Guines.

54. *How Arnold the Young was killed by his dependents in Fulbert's wood.*[206]

Meanwhile, however, a lamentable and forever dishonorable disgrace happened in the territory. When Arnold of Ghent was sitting down to eat at Guines on the feast of the Holy Innocents with Baldwin, the son of the lord of Ardres, and other of his knights, attendants, officials, and servants, lo, a swift messenger arrived, who announced that Arnold the Young, the lord of the citadel of Ardres, had been struck down and had his throat slit (or rather he was done in) [207] by his servants in Fulbert's wood near Northout. For shame!

Arnold of Ghent, therefore, arose as quickly as he could from table and commended the fortress of the castle of Guines to his most faithful subjects—
warning and ordering them to keep it upon peril of their life and honor—
and brought Baldwin of Ardres, now his confederate, to Ardres as quickly as
he could. He made the castle open its gates to him, and established him as
the prince and lord of the honor and dominion of Ardres.

*55. How Arnold of Ghent made war on Castellan Henry of Bourbourg at
Audruick.*

But Castellan Henry of Bourbourg, when the outcome of the matter became known through letters, no less than by messengers and rumor, swiftly
flew to Audruick with knights and an armed multitude of people, groaning
in anger and indignation. Hearing this,

Sprightly Arnold gathered every knight,
And cried, "*To arms! To arms! Now we must fight!*" [208]
His mouth and hand brought war; war was all rife;
For martial glory was to him his life.
He so loved war, his confidence was keen;
And through this war he hoped to conquer Guines!
He did not hide the hunger in his heart
To be the count; to those who took his part
He spoke his mind and with them made a pact:
They would provide the forces that he lacked.
The lord of Ardres and lord of Saint-Omer,
Matilda's noble sire (and brothers), were there.
These valiant people, simply for war's sake,
Did with free will war's dangers undertake.

Therefore, when he had gathered as many knights and footmen as he could,
Arnold of Ghent hastened to Audruick, where the first battle of the war
occurred and he manfully besieged the castellan of Bourbourg, Arnold of
Hames, and their supporters and encircled them with war in the castle.

Therefore both fought; harsh Mars was on the field.
Bourbourg kept safe the camps and did not yield.
He urged his men to battle for what's right,

Proclaiming the just cause: that they should fight.
To tear a rival's camps down, he implored,
Is just and right, when law has been ignored.
He stirred the archers to give it their all;
Like hail upon their enemies arrows fall.
Arnold, outside, desires nought but war;
He promises his comrades more and more,
Should he be victor. A soldier midst the rest,
With shimmering words, he promises them the best;
And so they all agreed and so did swear;
They acted thus; Mars rang out everywhere.
The gods contended to make victory yield
To each; at first Lord Henry held the field.
The virgin Justice fought on Henry's side;
Since he was right, to him she was allied.
Mars gnashed his teeth on all sides midst the foe,
But wild Bellona kept Ghent's camps from woe.

Then Arnold fortified the tower of the church with knights and arms, and he manfully entered that turret with them as though it were a war machine. And hence, when he had almost forced and compelled those who were inside the wall of the fortress—namely Castellan Henry of Bourbourg and Arnold of Hames and their supporters—to surrender because of the discomfort of war, Henry, fearing for himself and his followers, went away in the night with Arnold of Hames to Bourbourg and left the fortress deserted–for shame!—without its men or its forces. But Arnold seized the fortress and boldly occupied its rampart, and he alone ruled all the regions of the land of Guines as the count, and he fortified all the fortresses of the land with as many knights and retainers as were necessary.

But Henry could scarcely bear the injury caused him and the notorious shame and dishonor cast upon him. And so enraged with a spirit of complete malignity, he stirred up his bitter bile and let his wrath and indignation burn and devoted his entire soul to the depopulation and destruction of the wretched land of Guines. But although Arnold, as I have said, had subjected all parts of Guines to himself and claimed all the fortresses and Henry did not have any place in Guines where he might safely put his foot, Henry thought that if he somehow fortified Amaury's earthwork or Amaury's mound [209] and armed it with a war machine, by means of this fortification, he could doubtless conquer all of Bredenarde, and thus all parts of the land of Guines.

56. Of Amaurival.

There was a certain very rich man in Bredenarde by the name of Amaury who was descended from the lineage of Eckarde;[210] he was so confident in his resources and friends, that he presumed to raise an earthwork and establish a keep to the north of the village of Audruick, against the count of Guines. But although Amaury was driven from Guines by the count because of his bold and presumptuous rebellion (and not without warrant!), later on when the count had destroyed and torn apart the war machines and equipment on the rampart that Amaury had earlier raised, and flung them to the earth, the mound, despoiled of its fortification and wall, was left standing. For a long time afterward, therefore, and not without cause, that place was called Amaury's earthwork or Amaury's mound.

57. How Castellan Henry of Bourbourg had a tower built at Bourbourg by a carpenter and attached it to the earthwork at Amaurival.

So Castellan Henry of Bourbourg secretly sent surveyors and carpenters to Amaurival to go around the place with geometrical tools and measure and secretly build a tower and warlike bulwarks and other machines at Bourbourg that were proportionate to the height of the motte and the amount of space. While Arnold and the people of Guines were unaware, they were to move these fortifications (not without knights, men, and supplies) to Amaurival in the silence of the dead of night. Thus spoke Henry, and, lo, all things were done and prepared and collected and erected on high on this spot of his. Then he called the tower of that fortress "the Flower,"[211] not, as some people idly report, because a lance stood erected at the height of the tower and wild flowers were tied around the top of the lance, but because he introduced into the stronghold of that castle the flower of knights, archers, and other fighters to combat the people of Guines.

And so Arnold, rising in the morning and seeing the tower and bulwarks with the other war machines suddenly and unexpectedly raised and elevated at Amaurival, stirred his whole territory to arms. Thus came all the barons of the whole land of Guines who were on his side, along with many innumerable folk summoned from many places. When they had come together as one at Audruick, they besieged the tower called the Flower. And some of the men of Bourbourg sallied forth toward the men of Guines—not without much bloodshed on either side—and killed Gosso of Northout[212] and led many men away from there as captives. But when the people of Bourbourg saw the troops of Guines grow in strength, they returned to their castle at Amaurival as fast as they could.

58. *That Baldwin, the lord of Ardres, was shot in the head with an arrow at the Flower or Amaurival.*

Then, when the men of Guines followed and prepared and girded themselves to take and destroy the castle held by the men of Bourbourg, the archers of Bourbourg cried out. Lo, an arrow coming obliquely from the castellan of Bourbourg's side stood forth from the head of Baldwin, the lord of Ardres, and penetrated to his brain. Then Arnold and all of the men of Guines lamented and bemoaned him with inexpressible groans, because a prince of such lordliness had been gravely wounded to the point of death. Arnold, therefore, drew back his foot, and he and his men left the place and carried the lord of Ardres, Baldwin, to Ardres, not like a proud man, but like a wounded one. However, I shall until the right time put off writing about how this same Baldwin, after he had received this wound and was in danger of death, had a secret conversation and discussion with the venerable Abbot Thierry of Capella concerning the office of provost in the church of Ardres.[213]

The castellan of Bourbourg, hearing that Lord Baldwin of the citadel of Ardres was wounded to death, did not dare to linger longer at the Flower and ignominiously left again for Bourbourg with his followers. But Arnold and his men followed with an eager step. But when he came to the Flower and knew that the castellan and his men had left, he struck the tower to the ground, both the structures of wood and the bulwarks, as well as the earthwork, and he cast it down to earth and had it flung here and there and had most of the pieces carried to Audruick. And thus to this day Amaury's earthwork or mound remains as desolate and despoiled of its towers and war machines as it had been before.

59. *How Castellan Henry of Bourbourg devastated all of Guines.*

From that day, however, Castellan Henry of Bourbourg did not cease to harry and assail the soil of Guines. But coming with *a strong hand and outstretched arm* [Dt. 5:15; Ezek. 20:33,34], and having gathered men and collected his own forces and those of others, he began and undertook the de-

population and depredation of the wretched land of Guines, unmoved by
any prayer or calamity of the innocent poor folk, and he destroyed fortresses,
devastated villages, turned churches to embers, captured men, and carried
off animals and booty.

Baldwin, the lord of Ardres, recuperated, however, and when he was fully
cured of his wound and illness, he gave full thanks to God in the holy church
for the recovered health of his body. And now, following the advice of the
venerable father and abbot Thierry of Capella,[214] he no longer lent any military assistance to Arnold of Ghent, nor would he now advise Arnold against
the castellan. Hearing this, the castellan of Bourbourg rejoiced with Baldwin
of Ardres and congratulated him abundantly, and he sent legates with letters
to Baldwin at Ardres and gave him many thanks, because Baldwin rightly did
not intend to fight against the righteous side any longer. Baldwin, however,
who was in his heart and soul quite reasonably concerned about his own advancement, saw that Albert was idle and by no means either approached or
helped the territory. He sent messengers with letters to the castellan and asked
him whether Henry wished to have his daughter[215] separated from Albert and
married to Baldwin by correct and ecclesiastical ritual. Baldwin would be devoted to Henry like the son Eustace,[216] and, along with all his possessions and
friends, would very reverently and diligently offer Henry sincere service, and
he promised, boasted, and agreed to drive Arnold of Ghent from the land
and to liberate the land from this same Arnold. When he heard and understood this, the castellan was much happier. He sent messengers as quickly as
he could to Baldwin and announced and indicated and wrote back to Baldwin
that he wished all things to be according to Baldwin's desire in every detail,
just as Baldwin himself had said and proposed and, in fact, wished.

60. How Albert the Boar and Beatrice were separated and Beatrice married Baldwin, the lord of Ardres.

And so the castellan sent Bernwin, a priest of the church of Saint-Omer,
and others, both priests and knights, with his daughter[217] to Albert, and when
the cause of their journey had been explained to him, they laid before him the
illness of his wife, along with other sufficient considerations. When the day
had been agreed upon and set by judicial and ecclesiastical order, Albert and
Beatrice were separated.[218] And while Albert remained in England, Beatrice
returned to her father at Bourbourg.

When this was told to Arnold of Ghent, although he disguised the matter as best he could, he feared for himself and his followers. For the only thing he feared soon happened. Indeed, Baldwin, the lord of Ardres, now joined Beatrice, the daughter of the castellan of Bourbourg, to himself as his wife according to the law of matrimony, with the assent of Count Thierry of Flanders. Thus, the castellan of Bourbourg and the lord of Ardres became just like father and son, having one heart and one soul. And for this reason, these confederates attacked and disquieted Arnold's lands and despoiled the wretched poor folk of their possessions, however small, and preying upon them, left nothing to Arnold undespoiled save his camps or fortifications.

So Arnold feared for himself, and yet, penned in as he was and holed up inside the fortifications of his land and the enclosures of the citadels for longer than usual, he constantly persevered in his enterprise. One day, however, while he was listening to the mystery of our redemption at Guines in the chapel of St. Mary, and the clergy and chaplain were sweetly and smoothly singing the gradual, which is *"Place your thought upon the Lord and he will nourish you"* [Ps. 55:22],[219] and it pleased him greatly, he asked his brother Baldwin the monk (who was then, however, a knight)[220] the mystical interpretation of this very delectable song. When Baldwin had properly explained the literal meaning to him, the faithful interpreter also said to him: "My brother and lord, hope in God and He Himself will do it. *Do not fear*, for lo and behold, *soon you will be made a rich man*, and lo and behold, *the glory of your house will be multiplied.* [Ps. 49:16].[221] Have you never heard that

"*Though not expected, there shall come the hour,*[222]
In which the poor man may be raised to power?"

61. How Beatrice died.

As though he were speaking with a prophetic spirit, when the mass was just finished and sung, lo and behold, a messenger came quickly, and calling at the gate with a great clamor, he said that the lady of Ardres, Beatrice, had died that night.

As is the common custom among folk,
He mixed the truth with falsehood as he spoke.[223]

He said that late in the evening, when she tasted milk mixed with fat,

The milk was poisoned; on her marriage bed
Where late she dallied, now she rested dead.
Another pondered this in his own mind,
And speaking thus he left these words behind:
"O fickle Fortune! He who touched the sky
Now falls to earth; another goes on high.
The fleeting world resembles human fate;
It flourishes at dawn, then withers late."

And so Beatrice lived only for a few days with her husband, Baldwin, the lord of Ardres. Because she had stone and had been for a long time weakened and worn down by illness, as I have often said above, she died a miserable death at Ardres. And she was honorably buried, not without the lamentable ululation and weeping of her followers, in the chapterhouse of the monastery of blessed Mary of Capella (because monks had not yet been established or substituted for canons in the cemetery of the church of Ardres), so that she should be found at the last trump to have expiated her sins through the prayers of holy monks.[224] Her sister, Matilda by name, the venerable matron and abbess of Bourbourg, had a marble slab placed over her tomb after the space of some years.[225]

Thus, when Beatrice had died and had been long and greatly mourned by her father and her people, the castellan knew that nothing further remained except for him to give up the cause for which he had fought and the land which he had so long desired and that after he had troubled Guines for almost five years, he could not delight in or retain any expectation of Guines.[226] And so he made his way through the middle of Guines with torches and arms and was received in his own land at Bourbourg and he never again—O prudent, unchanging and immovable sequence of fate!—appeared in the land of Guines.

62. How Castellan Winemar of Ghent died.

In the meanwhile, however, Castellan Winemar of Ghent died. But as his son Arnold was set and intent on acquiring—or rather had now acquired—the county of Guines and was detained there, Thierry, the count and prince of the honor of Flanders, gave the castellany of Ghent to Roger, who was at that time the viscount of Courtrai, and entrusted it to him to hold.[227] He did so without consulting Arnold of Ghent (or rather, as he was now, Arnold of

Guines). Afterward, Count Arnold, remaining in peace, promised Roger to keep the peace as long as he lived, as Viscount Roger was to marry Arnold's daughter Margaret. Arnold confirmed this by both his words and his deeds.

63. How Geoffrey of Semur wished to have the county of Guines.

Arnold had gotten the honor of Guines with much labor and had done the rite of homage to the count of Flanders and had also reconciled the barons of Guines to himself and bound them to him with a pledge of security and established peace with them. Then when he thought he could live in peaceful tranquility, Geoffrey of Semur, his maternal kinsman and first cousin,[228] rose against him with an infinite multitude of his maternal relations, so that Arnold could truly say, "Faith is never secure, and some worrisome thing interrupts one's joys." And so Geoffrey hurtled into their midst and said that, according to hereditary succession, he had a greater right than Arnold to rule and succeed to the county of Guines by right of close relationship to his maternal uncle (namely count Manasses). For Arnold's mother Giselle and his own mother Adelaide were sisters, and Arnold's mother Giselle was younger than his mother Adelaide.

In reference to this matter, even though I reoriented my pen toward the people of Semur to write about this Adelaide and the children of this Adelaide—breathing hard, as it were, and assisting a second Hercules, while Atlas caught his breath!— [229] I speak so that I may not seem to have dreamed up one thing after another in the valley of Ascra,[230] while the people of Semur bluster against me. (I have become vehement because of rumors and I am in pursuit of the truth from truthful people and those who do not make things up.) When Geoffrey of Semur's mother had already died and been buried, her sister Giselle, Winemar of Ghent's wife, was still alive and her children, particularly Arnold (of whom I am speaking) and the others, were blossoming and flourishing in the flower of youth. And when Count Manasses of Guines, the maternal uncle of both men—namely of Geoffrey of Semur and Arnold of Ghent—went the way of all flesh, and both his daughter Rose and Beatrice, Rose's daughter, had died and were buried, and there was left no seed from the body of Count Manasses, Geoffrey of Semur impudently and irreverently plotted and in bold fashion made a calumny against his first cousin, namely Arnold, who was now beyond the shadow of a doubt the count of Guines. Geoffrey ignored the fact that his mother Adelaide was already dead and buried, while his aunt Giselle of Ghent, in truth, was still alive and surviving—God forbid Geoffrey should succeed his uncle in Guines, as though this were the hereditary order set out by proper custom![231] But when Geoffrey returned home and took advice concerning his injuries, with the same ease with which he had impudently and unjustly earlier slandered the land of Guines, he left Arnold, the just heir to the land of Guines, in peace, as was proper and as he ought to have done. Go to the people of Semur, if you need to know more concerning the family of Semur.

64. How Count Arnold called his followers to himself, honored them and exalted them.

Therefore, Count Arnold obtained the county of Guines after many altercations, assaults, and battles and lived peacefully and safely in the land, when all his adversaries, both those outside Guines and those living in his land, had been mastered, pacified, and made gentle. And since to most people

Rest is often found to be quite sweet,
When they've accomplished many an arduous feat,

he set his mind and determined upon peace and strove for it with as great zeal as he could. He summoned his followers in the land of Guines to him and looked after them. He gathered them together in his house and household and supported them. He married them off in the territory. Before all else and in every detail, he fully rejoiced in a glorious lineage of children, and he spurred and prodded himself with a most fervent goad and solicitude to promote them.

65. How Baldwin, the lord of Ardres, went abroad to Jerusalem.

Meanwhile, Baldwin, the lord of Ardres, went abroad to Jerusalem with King Louis of France, Count Thierry of Flanders, and other barons of Flanders, to wit in 1146 a. d.[232] Baldwin commended his land and particularly the castle of Ardres to Arnold Gohel of Surques, who was and was called the castellan of Ardres.[233] Baldwin made him his bailiff and provost, to take care of his affairs until Baldwin returned. But Viscount Arnold of Merck, who had married Baldwin's sister, namely Adeline, and by her had a single daughter, who was then an adolescent blooming with lily-like beauty, was angry and took it ill that Baldwin had not entrusted the land to himself. But when he had patiently put up with the situation for a time, rumor flew and announced now that Baldwin, the lord of Ardres, had perished of hunger at Satalieh, now that he had drowned in the sea, now that he was slain by the blades of Christ's enemies, but whether this or that, in the end that he was dead and buried beyond any hope of returning.[234]

66. How Viscount Arnold of Merck became the lord of Ardres.

When he had heard this, Viscount Arnold of Merck reconciled to himself and won for himself the love and good will of the count of Flanders, as well as that of the count of Guines, and became the lord of Ardres; Arnold Gohel gave his consent and other peers of Guines judged thus. Then Stephen, the son of Elenard of Seninghem,[235] saw and understood that Viscount Arnold of Merck had been promoted and raised to the lordship of the honor of Ardres, and saw that this Arnold's only daughter would in time be the future heir to this great honor and lordship by hereditary succession, and so he aspired to marriage with this girl. And for this reason, men and messages were sent running back and forth, and she was engaged and promised to him as his wife.

And so, when Count Arnold of Guines heard this, he feared for himself, or rather, he took care and forearmed himself and his posterity with the greatest discretion, as is prudent. He judged thus: If the now aforementioned contracted and confirmed marriage took place, it would be to the perpetual discord of the now pacified land and in a short time it would be the future destruction of the land. From that point, turning things over in his mind, he judged that if he could get the aforementioned young woman[236] and marry her to his firstborn son Baldwin by the law of matrimony, he himself and his people could enjoy lasting peace in the land. Thus, having humbled himself in accordance with the advice of prudent and older men, the most prudent count inclined himself toward peace, and when he spoke in secret with Lord Arnold of Ardres and his wife Adeline, he intimated and disclosed to them in a few words his reason for coming.

67. How Baldwin, the son of Count Arnold of Guines, married Christine, the daughter of the lord of Ardres.

And so the lord of Ardres and his wife, who were rather gratified and happy, called their daughter to give her consent to his proposal. Thus the girl heard what she was not displeased to hear and lo, as she was now present, she now expressed her assent with the happiness of her face. She leaned attentively with pricked ears toward the voice of her father and mother, about to answer more freely than to any other word before, as they asked for her consent. Consequently, the speech of each party was pleasing to the other party and the voice and will of all was unified as they said, "So be it! So be it!" Then Baldwin, the firstborn son of Count Arnold of Guines, married the daughter of Lord Arnold of Ardres, who was called Christine, both by right of her virtues and her own proper name. And let there be *glory to God in the highest* and *peace in the land* of Guines *to all men*. [Lk. 2:14]

And so that he and his might enjoy a perpetual peace, as I have just said, the firstborn son of the count of Guines (then the future count of Guines), was a little lowered from the height of the dignity and name of the count of Guines and diminished to provide an example and paradigm for many similar noble men (namely dukes, kings, and emperors) to humble themselves and marry for a similar reason. He worthily and joyfully lowered himself to take the daughter of his man as a wife according to the law of matrimony.

68. Of the construction of the tower and wall at Colvida and of the construction of the infirmary at Lostebarne.

Meanwhile, however, Arnold of Merck, the lord of Ardres, afterward raised a glorious tower into the air and erected it in the wood called Colvida—which took its name from coals, or perhaps from the cultivation or color of the ground.[237] He enclosed it with a wall all around on top of the earthwork, furnished it with buildings, and dedicated the place to God with a chapel built for serving God. Seeing that in his prosperity all things had fallen to him as he wished, he wished to please God, because he was not heedless of evangelical riches, although he pleased secular men and the world in every way and was rich in worldly terms. At the urging and request of his wife, the venerable matron Adeline, he built an infirmary or hospice for the sick and a chapel at Lostebarne outside Ardres, on what was at that time the royal road, which was frequented by a populous multitude of passersby. And he provided rents to support the sick or the leprous and also to support a chaplain in that place; by his forceful words and examples, he inspired the nobles and people of the whole territory to endow this most wretched congregation.

69. Of the founding of the infirmary at Espelleke.

Around that same time, Count Arnold saw that the lord of Ardres — earlier called Arnold of Merck, but now called Arnold of Colvida — had established a house for the sick at Lostebarne, inhabited by sick people and supported by rents. Moved by a not dissimilar pity in the presence of the poor of Christ who were missing the joints of their limbs and had become leprous, he himself established a poorhouse and leprosarium outside of Guines at Espelleke. Afterward, when his son Baldwin had become count of Guines, he enlarged it and furnished it with a chapel and enclosed it with a wall. He filled and enriched it with tithes and rents and, what is more, with his assistance and assiduous protection and visitation and donations of alms.

70. How leprous women were gathered at Lostebarne and leprous men at Espelleke.

When this same Baldwin had become the count of Guines and his son Arnold of Guines was the lord of Ardres and the castellan of Bourbourg, it was by reasonable and appropriate foresight decreed, established, and arranged concerning these two infirmaries or hospitals for the sick that all the women in all of Guines who became leprous should be brought to Lostebarne. There they might accept bread to sustain them so that they might live. But all the men in all of Guines, however many there were, who were similarly discovered to be touched or contaminated by leprosy should be brought or go along to Espelleke. There they might receive and eat the bread of sorrow, while they daily called with raucous voice for death, until they breathed their last.[238]

Then Count Arnold and the lord of Ardres, the man called Arnold of Colvida, were joined in such a pact of friendship, that they might be said to be a matched pair because of their friendship and were just like a new and recently revivified Theseus and Pirithous.[239] And just as two hands are employed for the sustenance of the body of one man, so these two were also joined in spirit in a single desire of the soul, as though they were in one body — although not in one body — for the consolation and defense of all of Guines.

Therefore, all the followers of each Arnold of either party rejoiced; now the plots of all the persecutors on both sides ceased. Guines rejoices and exults in peace; the court of Ardres rejoices and congratulates Guines. Nor do the people of Guines, on one side, and of Ardres, on the other, fight now. Let each defer to the other or feel obligated to yield, since each strives in turn to defer to the other. Indeed, the lord count tempered the dignity of his lordship toward the man subject to him, and the man, not pursuing the old rebellion against the counts of Guines, did not disdain to show his lord, his prince, and count respect and the submissive service he owed everywhere and at all times. And so Count Arnold and the lord of Colvida, called Arnold as I have just said, became as it were one *heart and one soul* [Acts 4:32]. Nor was there any difference in dignity between them in all of Guines, except that one was called count and the other lord. But although outside the territory the count was very frequently called simply a lord, through the integrity of his name and the dignity of his honor, he maintained that he had always been, was said to be, and truly was a count.

71. How Baldwin, the son of Count Arnold of Guines, sired Mabel of Cysoing and Arnold, his firstborn son, who was first the lord of Ardres and afterward also the castellan of Bourbourg.

Then Baldwin, the son of Count Arnold of Guines, knew his wife Christine; at Ardres she conceived and bore Mabel, who was married as a wife to John, the son of Petronilla of Cysoing.[240] Then later on and similarly at Ardres she conceived and bore Arnold of Guines, whom I called our lord and patrician at the beginning of the work, because of whom and for whom and concerning whom my labor and speech have been performed in this work.

'Tis he, whose love's my glory; who does give
His gracious grace by which he lets me live.

I judge it unnecessary to persist at greater length or more fully in his praises, since all the things I have said or ought to say in creating this work sing his praise and glory in every detail.

72. Of the procreation of his other sons, namely William, Manasses, and Baldwin the cleric.

Then at Ardres, where the venerable matron became the mother of all her children—let me tell the truth about this great and full progeny with brief eloquence—she bore William, a vigorous knight, but dead in the flower of his youth at Colvida and buried with his fathers honorably at Andres in the church of the Assumption of the blessed Virgin Mary. There was also Manasses,[241] who because of the outstanding quality of his wisdom and the force of his singular prudence by the particular privilege of love stood higher (but after Arnold, the firstborn) in his father's favor than the others. Consequently, his father gave him Rorichove with its associated rights, a breadth of spacious marsh, and many other benefices purchased and bought with money.[242] There was also Baldwin,[243] a cleric, a canon of Thérouanne and the procurator and parson of Nielles-lez-Ardre—not of the fields of Nestor, but of the church of St. Peter, the Prince of the Apostles, near La Montoire[244]— and similarly the provisor and parson of churches in England at Stevington, Stisted and Town-Malling, and Baicton.[245]

73. Of the death of Count Arnold.

Then it happened around this time that Count Arnold, who was now mature in years and burdened by old age, went to England so that he might provide for himself and the territory by looking after his affairs. While he was staying there for a few days in his own mansion at Newington (which along with its associated rights came to him from Emma, the erstwhile countess of Guines),[246] he was seized by a grave illness. As he was not unaware that the day of his death was approaching and thinking of the salvation of his soul, he set his house in order. Thus when he had called together churchmen and his household, he drew up and made an eternal bequest in the Lord, so that he might deserve sometime to be received in the eternal tabernacle. Therefore, he distributed and gave, not to the pimps or scoundrels who praised his name in the world, but to the members of Christ and the poor.[247] Although he gave many things to many people in alms there, he bequeathed his war weapons, his horse, his dogs, his birds, and whatever secular amusements he had to Saint-Ingelvert, where he had earlier chosen to be buried. Then Count Arnold of Guines died and was carried from Newington to Saint-Ingelvert and honorably buried there in 1169 a. d.[248] In this year, the daughter of the late king Stephen, sometimes called the countess of Boulogne, took the garb of religion at Messine again, and the churches, which were under interdict because of her, were freed.[249] In this year, the bones of the holy virgins were carried from Cologne to Licques.[250]

74. How Baldwin became the count of Guines.

And so Baldwin received consolation over of the death of his father as a wise man does, and when he had done homage to Count Thierry of Flanders, he became the count of Guines.[251] He was most eloquent in worldly wisdom and was, for his size, second to none in knighthood in the whole breadth of Flanders, so that he might rightly be said to be no degenerate heir of his father. As soon as he obtained the dignity of the honor, he shone with the rigor of justice throughout Guines, to the point that it was said that he was as just and judicious as a judge to the just when he was in judgment, that he was terrible, but nonetheless praiseworthy, to the unjust, and that he made marvelous judgments.[252] When he was still in his adolescence (before he was promoted to honor and responsibility in the county) he was frequently thought to be dissolute because of the carelessness of his years, to be frequently held back by the scantiness of his property and bodily support, and to be not at all careful or foresighted concerning the necessities of life. Although he appeared unwise to foolish men, however — or else he simulated foolishness — when he was raised to honor in the county, he at once held the foolish and malign (they always hate wisdom) in contempt as evil men, as though he had become a different man.

75. How Count Baldwin built the chapel of St. Catherine at La Montoire.

In the beginning, then, among his first works of piety, at the instigation and request of his most Christian wife, Christine, he built and constructed a chapel in honor of the blessed martyr Catherine at La Montoire. In that same chapel he placed the oil of that same martyr and holy virgin, Catherine, and relics of the blessed martyr Thomas, to whom more than any others he was determined to show a special and personal reverence.[253] Rather he was obligated to do so, because Thomas had administered the oath of knighthood to him and granted and bestowed on him the name and duty of a knight.[254] And in charge of this chapel, he appointed as the first chaplain Michael, whom the glorious martyr, Thomas, the archbishop of Canterbury, had ordained as a priest. He was a venerable man, well educated in letters, who originated from Louches and had once been the master of Ardres.[255] And Baldwin sufficiently, or rather abundantly, provided all things that he was instructed were necessary for the chapel and for the chaplain, both books and other ornaments.

76. How he built the round house at Guines and the chapel.

Then Baldwin built a round house over the keep at Guines with squared stones and raised it high in the air. He had it made flat and even in the upper part of the frame thus, so that a leaden roof, set on joists and crossbeams, could be placed on the peaks of the building and so that it would not be visible to those looking from above.[256] In that house, he constructed chambers, rooms, many lodgings, and many passageways, so that it seemed little different from the labyrinth, that is, the house of Daedalus. Further on outside the house, in front of the gate of the edifice, he built a chapel like the glory of Solomon,[257] with a marvelous floor of wood and stones. Furthermore, he undertook to enclose the outer fastness of the citadel with a stone wall. But he armed and adorned the entrance through the gates with both warlike towers and engines.

77. How he repaired the tower, buildings, and fish pond at Tornehem and sank a prison beneath the tower.

Then afterward, he repaired and rebuilt the tower at Tornehem, which his predecessors had earlier constructed. (It was gaping with fissures and threatening ruin with stones torn away and joints disjointed and broken down.) In the making of the repair, as a result, it seemed even to him (if the dialecticians will permit me to say so) to differ from its previous state. In this also he created a structure of labyrinthine form, and building on galleries one after another, he situated room after room and compartments along passageways like the Meander River. Indeed, in the tower, or rather underneath it, he buried a prison in the deep abyss of the earth, [reached] through certain secret drawbridges in the foundation. It was like a hell-pot to terrify guilty wretches and, to speak more truthfully, to punish. In it the miserable mortals slated for punishment, awaiting the day of terrible judgment, might hang onto their detestable lives and receive the bread of sorrow with the vermin in the shadows in squalor and filth. Moreover, at the exit of the tower, he also built a chapel in the stone vault, to which he appointed and authorized Siger as chaplain. Then he rebuilt, heightened, sharpened, and roughened the walls within whose sweep we have often seen fighters and athletes clashing, and he finished them with ramparts. Then he enclosed and fortified the village with a mighty and stalwart earthwork at the back side of the church. But to the west of the village, not without much labor and expense, he obstructed the waters of the river Reveria with a barrier of soft earth and stones like a sluice, and he enclosed the fish pond, which was full of the biggest fish, with well-defined banks.

78. That he moved the market of Zudkerque to Audruick and held it there at Pentecost and constructed a fortress and furnished it with a chapel and enclosed the village with an earthwork and dried out a marsh and made arable land.

His ancestors had ordained a market to be held on Sunday at Zudkerque by chance occurrence rather than prudent planning. He then moved the market to Audruick; he prudently changed the place but not the day, following the tenor of ecclesiastical and apostolic advice. There he brought the peasants of the outlying areas together by invitation and compulsion to reside like city-dwellers. And there he commanded and ordered a fair to be held during Pentecost and confirmed it by oath; it was to be solemnized more in a worldly than a religious fashion and to be attended by the whole people, the merchants, and other folk, who would come there because of the plenitude of goods for sale.

He also surrounded the town with a double earthwork and he built a motte in the middle with houses and necessary buildings. And he very diligently and reverently built a chapel in honor of St. Nicholas onto the gate at the entrance of the interior wall,[258] just as behooves and suits[259] a shrine of the saints. He procured and appointed a priest of the holiest life, Stephen, as the chaplain for it, along with books and other ecclesiastical ornaments to the sufficiency—or rather to the glory!—of the citizens of heaven. So also with Herculean skill, he dried out a marsh in that same place, having cut off the many heads of the Hydra.[260]

79. How Giles, Siger, Adeline, Margaret, and Matilda were born, and whom they married.

Meanwhile, around the same time, the venerable matron the countess of Guines conceived and bore Giles, who was first a cleric, then afterward a knight;[261] he married Christine, the daughter of the noble and prudent Eustace of Montgardin.[262] Then she had Siger, who similarly married Adelaide, the daughter of the similarly noble man Henry of Zeltun; Zeltun is near the Celtic tower built by the pagans when the lands were divided up, from which it took its name.[263] She also bore Adeline, who first married Baldwin of Engoudsent or of Merck (however, he was called Baldwin of Cayeux),[264] then later the most strenuous of knights, Hugh of Malaunoy. She also had Margaret (who married Radbod of *Ruinis*)[265] and Matilda, given as a wife to William, the son of Clarembold of Thiembronne;[266] she died without any bodily heir.

80. Of the wisdom of Count Baldwin.

Then the count, who was a most careful investigator of everything, did not leave Minerva undespoiled of any wisdom.[267] And although he was a layman and completely illiterate—Oh, he was an indescribable man of both wonderful ability and wit, a pupil of every philosophy, and a most learned son!—although he was, as I have just said, completely ignorant of the arts, he disputed with the doctors of the arts; he neither restrained his tongue nor kept silent, as he had made use of liberal tools more and more often. And since he was no deaf auditor of theological writing, he grasped and heeded[268] with his attentive hearing the pronouncements of the prophets and not just the literal meaning of divine histories and evangelical doctrine, but also their mystical power. And for that reason he showed reverence to the clergy with marvelous good will. Indeed, he received divine eloquence from them, and in exchange he told and related to them popular trifles that he got from story-tellers.

And thus it often happened that the count, as he was educated and instructed by his teachers in some little questions and was a most diligent retainer of what he had heard, answered his men as though he were a lettered man and inspired others to respond. And properly, since he was more instructed in many things than he needed to be by the clergy, he contradicted and opposed the clergy in many matters. He thus often provoked and made sport of them with the wonderfully clever eloquence by which he stood out in many affairs, however, so that after the argument of the disputation he might show them respect with a wonderfully honorable magnificence. And for this reason, many people heard him and broke out in admiration for his objections and responses and often said about him, "Who is this?" and, "Let us praise him. Indeed, he says marvelous things! But how does he know letters since he never learned them?" For this reason, he kept clerics and masters with him and asked them about many things and listened to them diligently.

81. How he had many books translated.

While the count was ruling the dominion of the honor of Ardres, since he avidly embraced all learning about everything and was not able to retain all knowledge in his heart, he had Master Landry of Waben, a most learned man, translate the *Song of Songs* for him from Latin to French and frequently read it to him; the translation was not only according to the letter, but also according to the mystical understanding of the spiritual interpretation.[269] Baldwin also diligently learned much of the Gospels, particularly the Sunday readings with appropriate sermons, and also the life of St. Anthony the monk as diligently interpreted by a certain Alfred.[270] He also learned the greater part of the art of physics[271] through the translation by Master Godfrey, a very erudite man, from Latin into the French that Baldwin knew.[272] Who does not know, furthermore, that Solinus,[273] who spoke of the nature of things in both a physical and a philosophical manner, was faithfully translated with the most careful and laborious diligence by the venerable father Simon of Boulogne,[274] the master of Guines, from Latin into the French language so well known to Baldwin? He presented it to Baldwin and recited it in public so that he might capture and gain Baldwin's favor for himself, or rather so that he could rekindle the grace he had earlier received. Just so did Baldwin have the holy books necessary in church for the cult and veneration of God copied and prepared for him and placed them in his chapels here and there. Hence he also acquired harmonious instruments of the musical arts and conferred them on the nuns at Guines for the inspiration and enjoyment of divine worship.[275]

What more? He was rich with such an abundance of so many kinds of books, that he might be thought to rival Augustine in theology, Dionysius the Areopagite in philosophy, Thales of Miletus, the fabulist,[276] in popular entertainments, and the most renowned troubadours in epic songs, whether the deeds of the nobles or even the fables of the common folk. If one had not seen and heard of it, who, moreover, would believe that Hasard of Aldehem, who was completely a layman, learned letters and in an entirely lay manner was similarly made literate by Baldwin? The man I just called Hasard, indeed, while keeping and guarding the whole library of the count, read and understood all the books he had that were translated from Latin to French. What more? Also while Baldwin was the ruler and guardian, when he governed Ardres and had just built the law court and guildhall building and covered it with a lead roof, the Master called Walter the Silent composed, drew up and adorned the book he called "The Silence," or "The Romance of the Silence" after himself.[277] The count gave him horses and garments for this and many little gifts in recompense.

82. How he freed Giles of Hazebrouck from the hands of Count Reynold of Boulogne.

With a strong hand [Dt. 5:15; Ezek. 20:33,34], he also rescued Giles of Hazebrouck from Etaples and returned him to his own lands, whether Reynold of Dammartin liked it or not. In accordance with the will and advice of the venerable count Philip of Flanders,[278] Giles was the prefect of Boulogne under Duke Baldwin of Lorraine;[279] Reynold had recently usurped the county of Boulogne unbeknownst to Duke Baldwin.[280] At the time of this memorable deed, Reynold, although he had always been deceitful and inimical toward Baldwin and his people, swore an oath by God's head concerning this matter. Speaking with the laudably truthful tongue of truth concerning Baldwin, he said that he had never before with his own eyes seen a little man of such great probity and manly greatness of spirit. Although in the pride and arrogance of his speech he used the diminutive in a derogatory fashion, he did not conceal Baldwin's magnificent probity. Upon hearing it, this most prudent count was not stirred to rage or ugly words, but offered and spoke this moral opinion:

I've often heard one may learn from one's foe.[281]
Thus may he test you, then commend you so.

83. The fortress of Sangatte and its description.

Who does not know that the armed tower, so near the sky, at Sangatte was then built by that same count Baldwin? He encircled it with earthworks and sharpened stakes and armed it with ramparts, so that it was more hidden from the enemy than exposed to him. Furthermore, so that the place Sangatte may be seen by some listeners and by those unfamiliar with the site of the place as more notable in reputation, and for that reason of more authority, I shall set down a description of this place, while the people of Calais and Wissant complain about me, or rather Sangatte.

From ancient times, then, there was a certain sandy place on the shore of the Britannic ocean near St. Bertin's Escales,[282] not far from Walter's Wood,[283] almost midway between the ports of Wissant and Calais. There the sea's swell broke through the middle of the dunes or through the back of the sandy ridge as far as solid ground by its natural impulse and violence and created a port in the form of a tidal basin, which received ships in a very safe harbor. Because the water that had frequently been driven here and there through the sand did not have a free path back into the sea, it stagnated there between the dunes and the edges of the solid ground of Sclive, making a very deep marsh;[284] it was thought to be the pagans' well by the inhabitants and was named after that characteristic. But later on, roving sand, mixed in with the bubbling of the fluctuating sea, was cast up; the wave begrudged the waters[285] to the port and took them away. The spine of the dunes that had earlier been broken by the waters' assault was now brought together and consolidated into a hill by the constant blowing of the sand and the marsh was cut off from the sea. For that reason, because the flow of the sea at first perforated and penetrated the sand of the dunes there, as I just said, the locals called that sandy place "the opening in the sand," Sangatte, in the vernacular.[286] They also called the marsh and village by the same name.

The magnanimous and most famous Count Baldwin made this once nameless place most well known. Although Count Arnold, his father, had scarcely a dwelling in which to lay his head with safe honor and dignified respect in the village called for the aforementioned reason Sangatte, as Count Reynold of Boulogne and the people of Boulogne were hostile on one side, and on the other the people of Wissant, Calais, and all the territory of Merck grunted, Count Baldwin of worthy memory built and established a sturdy castle in that same marsh, and raised a glorious tower from the depths of the earth into the air. This tower, moreover, which was highly fortified with ramparts and war machines, had as many stones as it had enemies. Wherefore, Trojan Ilium would now stand in glory, had it been armed with so many and such fine armed men, had it had, in proportion to the size of the realm and its affairs,[287] as many and the same kind of abundant resources as the tower of Sangatte:

Nor would the glory of the Trojan force,
Have been deceived by that Achaean horse,

nor would the palace of Priam nor the realm have fallen; the Greeks would not have enjoyed a day of victory upon conquering the Phrygians!

84. How Count Reynold of Boulogne wanted to make a fortress at Ostruicque.

Truly, when Count Reynold of Boulogne[288] saw and observed that the tower of Sangatte had been built and that Count Baldwin of Guines often amused himself in it with delicious banquets and feasts with his knights and arms and was glorified in an unprecedented manner, he feared for himself as well as for his territory and set every sort of rage and indignation ablaze. When he had gathered the knights and people of his whole land at Ostruicque, near Sclive region, he began to dig and build to construct a castle across from the fortress of Sangatte, so that if in any way he could, he might erase and destroy the name and the fortress of Sangatte. So on this site diggers, men with spades, laborers, wood-cutters, and other workers and masters of the fortress and earthworks worked; they piled up the earth as high as they could into a motte and dug and created an earthwork to defend the motte, while the princes and the knights of the whole land stood around.

The people of Guines and Sangatte, who were strong and warlike men, swelled with indignation upon seeing this. Crying out, their archers rained down deadly arrows and square shot upon the foe, to the point that their enemies' workers and those of the opposing side were terrified and agitated. They fled ignominiously, after the princes and knights had been put to flight, not without much bloodshed, leaving the work unfinished, as can be seen today. My zealous labor prepared these things concerning the site of Sangatte and its fortress, lest at some time the origins of the foundations of the site of Sangatte's long existence should vanish and disappear from the memory of posterity.

85. How Countess Christine died and was buried at Ardres.

Then, a year after the lord of Ardres, Arnold of Colvida, and his noble wife Adeline died, Countess Christine of Guines lay on her sickbed (as is the custom of birthing women) after she had borne her last child. Her husband, Count Baldwin, was staying in England taking care of his business, when he received and heard messengers announcing that the illness of the sick countess had become grave to the point of death. The count scarcely came to her where she lay at Ardres when her physicians and masters, namely Herman and Godfrey, despairing of her life, left her to the count to be cared for and consoled (or rather very soon to be mourned and lamented). Purgative remedies[289] did not benefit her, but only propelled her into death—oh!—and Christine, the most Christian countess of Guines, died on July 2 in 1177 a. d. The monks of the church of Andres assented and consented to the request of the family of Ardres; because she was born at Ardres and then died there, she was honorably buried at the feet of her mother, Adeline of Ardres, the venerable matron of Ardres, and placed in the floor of the church across from her fathers. The venerable abbots Godeschalk of Saint-Bertin, Alger of blessed Mary of Capella, Peter of Andres, Robert of Licques, and other priests, clerics, and innumerable lay people were present and celebrated her funeral liturgy with tears.[290] In that place, then, there was sorrow and the weeping of all the people and lamentation.

> Her children, knights, the count, with tearful eyes,
> Lamented her; *the ether rang with cries.*[291]
> They wrung their hands, mouths bled and then they called
> The lady's name. The folk of Ardres bawled
> All wretched, with their wretched ululations;
> Their weeping led to greater lamentations.
> Each single tear wept for the lady's demise,
> Inspired more; their mouths poured out their cries.
> The more the fire of love burned hot inside,
> The more assailed by grief the mourners cried .

Then when the noble matron, the countess of Guines, had been buried and honorably covered with a marble stone, I wrote these verses as an epitaph for her upon the masonry.

> Here lies the countess, born of thriving house,
> Christine by name, an equal to her spouse.
> Let all men note the sixth nones of July,
> Her death-day thus in memory shall lie.

A thousand years, one hundred, seventy-seven,
From Jesus' birth, she died and went to heaven.

86. How Count Baldwin fell gravely ill on account of his sorrow at the death of his wife, and how he recovered.

Then Count Baldwin, accepting no consolation for the death of his much beloved wife, fell without moderation on his sickbed for many days. He was said to have been so stricken in mind because of his great sadness and illness, that he did not know himself or anyone else for many days, but could not distinguish or discern good from evil or right from wrong. And consequently, his physicians, Herman and Godfrey, permitted no one to come to him except William of La Podenie and William of Colvida and a few others serving him in his illness.[292] Therefore, his knights and people near and far wept, and the sorrow that all had felt at the death of the countess was renewed, because of the miserable illness of the count.

But the Lord, assailed by the prayers of His people, took account of Baldwin's humility and showed His mercy to the count (or rather to His servant) and granted him health and well-being. Then the count recovered from his illness and *was renewed*, like an eagle, in *his mind's spirit* [Eph. 4:23], in *acknowledgment* of the body of Christ and of the church [Col. 3:10]. And so his *heart grew warm* toward all [Ps. 39:3], but particularly toward members of his household, as was clear from his innumerable works of piety. Thereafter he became a pious auditor and consoler of orphans, a ready defender of widows against their enemies. Furthermore, with as much zeal and charity as he could, he restored noble orphans to their inheritances; he reestablished those who were bereft of their parents and frequently those who were deprived of their inheritances or possessions through their own prodigality or that of their parents. He even kept many of them near him, honored them, promoted them, and joined them in legitimate wedlock to wives great in riches and honors. What more? He was steeped in and notable for every kind of liberality, generosity, and cheer in receiving and gathering guests together — the kings, dukes, counts, knights, burgers, archbishops, bishops, archdeacons, abbots, priors, provosts, archpriests, priests, canons, clerics, and people of clerical professions, and prelates who took the road through his lands.

So that it may be more easily believed and proven by a truthful example how he behaved toward all people in every way and on all occasions, let me disclose with respect to one guest of memorable name with how much liberality and cheer Baldwin received him as a guest at Ardres and with what heartfelt desire and humane diligence Baldwin showed respect toward him and his followers. That guest was Archbishop William of Reims, the maternal uncle of King Philip of France.[293]

87. With what great liberality he received Archbishop William of Reims as a guest at Ardres and St. Thomas, the archbishop of Canterbury.

So one time, when Archbishop William of Reims of venerable and noteworthy memory, the son of Count Thibaud of Champagne, was on pilgrimage to the most holy martyr, Archbishop Thomas of Canterbury,[294] he was invited in by Count Baldwin of Guines of worthy memory. He sat at table to eat in the hall of Ardres, and dishes innumerable to the point of extravagance were liberally set down and joyfully accepted and one wine after another — Cyprian, Megarian, spiced wine, and claret — flowed into goblets here and there throughout the courtyard. The French asked for and requested the living water of the fountain, so that they might restrain and temper the strength of the wine somewhat. The servers and waiters, who were instructed and trained by the butlers (or rather by the count), poured the precious wine of Auxerre into glasses and small vessels from flagons; they lied and said that they would bring water. The clergy and knights did not know better and everyone was eating with pleasure.

When this finally became known to the venerable and pious lord archbishop — indeed, *nothing is covered that will not be revealed* [Mt. 10:26] — he almost substituted ingratitude for the thanks the faithful count and prudent dispenser deserved for showing the archbishop respect, because the count had so exceeded moderation with his liberal and generous hand. But since the venerable bishop as he ate had belched up into his memory the words of the apostle, "*Practice hospitality ungrudgingly to one another*" [1 Pet. 4:9],[295] he summoned the count to him and, as though he were ignorant of the affair, he asked the count to bring him a flask of water so that he might taste and imbibe the pure liquid element, water. Then the count withdrew smiling, as though obeying the orders of the venerable bishop and, in front of his servants, foot-soldiers, and men-at-arms, he broke as many water vessels as he could find. He kicked them with his foot, and with an exuberance beyond joy, pretended to the servants and the drinkers to be drunk, so that in all matters he might seem cheerful, pleasant, and jocular on account of the archbishop's reverence and presence. But the venerable bishop, his table-fellow, seeing the great liberality and cheerfulness of the man, promised to do all things that the count might wish that were in his power.

Let this case concerning his reception of one person or guest suffice us, then, so that whoever is listening may gather and comprehend from these manifest and authentic events that this count granted the benefit of a similar reception and hospitality to many others, in proportion to their personal status and his love for them. And so when that pious pastor, who by his name and deeds was worthy to be called archbishop, departed, the count offered and gave the archbishop two vials full of balsamic liquor to remember him by. With the same hilarity of face, as I have just said, just as he wanted and knew how to act, he received many people as guests and made and forced them to stay until the morrow with him and receive hospitality.

For that reason, I do not judge it necessary to write with what assiduity or with what honorable reverence, in what great magnificence and glory he received the most holy archbishop Thomas of Canterbury as a guest at Guines when he was returning from his exile to the place of his martyrdom. For if Baldwin showed a joyful and pleasant face to the venerable archbishop William of Reims as a lord, as a father archbishop, and as man ennobled by a glorious French family—or rather, if he acted with zealous respect toward many men not as worthy as that—what sort of cheerful and generous face might he be thought or believed to have rightly shown a wise man? A man whom he already knew to have, through his words and deeds, built his house *upon a rock* [Mt. 16:18]? A man dear to God? A holy and chaste man? A man born to reprobates in scandal?[296] A man elevated by the promotion of the holy church? A man who worked marvels in the land of Egypt, terrible things upon the sea, marvels in heaven and on earth? A man who pacified monsters? A man who did not fear the threats of persecuting enemies? A man heard by God in all things? A man, I say, a man—Oh Archbishop Thomas, a man of worth in all matters beyond all others and holier than the others!—who once hung this same count's sword at his side as a sign of his knighthood? And put the spurs—Oh, the humble virtue, worthy to be praised in every way, of this outstanding priest of Christ!—on the feet of his own knight? And gave him the accolade on his neck, which, nevertheless, Baldwin repaid on the day of his promotion to knighthood with various little gifts and expenditures more splendid than royal ones?[297] Lest Baldwin be thought unmindful of the benefit he had accepted, lest he be judged ungrateful and unworthy of such a great gift and honor, Baldwin showed himself to be such a man as he had never previously shown himself to be to anyone, and never wished to show himself to be afterward, in order to give thanks to the holy man for his grace not cheaply, but worthily, as was proper.[298] So holy Archbishop Thomas greatly enjoyed the cheer, presence, and liberality of the count, and when he had given thanks, he crossed to England, where after a few days he underwent and received martyrdom in the church and for the church.[299]

88. Of the prudence of Count Baldwin and of his negligence.

In the council of princes, this same count was said to be so prudent in counsel and wise in judgment, that he shone like a precious gem in the crown of the realm of France, and in the diadem of the king of England he sparkled like a precious ruby.[300] What more? If I could persist and write every detail in praise of this great count, I would sooner lack life than appropriate material to praise him. The ink would sooner dry up in my pen than his wonderful deeds would fail the writer. And so I have rightly said that in all things and in every way he was a praiseworthy man.

Those who envy him and us, however, say this about him, as though they were telling the truth: that in the rosy dawn he listened with a more attentive spirit to the hunter's horn than the priest's bell; that he heard the greyhound's voice more eagerly than that of the chaplain or his vicar; that he roused his austringers from sleep earlier than the keepers of the temple; and that he applauded a hawk or falcon circling and beating the air more than the priest giving a sermon. Then they also add true comments, as though they had been in no way deviating from the truth, and they try to show (and in a manner of speaking they do show) that because of the intemperate tumult of his loins he was of ungovernable lust from his first adolescent impulses to old age.[301]

89. Of his procreation of children after the burial of the countess.

He was, in fact, so ardent, as they say, toward young girls and especially toward virgins, that neither David nor his son Solomon is believed to be his equal in the corruption of so many young women, nor even Jupiter (as long as his sophistical flatteries fell upon girls).[302] Those hostile to him and us say these things. But far be it from the minds of discreet men that they should think it acceptable or appropriate for our enemies, who wrinkle their noses in derision at us, to be appointed or to be our judges.

So around the same time that Countess Christine of Guines died and was buried, he sired Giffard, a canon of the church of Thérouanne and Bruges and a procurator and parson of many churches in England, at Guines; also Bolde-kin the Bastard; Eustace and Willekin (a bastard in name and fact); Eustace, a cleric and a native of the citadel of Ardres; and innumerable other sons and daughters of many sorts, who were, for the most part, married to noble men here and there by their father's foresighted industry and care. How-ever, concerning the boys, some prepared themselves for the life and deeds of knighthood, and others indulged in the games of youth. Some were entrusted to teachers to be looked after; others were given into the care of masters at schools to be educated, and others were left here and there to be raised by their mothers or nurses, all this as the innate nature of their ability prompted. Since I am unsure of their number—and indeed even their father did not know all their names—I shall pass up saying anything more about them.[303] If I were fully to follow truth's report concerning them, I fear I would offend more than please.

90. How Arnold, his son, stayed with Count Philip of Flanders.

Let me turn my pen, therefore, to Arnold, his firstborn son, to whom my words are addressed. So then after Arnold had spent his childhood in his country with his father, he began to mature in manly strength and he went to bohorts and tournaments all over,[304] until he was commended to the ven-erable prince of Flanders, Count Philip of worthy memory,[305] to be trained in morals and to be diligently introduced to and steeped in military respon-sibilities. When he was with Philip, Arnold was named first in number and merit among the most prominent youths of the Flemish nobility. Although he had not yet received the knightly accolade, everyone said that in all things and every detail he was vigorous in arms and outstanding in his character and skill, gifted in every sort of courtly foolery, prompt in service, almost prodi-gal (if I dare say it) in generosity, cheerful of expression, more handsome in face than all those of his age at court, gentle and affable to all, and gracious. And he was all these things.

Meanwhile, after some years had rolled by, he then decided to take the oath to join the knights, as both his age and the superiority of his future, or rather his current, skill demanded. He wished above all else and in every way to please his father and to reserve for him the new glory of his knighthood, even though Philip, the most reverend prince, the chief glory of Flanders, fully wished to make him a knight and reverently to show him military honor through gifts and arms. So once Arnold had received permission from Philip, as befits a man of prudent and good disposition, he hastened with his man Eustace of Salperwick to his father in Guines.

91. How this same Arnold was made a knight.

Then the count of noteworthy memory, his father, showed with most evident signs how much joy he felt at Arnold's coming. In fact, he called his sons and acquaintances and friends to his court at Guines on the holy day of Pentecost in 1181 a. d. and the man who must not be struck in return gave Arnold the military accolade,[306] and initiated him into full manhood with oaths. Along with Arnold, Baldwin also honored Eustace of Salperwick, Simon of Nielles-lez-Ardre, Eustace of Nord-Ausque, and Walo of Preures with oaths, military equipment, and supplies,[307] and they spent the solemn day with noble and refined food and drink, whiling away and passing the day of sempiternal joy in as much pleasure as they could. Then Arnold, newly clad in knightly garments, jumped into their midst and gave money to the minstrels, mimes, players, clowns, servants, attendants, and performers, and all those who called and cried out his name, until he received the reward of their praise and their thanks as recompense. In fact, he gave away with a generous hand whatever he could own or acquire as though he were throwing it away and as though he were made of pure and naked intellects (they are found on Porphyry's first page).[308] In consequence, as he gave away great possessions along with small ones, his own as well as those acquired from his followers and those taken from foreigners, even his own person scarcely remained his.

Then the next day in his Ardres, he was received in church with a procession and with bells ringing, while the monks and clergy in joy intoned "Virtue and Honor to the Highest Trinity" in his praise, and the people also called out and exulted in joy. And so from that day, for almost the next two years, he travelled around many provinces and regions participating in tournaments — not entirely without his father's help and support — and Eustace of Salperwick always clung to him as his companion.

92. How when Arnold had become lord of Ardres, he kept Eustace the Razor as his associate and fellow soldier.

Philip of Montgardin, who was in Guines, was Arnold's adviser, although the count, Arnold's father, disapproved.[309] And Philip frequently (or rather incessantly) urged Arnold to ask and beg his father for Ardres and the properties that belonged to him through his mother's side. This came about at last, although they had first had many lengthy discussions and words and many days had passed; he subsequently got Ardres and Colvida with some, but still not all, of the associated rights.[310] His father was at first somewhat ungracious toward him; then his fatherly mood toward Arnold was softened, so upon his father's advice, as well as that of Count Philip of Flanders, Arnold accepted the noble man Arnold of Cayeux as his advisor in tournaments and when he disposed of his possessions and as his guardian and, as it were, his teacher. Arnold of Cayeux was a man learned in arms, prudent and discreet in advice. Because he could not always be on duty everywhere with him and because he could not fail to overlook something,[311] he left his nephew with Arnold of Ardres as a teacher and instructor in arms; the nephew was a man vigorous in arms, who had previously been a fellow soldier and associate of Henry the Young King of England.[312] After a few days, without consulting his father and brothers, Arnold gave this man Hervelinghem near Licques as a perpetual fief. Eustace of Salperwick and Hugh of Moulle were also Arnold's inseparable companions and comrades in arms.[313] And Henry, the son of Henry of Campagne,[314] and all of the tourneyers of the land of Guines also flowed to him as their lord and the principal member of the capital. To all of these, he showed as liberal a hand as he could, and even more, and he led them to tournaments and back again. Philip of Montgardin, however, conversed with him when he was in his country and urged him to moral actions with witticisms and jokes.

93. How Arnold, while he was going to tournaments, delighted Countess Ida of Boulogne because of his very great liberality.

So he was entrusted to the keeping and care of Arnold of Cayeux, as I said, and associated with Eustace the Razor, Eustace of Salperwick, and Hugh of Moulle, who were members of his household and his cronies, and Henry of Campagne, and many other noble and illustrious knights, and he preferred to go into exile in other places for the love of tournaments and for glory than to spend time in leisure in his homeland without warlike entertainments. He did this principally so that he could live gloriously and attain secular honor. With such great skill, Arnold thus became the hero and glory of the name of Guines, that he acquired and won a famous name for himself in many regions and came very much to the notice and into the mind of Countess Ida of Boulogne. She was, in fact, the daughter of Count Matthew of Boulogne; her father having already died, she assumed the name and dignity of countess.[315] She had earlier been betrothed to Count Gerard III of Ghelria,[316] and then afterward, upon the advice of the venerable count Philip of Flanders, her paternal uncle, to Duke Bertulf of Zeringhen.[317] Events intervened around this time so that she was bereft of both, and she indulged in pleasures and worldly delights of the body, like a widow without a husband.[318] And hence she enticed Arnold of Guines as much as she could and loved him with a sexual passion, or at least, she pretended she did out of feminine frivolity and deception. Thus, as messengers and secret signs went back and forth between them carrying tokens of true love, Arnold loved her with a similarly loving return—or pretended to love her out of manly prudence and caution. But he did aspire to the land and the dignity of the county of Boulogne once he had won the favor of this countess through this exhibition of real—or feigned—love.

94. How Reynold of Dammartin, having deserted his wife, the sister of Walter of Châtillon, carried Countess Ida of Boulogne off into Lorraine.

Meanwhile, Reynold, the son of Count Albert of Dammartin, had deserted his wife, who was the sister of Walter of Châtillon.[319] (Walter was now married to the daughter of Count Hugh of Saint-Pol.[320]) He sent messengers over and over again to Countess Ida and sought her very boldly with a not dissimilar effort and expectation and he labored and strove to attract her love with great industry. And inflamed and alight as she was with women's frivolous love, she would have satisfied both her desire and Reynold, if she had found her uncle, the count of Flanders, ready and willing to consent. But prudent Count Philip, a man of worthy spirit, had gotten the county of the land of Boulogne and held it in hand and received and dispensed its fruits at will; he saw the French as hostile and dangerous. He knew that Reynold was a slanderer and was both related to and had the ear of the king of France[321] and helped and obeyed him in every way and in all things in his council. The count knew that the king of France had made peace with him, but was, never-theless, not reconciled to him, and so Philip refused to marry his niece to any Frenchman, much less to Reynold, who had never pleased him.

But because Ida was full of stupid female instability, she despaired of procuring Reynold's love for herself and again burned and was set afire with love for Arnold of Guines. She therefore often sent for him at Desvres, and more often at Merck,[322] where they had secret counsel concerning their pri-vate business in the rooms and in hidden places. But even this did not satisfy her. So when she had sent to the hero at Ardres, it happened that the messen-ger and person in her confidence fell sick three days later and then died there. Hearing this, the countess took the opportunity to see Arnold of Guines in his Ardres and to bury her dead servant there. But Arnold, knowing ahead of time about the countess's arrival, solemnly received her; when the dead man had been buried, he had her dine with him and when they had spoken of many things, the countess went away. Still, Arnold would have detained her, but he believed the woman when she promised that she would come back to him after a short while.

But in the meantime, Arnold spoke about this and other matters with the venerable count of Flanders, and the count promised him that he would be favorable toward Arnold's request. Then Reynold, who was always vigilant and feared Arnold of Guines more than anyone else, secretly came to her with his henchmen and—Oh, the perfidy of female instability!—without really using force, he brought force against the willing woman, just as he wished to do; he abducted her and carried her to the fortress of Riche in Lorraine without consulting Count Philip of Flanders.[323] However, she asserted that force had been brought by Reynold against her while she resisted and was unwilling—Oh, the machinations of feminine treachery!—and secretly sent for Arnold of Guines. She announced to him that she promised and swore that she would leave Reynold and marry him, if he could come for her.

95. How Arnold of Guines, who had gone to Verdun for the sake of Countess Ida of Boulogne, was captured and made prisoner.

And so Arnold, hearing the fanciful tale less than prudently, believed that the straying woman was the picture of female fidelity. He gathered his most faithful friends and companions to him—the knights Eustace of Sal-perwick and Hugh of Moulle, the men-at-arms Baldwin of Moulle and En-guerrand of Brunembert,[324] also Thomas Bach, the provisioner of goods and

funds, and also the mercenaries Drogolin and Willemot the Englishman—
and taking the road into Lorraine, he came as far as Verdun. There he and
his men were captured by the prince or the commander or dignitary of Metz,
upon the request and urging of Reynold, who had been forewarned about
Arnold's coming through the countess's treacherous report, and Arnold was
a long time kept prisoner in unyielding shackles.[325] (The bishop-elect of the
city of Verdun gave his consent or, more exactly, urged that the deed be committed and carried it out.[326])

This shame and misfortune fell to him, I have no doubt, or rather I truly
believe, because he had recently accepted a tithe of the land of Guines to serve
the living God in Jerusalem, along with King Philip of France, the son of the
reverend Louis,[327] and the noble count of Flanders of the same name, Philip,
and innumerable other nobles of many nationalities.[328] As a bearer of Christ's
cross he was to fight the enemies of Christ's cross, and to put the filthy pagans
to flight from the tomb of the Lord. And he neither began nor completed
the pilgrimage, nor had he even, in fact, been absolved of the vow of pilgrimage he had undertaken, but he did not *give to the poor* and needy, but
spent the tithe in prodigal and luxurious living [Ps. 112:9]. But concerning
the money he collected for the visitation and liberation of the Lord's tomb,
if anything (given the excess of his dining and clothing of himself) was left
over after worldly and secular entertainments and food—on account of the
crusade, tournaments were forbidden everywhere in the world at that time—
he irreverently and imprudently distributed it. He gave one hundred marks
to someone, the same number of pounds to someone else, a silver chalice
from his chapel to another, in the same fashion silver goblets to someone else,
to another shields and spurs made of the same metal, to another changes of
clothing, to someone else painted coverlets, tapestries, and things similar to
these, and to one man and another the arms and horses prepared for the service of God. Thus this imprudent man scattered and sowed for the sake of the
world, where nothing is ever harvested or gathered except the world's foolish glory or favor. Nor, indeed, could those people whom he kept with him
unto death for the sake of worldly favor help him, when he was shackled in
chains at Verdun, nor could the others, to whom he had given with excessive
prodigality on many occasions.

However, *the Lord God, who chastises and beats the son that he loves*
when He wishes [Heb. 12:6], nevertheless had mercy on His son and servant
through William, the reverend archbishop of Reims. He intervened and sent
letters of the most efficacious strength to the archbishop of Trier,[329] when
the archbishop of Trier went, like a good shepherd, to Verdun to consecrate

Albert, the bishop-elect of the city. The archbishop of Trier asked the bishop-elect constantly for Arnold of Guines and when the bishop-elect ceased out of sorrow to answer the archbishop, the archbishop responded that never could or would he consecrate the bishop-elect until Arnold of Guines and his men were completely set at liberty and released. And thus liberated, Arnold and his men returned to their land, while Reynold and his followers groaned. And he was received with joy into his Ardres and all the knights and people of the whole territory ran to him. I shall leave it, however, to the writers of Boulogne to write it down how Reynold was received as count of the land of Boulogne, without the knowledge of Duke Baldwin of Lorraine,[330] when Count Philip of Flanders went to Jerusalem, because this certainly contributes nothing to my project.

Because I have thus far composed the deeds of the family of Guines in some fashion, accordingly, so that I may complete my project to the degree that I am able, I shall turn my authorial pen to the history of Ardres. Following the order discussed in my proposal, I shall adapt the execution to my intention; using an artful order of narration, I shall insert it within the history of the family of Guines and continue it and then, just as the facts demand, join them together as though in one body and to complete one work.

96. How Arnold of Guines behaved, after he returned from Verdun to his father's power.

And so when Arnold of Guines came to his right mind afterward, he understood the inconstancy and falsity of women. Leaving behind the confines of Verdun, he returned to his country. He made peace and became reconciled with his father and behaved according to his father's will in all ways, except that he is said to have had more knightly companions than his father, and to have made more lavish expenditures than the extent of his possessions demanded, since he persisted in giving larger gifts than his father's advice taught or recommended. Indeed, he gave more than he owned or kept for himself. He went to tournaments wherever he could with those knights he loved with such marvelous affection. Then when he was returning to his country from tournaments, he often stayed at Colvida, but more often at Ardres, where, as youthful years require, he indulged in games and pastimes with his knights and members of his household. For that reason, he loved to converse both with youths and with men his own age. But he respected old men and even decrepit ones and kept them with him, because they told him the adventures, fables, and histories of the ancients and added serious matters of morality to their narrative and included them.

For that reason, he kept these men with him as members of his household and as his cronies, and he willingly listened to them: a certain old soldier named Robert of Coutances, who instructed him and pleased his ears on the subject of the Roman emperors[331] and on Charlemagne, Roland and Oliver,[332] and King Arthur of Britain;[333] and Philip of Montgardin, who told him to his ears' delight of the land of Jerusalem and of the siege of Antioch and of the Arabs and Babylonians and deeds done overseas;[334] and his relative named Walter of Le Clud, who diligently informed him of the deeds and fables of the English, of Gormond and Isembard,[335] of Tristan and Isolde,[336] of Merlin[337] and Morolf,[338] of the deeds of the family of Ardres, and of the first construction of Ardres, because Arnold of Guines, whose kinsman Walter was and in whose household he was, himself took his origin on one side, as I have said above, from the family of Ardres.

Then, roughly around the same time that Arnold of Guines was engaged to Eustacia or Eustochia, the daughter of Count Hugh of Saint-Pol, called "White-straw" or "Field-straw,"[339] it happened one day while Arnold was staying at Ardres that the winter rains increased and the windbags of Aeolus opened, that the clouds battled each other in the air and the winds blew in the heights and wandered whistling everywhere through the land. Arnold was confined to the house at Ardres for two days and one night with his knights and members of his household on account of the inclemency of the weather. He had heard much concerning the Roman emperors and Arthur from Robert of Coutances and much more about the land of Jerusalem and Antioch from Philip of Montgardin, so finally Walter of Le Clud was asked by him and me and all the members of the household to tell and relate for us something about the family of Ardres and the deeds of the men of Ardres. The rains had not yet ceased, but as he began the wildness of the winds eased and softened a little, as if to let us listen. He put his right hand to his beard and combed and carded it with his fingers as old men often do; he opened his mouth in our midst, before me and all who were listening to this very thing and said:

97. How Walter of Le Clud narrated the history of the lineage of Ardres.[340]

Reverend Fathers and Lords, since, then, your purposeful will is that, until the rains cease, I should recall to mind the history and deeds of the family of Ardres by this present narrative, as I have heard and known it from my fathers: There was once a father of reverend memory, the bishop of the church of Thérouanne, Frameric by name.[341] Now Frameric had a niece living in the place which is called to this day by the ancient name of Selnesse, near the marsh on the estate of St. Mary of Capella. She was named Adele and she was of great and famous name in the land of Guines. She was born of out-standing local forebears and was, in fact, fairly rich in estates and possessions, but she lacked the advice and solace and help of a man; she had been left alone and abandoned through the neglect of her parents, although they were noble. So this Adele, deprived and dispossessed as she was, as I have said, of the solace of parents, was entreated day in and day out by Count Eustace of Guines to marry according to his advice and to accept a man who did not suit her. Since she did not dare to refuse the petition of the count completely, she put off agreeing as long as she could and from day to day dragged matters out for many days.

98. How Adele of Selnesse gave all her allods[342] to the bishop of Thérouanne and received them back from the same bishop as a fief.

But when she was pressed, as though with a great spur, more harshly than was suitable or appropriate (or rather, more than was just) by the afore-mentioned count (he was her relative) for what he had asked and for her to marry whether she wanted to or not, she resigned all her estates, wherever she held and possessed them, in the name of the Lord into the hands of her maternal uncle Frameric, the bishop of the church of Thérouanne, because she was a wise virgin and belonged to the number of the prudent virgins and had no manner of concern for any fleshly relationship.[343] And when she had done and shown him homage, she received them all back intact as a perpetual fief. For she had often heard and learned from her fathers that after Walbert of reverend and worthy memory, who had once been the count of Ponthieu and Saint-Pol and Guines, bid farewell to the world and left Guines to infirm and incapable heirs, many nobles of old who lived in Guines received their estates, by a gift of a similar sort, as fiefs from noblemen, bishops, abbots, provosts, even some kinds of prelates of churches, or parsons. They might thus fight under the authority of a greater name and live in the secure peace of a greater protection.[344]

These, then, were the properties which Adele converted from allods and estates into a fief through this same bishop and for this same bishop: whatever she owned in Peupelingue, whether land or tithe; whatever she had in Inghem near Wissant;[345] whatever she had in Guemy, in Welles, and in Nord-Ausque; also the altars of Bonningues-lez-Ardre and Zouafques, not leaving out any tithes that she held in the land of Guines or that happened to be held by her as fiefs; whatever she had in Hondschote, whether marsh or customary right or land or altar. But you should know that the abbot of Saint-Vaast in Arras had formerly granted her predecessor the property she possessed in Hondschote, because he had at one time undertaken a judicial duel to preserve a certain bequest to Saint-Vaast. He became the faithful man of this church, and when the inheritance of the church of Saint-Vaast had been preserved and its honor recovered in this duel, he enjoyed a day of victory.

99. How Herred married Adele of Selnesse.

Then the bishop, seeing the devotion and noting the intention of Adele, who was a most Christian woman and one dear to God (and also his niece), married her to a man of memorable nobility and wisdom, a strong and vigorous knight, according to the marital law of wedlock. He was descended from the Flemish nobility and was the first and most important among the people of Furnes. He was called Herbert among his followers, Herred among us.[346] He had been tagged with the surname Crangroc in the vernacular[347] by the boys in childhood, when he was of boyish years, because his tunic was inside out. And furthermore, Frameric increased and augmented his fief, not so much because he had married Frameric's niece as for this reason, because Herred was to be the faithful man of the church of Thérouanne in Guines and also everywhere else. And so he gave Herred Clerques and Cormette and Bouvelinghem with their associated rights as a fief and also West-Bécourt near Acquin. (This was namely the village of West-Bécourt that Count Baldwin II of Guines later on gave his brother William as the perpetual gift of a fief to confirm the peace between them; Baldwin's firstborn son, Arnold, gave his assent because the village was supposed to belong and appertain to him by hereditary succession from his mother's side.)[348] In this same donation, this Bishop Frameric also gave Herred and Adele Hubersent, the village near Longvilliers, as a gift of the status of fief (it was named after Eilbod by the inhabitants),[349] and certain lands and tithes in the land of Boulogne, which Stephen and Anselm of Cayeux and their heirs are supposed to hold from the lord of Ardres as a fief. And thus Frameric made him a peer and a baron of the court of Thérouanne.[350] He added this to honor and promote Herred, that at the enthronement of the bishop of Thérouanne, Herred himself and his heirs were to transport and bear that same bishop from the place of election to his throne, along with others assigned to this same office and fellow peers with similar fiefs.

Now this is the reason why Herred, the progenitor of such nobility, who was worthy to be called by the more proper appellation Hercules, was called by the vernacular surname Crangroc because of his inside-out tunic. It was not because when he had married the noble woman Adele, the faithful and prudent administrator of her possessions was sparing of his clothing and wore[351] them to the point that on feast days he turned his tunic inside out and belted it because of the cheapness of the garments and because he had carried out hard work in them, as those envious of the nobility of Ardres mockingly fantasize. It was instead because, when Herred (or rather Hercules!) was still an adolescent, his father was deeply enthusiastic about hunting with dogs. And so on account of this zeal his father sometimes rose very early in the summer time and roused his son, still heavy with sleep, to come with him into the woods and dunes at the seaside near Furnes. Herred, who had been asleep until then, got up at his father's voice and put his tunic on inside out, unaware of what he put on himself or how. And thus, when he came to his father, and his companions saw him dressed in the inside-out tunic (he was himself unaware of this, as I have already said), they cried out and called him by the vernacular name Crangroc. I know and proclaim that from that time to this day he was called Crangroc for this reason.[352]

And so when he had taken Adele as his wife, Herred manfully took himself off to go into the land of Guines, following the advice of the venerable bishop, and he began to live at Selnesse where his wife's predecessors and his wife herself had resided earlier. He was reconciled to Count Eustace of Guines through the mediation of his friends and relatives and the bishop of Thérouanne and performed homage to him for certain tenements lying adjacent to Ardres, and at length Herred recovered his love and grace. And so Herred stayed at Selnesse, as I just said, between the wood and the marsh in that place. To this day one can find there the relics, as it were, of the pagans, namely ruddy roof tiles, shards of vases the color of cinnabar, and fragments of glass flasks. A track or a hard and stony road trodden from the marsh into the wood can now be discovered there by the plunging plow.

100. How the town of Ardres was first built and how it got its name.

Still, the place that is now inhabited by the multitudinous arrival of the people of Ardres was pasture and was cultivated by only a few inhabitants. Nevertheless, a certain brewer of beer or maltster lived there near the road in the middle of the pastureland, in the place where the commercial market of Ardres is now held, where simple and rustic men used to gather to drink, loiter,[353] or even carouse because of the broad and wide flatness of the pastureland. Then this place, as yet unnamed, since it was pasture up to the mountain the inhabitants call Agomelinda, was called "Arda" in the vernacular after the pasture, as the inhabitants say.[354] The shepherds and others who used to gather there, in fact, egged each other on and because they did not know the name of the tavern-keeper, said, urging each other, "Let's go! Let's go and meet in the pasture, that is, in Arda."

But afterward, men came to this place from another dwelling place and began to live there. Then as the number of people, both locals and newcomers, grew there, the settlement coalesced into a village. Then later on, when certain Italians, who were passing through that place to do business in England, asked and heard the name of the place, they thought that the village was called Ardua. They looked and saw a certain bird, namely a heron, flying toward the marsh to the north. The Italians, therefore, exclaimed that they had come from and left Ardea, the city of Turnus, and named this place after their city or after the heron which they had seen: Ardea.[355]

Thus, as the people there multiplied, the size of the place grew, and the breadth of the site of the village grew, and the goodness and fame of the name of Ardres grew to the point that Herred right then decided to move his buildings there from Selnesse. But the family of Furnes noted that the site of the place of Selnesse was a fortress surrounded and enclosed on almost every side by a broad and deep marsh and dense woods. They and other people as well, his relatives and friends, inasmuch as they were strong and warlike men, and, if I may dare say it, the fathers and progenitors of the Blauwvoets,[356] dissuaded Herred from his proposal. So he remained in his most fortified Selnesse with his wife Adele, living delightfully in wealth.

101. That there were certain liars who said that Herred came from Peupelingue.

But it ought to be known that, although I knew and have asserted for certain that Herred truly came from Furnes, as the chronicle writings of the people of Furnes attest, nevertheless, there were certain others to whom the past has left, as it were, some small recollections about Herred. They, ignorant of the true story concerning Herred, distorted and obscured the true story with poetic fictions out of verisimilitude;[357] they said and asserted that this Herred came from Peupelingue near Cauquelle. Now they have said against me (but really they murmur against truthful ancestors), that there was once a certain rich man at Peupelingue named Arnulf, the lord of that same village. He was said to have had two sons, Herred and Haket, and the lords of Ardres took the beginning of their lineage from Herred and the Hakets of Peupelingue from Haket. When Arnulf died, however, the sons divided their father's inheritance and his allods in two portions, but not equal ones; the larger part fell to Herred, as the elder by birth, and the smaller to Haket, the younger. Because these two brothers were constantly harassed, on one side by the count of Guines and on the other by the count of Boulogne, to do and perform homage for their estates and themselves as a sign of subordination, Herred, the elder by birth, who neither bowed nor consented to either count, went to the bishop of Thérouanne at a rapid pace, and from him received whatever land or tithe he possessed in Peupelingue as a perpetual fief. But the other one, namely Haket, who feared men more than God, hurried against his brother's will to the count of Boulogne, and when he had done the count homage, he received his land as a fief. His brother Herred was present and fully protested this as best he could, because the authority of the county of the whole land of Peupelingue, of all law, and of lordship belonged to him. But in the end, the generous and pious good will of another very religious count of Boulogne, namely Eustace,[358] the husband of the most holy lady Ida, gave the lordship of this piece of land to the monks of Cluny, this land which cruelty had earlier seized and confiscated from Herred, or rather from God and the bishop, so that they might build a monastic cell or a priory at Le Waast.[359] Moreover, they assert that this Herred was such a grasping and such a stingy lord to the people of Peupelingue that when pulling the handle or end of the plough, he turned his tunic inside out, because of the cheapness of his clothes, and belted it, paying no mind to his great lordship.[360] Hence wrongly slandering his name,[361] the farmers called him by the vernacular name of Crangroc, after his inside-out tunic. And so they similarly lie in saying that this Herred acceded to the lordship of Ardres at some time through the law of marriage.

102. A refutation of the falsehoods of those who think this.

Just so do our adversaries argue, who are envious of the nobility of Ardres and mix the truth with fables as though these fables were true. But these statements shall lose their credibility; and fables of this kind shall blow away in the light breezes. And so far be it from the minds of true believers that I would embrace doubtful things over certain ones, or rather any sort of fictions entwined with some sort of truth over the truth itself. For indeed, our Herred, who might most worthily be called Hercules, was not called Herred among his own people (as I have just said), but Herbert, and also he did not take his name from his tunic being turned inside out because of the cheapness of his clothes, but by chance, as I have noted. Nor have the semi-educated or those envious of the truth been given the ability to investigate the certainty of any sort of truth by any judicial decree or any arrangement that proceeds properly, nor will it be given them; rather it shall be given to the devout and well-intentioned, those without any mark or taint of corrosive envy, who follow their truthful ancestors along the proper path.

Let me pursue the truth with true speech and testimony, just as I have already put down: So then Herred, a man by his nobility and nation of the blood of Furnes, was an inhabitant of Selnesse and had made a dwelling there. When he was living at Selnesse in tranquil peace and delight, according to what I said about him above, he knew his wife Adele and had two daughters by her, the first named Adele after her mother, the second Adelaide. The first of these was wed in legitimate matrimony to Eustace, the first of that name, the father of Eustace the Old of Fiennes.[362] The second was married to Robert, the lord of Alembon, surnamed Putepelisse,[363] the father and forebear of the lords of Alembon. Guy succeeded him; he was killed before Guines, because he attacked the count of Guines with the people of Ardres. Guy II succeeded him; Count Manasses of Guines had him undergo a capital sentence of death. Guy III, namely the father of Guy the Older and the Younger, succeeded him. But after many altercations between the two Guys in both ecclesiastical and secular courts, in the end, when the older Guy died, Guy the younger survived as the heir and lord of the people of Alembon.

103. How when Herred died, Adele married Eilbod of Bergues.

Then, when the span of a few days had passed, Herred died. And Adele did not remain a widow for many days. Upon the advice of the bishop of Thérouanne and of her friends, she married a certain noble man named Eilbod, the brother of the castellan of Bergues,[364] and never married again. On the first night she was known by her husband, as they say, she at once conceived, and she bore Arnold, no less noble and handsome in soul than in lineage, and she bore other daughters and sons. I shall forego writing about these last, but will leave space for Arnold, for I will discuss him at greater length in what follows.

104. How Eilbod created a fish pond and a mill while he was living at Selnesse.

Then Eilbod, a man midway between maturity and old age, was pleased by the abundance of his noble offspring. Since he felt himself more and more to be approaching the downward slope into old age, after he had renounced secular amusements and tournaments, he lived in his house at Selnesse and remained near the house and near his family with his household members and was a faithful and prudent administrator and manager in taking care of his business. And therefore, he had no wish to leave his country, when he could put this off or defer it. Instead, he tarried often at Selnesse with his wife, children, and household and instructed his children with pious care, employing salutary documents or with farsighted solicitude in the management of his affairs, he made the rounds about the confines of his land, as much for the preservation of his own honor as to preserve that of his people.

But since he had heard at some time from his servants that his predecessor Herred had proposed to move his buildings from Selnesse to Ardres and to build a new mansion there, he was also seized by a similar turn of will. He uprooted the alders between the spring of St. Folcuin up to the foot of the courtyard of the original mother church of Saint-Omer of Ardres (the venerable confessor, St. Folcuin, the bishop of Thérouanne,[365] once rested at the spring, when the pious pastor was going around his diocese and visiting the churches, as is the pastoral custom) and he built a sluice or earthen mound in the middle of the marsh.[366] When he had brought together and collected and dammed up the waters of St. Folcuin's spring and the other springs, he made a very deep fish pond there and constructed and erected a mill on the near edge of the village weir, with as much skill and foresight in these matters as he could.

105. How his son Arnold, called the first lord of Ardres, sired Ralph, the canon, and Libert, the father and progenitor of the Bothet family; and of the death of Lady Adele of Selnesse.

When Eilbod's son Arnold was returning one time to his father and country from the glory of tournaments, to which he was completely dedicated, he played and made sport, as young years commonly do, with a certain most beautiful girl from Saint-Omer, and by her he had Ralph, afterward a canon of Saint-Omer. Now this Ralph fathered Ralph, a well-known and forceful knight. Later on, when he had been severed from the love of the family of Ardres, he attacked them, with Philip, the son of the lord of Ardres,[367] and with the help of Reynold of Saint-Valéry.[368] He continued to carry off their possessions, until he recovered their love and again made peace with them. The aforementioned Ralph the Canon also sired Eustace, the canon of the church of Ardres, and Walter, surnamed the Knight (Walter was the father of Raulin du Bois), and Eve, and Adele,[369] the mother—if it does not embarrass you to hear it—of the person telling you this story.[370] Then, when this same Arnold was returning from England to his country and came through Boucres, he got himself a girl with a most gorgeous body.[371] After he deflowered her, he fathered by her Libert, the father of Drogo Bothet; Drogo fathered Eustace Bothet, the father of William Bothet; William married Agnes, the daughter of William of Colvida.

Now afterward, Adele, the lady of Selnesse, died. She was honorably buried in the cemetery of Saint-Omer of Ardres, where she had earlier chosen to be buried and should have been buried.

106. Of the chapel of St. Quentin of Cappelhove.

After the small chapel of St. Quentin (the one the monks now inhabit) was built in the place which to this day is called Cappelhove, and the courtyard of this small chapel, where the elders of Selnesse were buried, and the cemetery had been created, it was unvisited by the clergy or the people for worship.[372] From that time, in fact, the place remained desolate and was visited by no men and there remained there no vestige of the former worship or religion, except that in that place one might find great stones placed like an altar and joined without mortar among the thickets of the woods, and very old images and figures of the saints on that altar. But later on, a certain hermit of the most holy reputation, named Abraham, stayed in this small place of ancient religion, which lay isolated and desolate among the thickets of briars and thorns. He baptized the lord of Northout's son, and gave him his own name of Abraham. The boy was already ten years old and, in imitation of pagan depravity, was as yet unbaptized, because of his parents' negligence.[373] Up to that time and for that reason, he had been called Pagan; nevertheless, he was called Pagan of Northout as long as he lived.

After this, the holy hermit fled because of a horrible infestation of frogs, toads, lizards, and other sorts of vermin and to the end of his days secreted himself, as though fleeing to a safer and cleaner place, in the deep wood at Selnesse (to this day it is called Dickebuch).[374] Then two devout sisters came from St. Mary of Capella to the aforementioned little spot of holy worship, and led a solitary and eremitic life as nuns for the course of some years. They inhabited and occupied that place, until, because of the horror and filth of the vermin, they also were forced at the urging of necessity to retrace their steps to the place whence they came.

107. How the families of Fiennes and Alembon requested allods from the family of Ardres and how Eilbod died.

And so when Adele had died and was buried, the families of Fiennes and Alembon came to Eilbod and to his children, asking for a portion of the allods which ought to belong to them through Adele, from whom they were descended.[375] But when Eilbod and his children absolutely said and constantly repeated that they had or had gotten no allods from Adele, because Adele had received all her allods in fee from the hand of the bishop of Thérouanne, the family of Alembon agreed and went back to their own place. The family of Fiennes went back to their own place and put up with this situation for the time being, but they complained about it.

Eilbod, a man mature in years, was broken down by old age and full of days, and afterward, having entered upon the way of all flesh, he left the world. His body was buried near the wall of the shrine of Saint-Omer of Ardres, not without the tearful weeping and lamentation of both his men from Bergues and those from Ardres.

Now let me pursue what I have planned, leaving out, as though they did not exist, almost all the sons and daughters of Eilbod and following Arnold alone, as is worthy and right.

108. How Eilbod's son Arnold became the seneschal of the count of Boulogne, Eustace, and also became the lord of Hénin-Liétard and Ecluse.

And so after Arnold had been promoted to the honor of the lordship of Ardres, when his father Eilbod was already dead, he went around the provinces and regions everywhere with the spirit of Hector. He groaned, as though he were calling out with Ajax, *"Men, to arms! to arms!"*[376] and professed that he had accomplished nothing praiseworthy in tournaments, unless the burden and the glory of the tournaments was said to be granted to him alone. By loving tournaments and attending them, he became known in many regions and thus was very intimate with and very close to Count Eustace of Boulogne,[377] the father and progenitor of a most noble son, Eustace, and also Godfrey and Baldwin.[378] As a result, because of his outstanding strength in knighthood, his temperance, and his wisdom, the count set him in his own place, as the seneschal and justiciar and bailiff of his whole land.[379] In his responsibility for this office, he was not only beloved, well-known, and gracious to the people and the count of Boulogne, but also to kings (namely those of France and England) and other princes and dukes of the land.

Although he thus ruled in a foreign land, let it not be forgotten how he behaved at his Ardres. For whatever little gifts he got in foreign parts, at the right time and place, he gathered them with the greatest devotion in the environs of his land and of Ardres. The aforementioned count Eustace, moreover, held Lens and Hénin-Liétard and Ecluse near Douai. But since this same count of Boulogne owned nothing of his own in Hénin and Ecluse except homage, and the lords of Hénin and Ecluse were wild men and were proud and rebellious against the principality of Boulogne, he forever granted and gave whatever he had by right in Hénin or Ecluse to his seneschal, Lord Arnold of Ardres, once his homage had been received, as a fief to remunerate him for his service. Then Eustace, the lord of Hénin, and Baldwin of Ecluse did him homage and promised him service at the instance of the count of Boulogne. And hence, some inhabitants of Hénin and also of Douai and of Ecluse came of their own free will to Arnold at Ardres, because they found him favorable to them as a lord; with his assent, they chose a permanent residence among the people of Ardres. But at some later time, when the people of Ardres were wrangling and quarreling with them, the people of Ardres said tauntingly, attacking them with ugly words, that they were upstarts and well-known for the taint of their servile condition. So it was that their heirs got the name and dishonor (albeit unjustly and unfairly) of being serfs, because of this shameful and abusive name-calling, done solely once upon a time in anger and strife by their ancestors.

109. How Arnold moved all his fortifications from Selnesse to the keep of Ardres.

Arnold, therefore, seeing that all things smiled upon him and resulted in prosperity as if they followed his will, made a sluice in the marsh near the mill at Ardres, and another sluice about a stone's throw away. He established a high motte or prominent keep between them in the depths of the mirey marsh and the gurgling depths, almost at the foot of a nearby hill, as the boundary mark of his fortification, and he amassed an earthwork. As the locals say, a domesticated bear—not the one for which the oven dues were exacted[380]—raised that fortress's keep between the foundation and the height. (Oh, the industry of mortal men! Oh, the gentleness of untamed beasts!) They say that a good luck token, a gem set in the finest gold, was placed in the most secret corner of the mound to remain forever buried. And he surrounded the space of the external wall with a stout ditch; the mill was within the wall. Soon, when all the buildings at Selnesse had been taken apart and torn down, as his father had once planned, he fortified the keep of Ardres with gates, drawbridges, and necessary buildings. And so from that day, once the great place of the mansion of the people of Selnesse had been dismantled and taken down and the buildings dragged and carried to Ardres, any recollection of the family of Selnesse was destroyed along with the castle, to the point that Arnold was named after Ardres and was everywhere called the protector and lord of the people of Ardres.

110. How Arnold married Matilda, the daughter of Gonfrid of Marquise, and had sons and daughters by her.

After Arnold armed his place at Ardres with this sort of fortification and castle, Gonfrid the lord of Marquise died, so taking the advice of Eustace the Whiskered of Boulogne, for whom Arnold fought, and that of his other friends, Arnold married Matilda, that same Gonfrid's daughter. Gonfrid had left her behind as his only child and the heir to his whole land.[381] And when he had received from the count of Boulogne leave to go, as well as many gifts, Arnold withdrew with his wife to Ardres.

Then Arnold knew his wife and by her he had Arnold, afterward called the Old, and Gonfrid, afterward the lord of Marquise; namely he was the father of Baldwin the Old of Marquise, whose son Baldwin afterward married Adeline, the daughter of Count Baldwin of Guines.[382] Arnold also sired Ermentrude, the mother and lady of the lineage of Northout; and Avice, the wedded wife of Humphrey, the lord of Ordres; and Jocasta or Ivisia, who was joined as a wife to Lord Stephen of Brunembert; and Emma, wed in legal marriage to John of Bellbrone.[383]

111. How Arnold made the village of Ardres a free town and established twelve peers and aldermen in it and confirmed the market by oath.

Then this Arnold, after he had acquired a glorious name and the tribute of praise in all the tournaments in the crown of England no less than those of France, resided safe in his Ardres, prudently examining and diligently considering how he might elevate Ardres in name and honor as much as possible. He therefore petitioned Baldwin, then the count of Guines (that is, the founder of Andres),[384] and asked he might make his village of Ardres, even though it was small, into a small free citadel, or rather the freest possible small castle. The count granted this; Arnold freely offered a basket full to the top of pennies to the aforementioned count as thanksgiving for all things whatsoever that Arnold had asked of him, and the count accepted it. Then Arnold, the lord of Ardres, appointed twelve peers or barons, who were attached to the castle of Ardres. When he had prepared a strong earthwork outside the wall in a circuit like a crown, he established a market for selling things in the middle and ordered that it be held and attended on Thursdays in perpetuity. And he ordained aldermen in that same place, and in the church of Saint-Omer of Ardres with the twelve peers of the town of Ardres, the rear-vassals, the knights, the burgers, and the people, he swore with his hands on relics and confirmed that the judgments of the aldermen would be preserved and upheld forever, as they were in the jurisdiction and custom of the aldermen and burgers of Saint-Omer.[385]

112. Why Arnold was called "the Advocate" and how his wife Matilda died.

Since this Arnold had received the office of steward or provost of Saint-Bertin in the land of Guines from his ancestors by hereditary right, from the time of the venerable father and count Walbert, he so much pursued the greatest intimacy with the monks of that place that they named and made him their church's faithful man and their advocate for all affairs in the land of Guines. And for that reason, he received the title of advocate for their lands everywhere. And so because this name and charge were bestowed on him, Arnold is found in many authentic charters and privileges of the churches of Ardres, Saint-Bertin, Saint-Omer, Thérouanne, Boulogne, Hénin, and also Saint-Pol as the advocate.[386] This faithful man, who owed homage and was the defender of the abbot, namely, the abbot of Saint-Bertin, was appointed, moreover, for the reason given above, because he held Corlis and certain lands in and around Saint-Omer and Wacquinghem and also certain other lands of that same abbot.

Then his wife Matilda, who was staying for a time at Ardres while the hour of her giving birth approached, barely had produced a son in pain and danger of death, when she died together with the boy and was buried at Ardres with lamentation and groaning.

113. How Arnold, Arnold's son, won land in England.

Then Arnold, his son, who at that time had passed through his adolescent years, began to grow in manly strength. And now that he had become a knight, he followed in his father Arnold's tracks and character in every way and seemed to differ little or not at all from his father in the glory of his knighthood. Arnold's son Arnold was, indeed, a most vigorous knight at arms. And for that reason, with the help of Count Eustace of Boulogne, he stood first among the soldiers of King William of England, who assailed and won England with war and arms and troops of men, and he served William for many years.[387] Then Arnold's brother, Gonfrid, was also called up by that same king William; they served him together for a long time behind a shield of skill like Hector's. And so while they were serving the king, both brothers, namely Arnold and Gonfrid, were so much taken into his favor that in addition to the daily stipends and the innumerable gifts he conferred upon them, he also conferred on them and granted them Stevington, with its associated rights, Duxford, Trumpington, Ilford, Tolleshaut, and Holland in perpetuity.[388]

Then in the meantime, while he was staying in England in the service of the king, Arnold had three sons by three girls. Helinand and William were knights, but Anselm went off and arrived and stayed in Outremer.[389] He was finally captured by the Muslims and apostatized from the Christian law and faith and the traditions of his forefathers. But he escaped the hands of the Muslims after many years, returned at length to his relatives in his country, and stayed with them for a time. But although he was staying with Christian relatives, he ate meat every day, not even excepting Fridays, nor did he ever hide that he was formerly an apostate and that he had once lapsed into Muslim depravities. And as he was hateful for this reason to his Christian relatives, he left Ardres to go overseas again and never again appeared among his family.

Then one time when Arnold was returning to his father, he had Philip by a noble girl from Louches. This Philip was a knight no less noble in arms than in family, so he collected robbers and henchmen for himself and frequently harassed the lords of Ardres with raids and arms, because the lords of Ardres denied him the fellowship of a benefice that they owed him by right of kinship.[390]

114. How Arnold I married the widow of the count of Saint-Pol.

Then, while Arnold and his brother Gonfrid were fighting for the most gloriously remembered king of England and after their father Arnold had married his daughters to the men mentioned above, their father Arnold was no less famous and celebrated throughout all of France, England, Normandy, and Burgundy than throughout Flanders. Indeed, he was a Nestor in counsel and in his clever foresight a second Ulysses—although he did not have the consolation of a Penelope.[391] He was in judgment a shepherd Paris—although there were no snares of Venus.[392] He was, to the degree that this rather envious and showy age permits, an Absalom in his beautiful elegance.[393] He was, not another Triptolemus, but an Achilles in the glory of his knighthood,[394] as he presented himself in arms against all enemies. As to what remains, he was in wisdom and in the restraint of his rule, a Solomon.[395] And so he seemed to be more a hero of the kingdom than the heir of Ardres.

Meanwhile, the count of Thérouanne or of Saint-Pol, namely Hugh the Old, went the way of all flesh. He had had children by his wife Clemence, although these children were still incapable and needed a guardian. Because of the eminence by which Arnold, the lord of Ardres, outshone all other fighters in wisdom, strength, and the glory of his knighthood, the Countess Clemence of Saint-Pol[396] was joined in legitimate marriage to Arnold, following the advice of the barons of France and Flanders, with the help of the count of Boulogne, and with divine guidance always leading the way. And it happened in the same way one time, that when the count of Aumale died, Baldwin, the noble son of the advocate Robert of Béthune, because of his eminence in knighthood (by which he excelled many) and the praise and glory of his nobility and skill, impregnated the widow.[397] With the help (or rather upon the order) of the English king, Richard, for whom he had fought for a long time, he married her and was appointed and became the count of Aumale.

When Arnold thus became the count of Saint-Pol, he gave and granted in all things as much thanks as he could to the Lord Christ, the author and architect of this great gift and honor. Although he was raised to the honor of such a county through the demands of his own merits, he was not swelled up by human praise or glory, but having weighed and maintained the high magnitude of this great honor with discretion, he showed himself to be humble in the rigor of his justice and unbending in the force of his humility, as the situation of the time or the action of the persons involved required. He had, indeed, once heard and learned, "*However great you are, abase yourself in all things.*" [Sir. 3:20][398] So he did not wreak a tyrannical rage upon his subjects but acted with all gentleness and benignity, with as much eagerness as he could, as though he imagined himself to be the hereditary count and lord of the people of this land. Nor did he disperse what had been gathered, as is increasingly the custom of those taking over, but took pains to gather what had been dispersed with as much care as he could. And since he once heard that "A short reign does not spare the people," he ruled and protected that county with the unbending sword of solicitude, as though he would endure and rule in this county with his heirs forever.

He did not, nevertheless, drive from the small chamber of his memory how his Ardres was doing, how it viewed him, and how it went on, nor how his sons in England behaved or his daughters, whatever the country they resided in. Consequently, he sometimes stayed in the county of Thérouanne, sometimes in Ardres. Now he halted his journey's progress in Hénin-Liétard, now in Ecluse. Now he took comfort from his sons in England, now he showed his love for his daughters and their children. Now he went around the county of Thérouanne and acted diligently in the count's stead. Above all others and in everything, however, showing his wife respect, he did her reverence and service not so much as a wife, but as his lady, and he enjoyed himself with her as was proper and wished her joy. But since he was not ignorant that he could not and ought not to transfer the county of Saint-Pol to his heirs, he took care to carry off whatever he could without violating his honorable reputation[399] from the place he had taken charge of to the place he owned at Ardres. He made such provision for his secular affairs all around, that he might know each day how he should act in the Holy Church.[400]

115. How Arnold I built the church of Ardres and established canons there.

And so, since all the people applauded him and almost the whole world smiled in prosperity upon him, he began to contemplate *things to come* [cf. Sir. 28:6], following the advice of the wise man. And hence, when he had at length received a divine response, he began to negotiate with Drogo of happy memory, the bishop of the church of Thérouanne,[401] about how and in what manner he might build and establish a small conventual church at his Ardres. For at that time there was in Ardres a certain parson or representative named Walter, who was appointed under the direction of the bishop of Thérouanne; he had procured the church of the village of Nielles-lez-Ardre and of Autingues under a similar condition. Arnold, therefore, spoke with this Walter about the things he had decided to bestow in the church at Ardres and voluntarily yielded and adopted Walter's every wish. For Arnold had, as I have already said, a certain son by the name of Ralph, who had been born and raised in the town of Saint-Omer and was now a canon in this same town in the church of Saint-Omer.[402] Then, on Ralph's advice and also that of the aforementioned Walter, he went to the above-named bishop Drogo of the church of Thérouanne, and when he had often and for a long time spoken with him and with the chapter of that place, he established some prebends in that same church. And consequently he received more important things from the bishop and the chapter than he had desired. The bishop knew, in fact, because he was forewarned and forearmed, that Arnold intended to make a conventual church in Ardres; in the presence of Walter, the parson of Ardres, and with his agreement, the bishop offered ready and gracious assent to his doing this and gave him the altar of the small church of Ardres, with all rights associated with the altar, and the whole church of the same place, free just like the church of St. Mary in which the body of Blessed Omer rests.[403]

So then Arnold rejoiced richly and exulted in the Lord and hurried his steps toward his Ardres with the aforementioned two men and other canons of the church of Thérouanne. As quickly as he could, he called together his sons and daughters and the nobles of his land, and also the clergy and men of religion, and he entered the little church, whose ancient paving stones are now joined and adapted to the new work or the chevet. There before God and St. Omer, in whose name the little church was founded from the beginning, and before all the saints, while all those who were present and standing by granted their consent, he offered a green olive branch, which he placed on the altar of that same little church in the symbol of the holy Cross. He conferred [the following things] on it in free alms, to support ten clerics or secular canons who were appointed to serve God and St. Omer in that place forever. First, he gave the altar of this same place in the same liberty in which he had asked for and received it earlier from the bishop of Thérouanne, along with the associated rights of the altar, and all the tithe of the parish, both of the new lands and of those cultivated by the ancients; this did not exclude or except wood or marsh, but included everything whatsoever that the sacred canons and the decrees of the holy fathers established and ordained should be tithed. He also gave the tithes of Ferlinghem, Rodelinghem, and Welles, and the mill in that village and one little farmyard near the mill; a carrucate of free land in Nord-Ausque; also the altars of Zouafques and Bonningues-lez-Ardre; also the altar of Hondschote and the figures around the hall of that village[404] and the moor and marsh rights; and a carrucate of free land in Blendecques.[405]

Since it was unknown to the possessors of the church of Ardres of this time where this land in Blendecques is or how it was alienated from the church of Ardres, some opined that it lay forgotten during the time when the canons of that church were replaced by monks.[406] At last the land passed down to a certain Boidin, the dean, as though by hereditary right. Since he knew from his ancestors that this land belonged to the church of Ardres, and since he could not and perhaps did not wish to restore and return it to the church of Ardres as he ought to have done, he knew himself to be wrong. So as if he had taken wiser advice, he established a monastery of nuns, now called Sainte-Colombe, on the same land,[407] in which he gave himself as a brother, like a canon or monk, along with all the land.

In Ardres, Arnold also granted the land of the cross and the mill on the east side of the castle, and he conceded one free farmyard near the courtyard to each canon whether resident in the village or not.[408] And the other nobles of the land, the barons of Guines as well as those within Ardres's jurisdiction, hastened with similarly fervent devotion to support the canons and offered their lands and whatever tithes or small estates they had. This one offered a basket or bushel of grain, this one two or more. That one offered as many of oats, another so many pennies. This one offered a little property of such a size, the other the judicial rights over another piece of land.

When this had been done, Arnold first summoned Walter, who had earlier been the parson of the small church of Ardres, and gave him the first prebend in the name of the Lord and of St. Omer. He gave the second to Ralph his son, and thus similarly gave the prebends to all the others. At length, in the presence of his sons and daughters and many nobles and the clergy and the people, who all called upon God and St. Omer and raised their laudatory assent on high and rejoiced, he installed and established the ten canons. He did this so that whatever sin he had committed against the ten commandments through secular negligence and worldly excesses he might expiate through the prayers of the ten canons, as the merits and intercession of St. Omer before God would aid him. And so ten canons of the church of Ardres were created and installed in 1069 a. d., during the reign of King Philip of France, when Robert the Frisian was governing Flanders after he triumphed over Richilde, and when Baldwin the count of Guines was in power, when this same Arnold or Arnulf the advocate was presiding over the county of Thérouanne and ruling the people of Ardres, and while Drogo was holding the staff of the church of Thérouanne.[409]

116. How Bishop Drogo of Thérouanne confirmed the church of Ardres with its associated rights.

And so, when Bishop Drogo of Thérouanne had received privileges and letters of confirmation concerning the church of Ardres from Arnold, in full synod he granted the aforementioned church along with its associated rights and attachments and possessions to Arnold and his successors and the canons who were to serve in that church forever and he confirmed it in this manner:

In the name of the Father and the Son and of the Holy Spirit, the one true God. I, Drogo, by the grace of God the bishop of the church of Thérouanne, wish to notify the faithful, both present and future, that at the prayers of our faithful man, namely Arnulf the advocate, who asks things that ought not to be denied, I have granted the altar of Ardres with a liberty like that of St. Mary in which the body of St. Omer rests, to wit under this condition: that it shall remain under his protection and that of his successors forever free of the demand for any regular payment, while, nevertheless, they shall annually pay to us and to our successors two shillings on Maundy Thursday at Thérouanne. Two parts of the offering of that altar, however, shall be given to the canons serving God there, but the third with all the wax[410] shall go for the lighting and repair of the church.

These are the things, therefore, that this same Arnold gives to God and the canons for the sake of his soul and those of his wife and of his children and of his mother and father and his ancestors and successors: the tithe paid by all persons of the same village; all the land, as one free carrucate; one free farmyard in the same village to each canon; the tithe of Ferlinghem and Rodelinghem; in Peupelingue, the tithe of that same village and one free carrucate of land; the tithe of Welles and one mill and one free farmyard; in Nord-Ausque, one free carrucate of land; the altars of Hondschote and of Bonningues-lez-Ardre and Zouafques, which belonged to his benefice, for which five shillings are to be given in our honor and that of our successors to support a dean who will come to synod; also, the mill which is in the east part of the castle of Ardres and a meadow with land at Blaringhem and one free carrucate of land in Blendecques.

If anyone shall try to go against this charter of ours, first he shall incur the wrath of God and then, under the penalty of law, he shall pay ten pounds in gold. Enacted at Thérouanne in 1069 a. d., the second indiction, in the reign of King Philip, in the presence of suitable witnesses, whose names are written below. The sign of bishop Drogo; the sign of Hubert, of Warner, archdeacons; the sign of Gerald, dean; the sign of Girmoland, cantor; the sign of Jodo; the sign of Odo; the sign of Arnulf; the sign of Walter; the sign of Richard; the sign of Gerhard; the sign of Arnulf the advocate; the sign of Sichard Descoches; the sign of Gerard Godnach; the sign of Adelo; the sign of Rainier; the sign of Baldwin of Uphem; the sign of Arnulf; the sign of Hibbert; the sign of Galand; the sign of Frumold; the sign of Eustace.[411]

This, then, as well as I can remember, was the tenor and form of the privilege of Bishop Drogo of Thérouanne. Nor should you wonder, fathers and lords, and particularly you chaplains and clerics, if in laying out this privilege, translated from Latin into our mother tongue for you, I have not interpreted it very well or very elegantly. But may your capacious understanding or discreet attention or certainly your rational discretion grasp and understand in whatever sort of words I have offered what our lay language is not able to express.[412] In a similar fashion and with devout intent, Arnold requested and sought privileges from the archbishop of Reims and from the pope in Rome.[413]

117. How Arnold placed the relics of many saints in the church at Ardres.

After these events, Arnold went around to many churches, and, seeking and acquiring the relics of as many saints he could get, he gathered them in the church at Ardres. For that reason, the canons of Saint-Omer of the chapter of blessed Omer extracted a tooth of their father and patron and gave it to him; he encased it in the purest gold and precious stones and placed it in his church with the greatest reverence. Then, the abbot of Saint-Bertin,[414] whose faithful man he was called (and was), gave him a small cross in which were hidden some small cuttings of the hair and clothing of the blessed Virgin Mary, of the beard of St. Peter the apostle, of God's manna and of the dust of St. John the Baptist. The same abbot also gave him the arm of St. Pancras the martyr and a large part of the relics of the holy martyrs Nereus and Achilleus,[415] in exchange for which, they say, Arnold gave the abbot and monks of Saint-Bertin rents and prebends that could support four monks forever, and the same number of canons in the church of Saint-Omer at Sythiu. And with the consent of some of the canons and of the bishop, he transferred the relics of many saints, books of the Old Testament, passionaries, and some other books and many ecclesiastical ornaments from the church of Saint-Paul to his church at Ardres.[416] And while he was thus going around to many churches with the same purpose and enriched his church with relics and ornaments received here and there, his wife, the noble countess Clemence, died.[417]

118. How Arnold built a bigger church at Ardres and moved the canons to it.

Then, when his wife Clemence had died and was buried in the church of Saint-Pol and was most dutifully mourned, Arnold took himself off to his Ardres, quite prudently bidding the county of Saint-Pol farewell and relinquishing it. And in the middle of the market, before the gate of the interior wall, he built a great new basilica in honor of the blessed Virgin Mary and of St. Omer, the confessor and also the bishop of Thérouanne, and of the saints whose relics he had sought out. And he called the canons from the cemetery church with their shrines and relics and all the books and ornaments of the church and he established them in the new church, as if in his chapel, to serve God forever. He procured a priest for the cemetery church to serve God unceasingly and to celebrate mass for the faithful. Thereupon, he conferred and granted a free manse around the market and around the new church upon

each of the canons resident and living in the village. But after he introduced
the canons into his new church, he ordained and confirmed by oath, both
by his own hand and that of the chapter of canons, that any canon who did
not earn his prebend in church in his own person would not obtain more
of the prebend than one hundred shillings—his vicar would get everything
over that. Nor might any non-resident canon appoint his own vicar there, but
only the dean of the church, with the advice of the canons who daily resided
in the church.

119. How this same Arnold became one of the peers of Flanders, and how he could receive outlaws.

It ought to be known, moreover, that Arnold or Arnulf, called the advocate, the provost and founder of the church of Ardres, the erstwhile count of
Saint-Pol, disdained and refused to submit to Count Baldwin I of Guines as
his lord, and that because of this he was frequently attacked by the count of
Guines and persecuted with lawsuits and arms. So on the advice of his son
Arnold and of some others, he received the keep of Ardres and other of his
allods as a fief from Count Robert of Flanders, the son of Robert the Frisian,
of whom I have already spoken, and Arnold did him homage and promised
him obedience. (Later on, when Antioch had been vanquished, Robert captured Jerusalem.[418]) And hence, the count of Flanders granted it to him by
hereditary right that he might sit in judgment with the twelve peers and barons of the court of Flanders and that he might glory that he was a peer and
a participant in their honor and dignity in every detail. He also granted it as
a hereditary fief that Arnold might for a year and a day keep anyone safe at
Ardres who was proscribed for any reason, in opposition to any men whatsoever of the count's jurisdiction, as long as this person did not openly work or
conspire against the person of the count or countess of Flanders. And if the
banished man did not wish to stand judgment, he could produce this man
safely in any court of the count's realm before any judges and then, as long
as he did not wish to stand judgment, Arnold could lead him back and keep
him in his own territory.[419]

Thus laudably performing worldly acts with secular men in the world,
he then began to grow sick. And when he had called the abbot of Saint-Bertin
to him,[420] having called his sons and the clergy of his church to him, he said
goodbye to the world before all of them, became a monk, and was carried to
Saint-Bertin. Lamenting the negligence of his sins in penance there for a few

days' time, he sloughed off and relinquished the burden of the body together with its miseries and was received, beyond the shadow of a doubt, among the ethereal thrones. His body was buried honorably by the monks in their cloister and was carefully housed in a memorable tomb forever.

120. How when Arnold died, the lords of Hénin and Ecluse did not want to do homage to his son Arnold.

But when Arnold or Arnulf the advocate, the lord and provost of Ardres, died, Eustace of Hénin and Baldwin of Ecluse flew to Count Robert of Flanders and did homage to the count of Flanders, the homage that these men ought to have done to Arnold, the lord of Ardres. (Oh, the perfidy of evil counts! Oh, the evil hands of subjects! Oh, the perpetual shame of the people of Hénin and Ecluse!) They were unashamed and unembarrassed about this act of submission. And although many rebuked and blamed them because of the perfidy of this great crime and spit on them in their disapproval of reprobates and of men who transgressed in treacherous fashion, yet they steadily refused to be bound to the count of Boulogne or the lord of Ardres by any title of subordination or obligation. And Arnold, the lord of Ardres, the son of Arnulf, was stirred to rage and so if there were any inhabitants of Hénin or Ecluse staying at Ardres, he considered them traitors and party to the disrespect and shame of the disloyal lords of Henin and Ecluse, and he forced them into and bound them with servile shame.

121. How Arnold the Old gave the land of Marquise to his brother Gonfrid and how Gonfrid left him part of his land in England.

When the son of Arnulf the Advocate, Arnold, who was called the Old or the Old Man, had very wisely accepted sufficient consolation upon the death of his father, he became the lord of Ardres and the provost of the church of Ardres. And as quickly as possible, he purchased and transferred from his brother Gonfrid the land in England that they had together acquired and received from the aforementioned king of England as a reward and recompense for their knightly service. And he granted his brother Gonfrid the land of Marquise with its associated rights to be held by hereditary right; it belonged to him from his mother's side.[421] And thus Marquise was allotted to Gonfrid and his heirs.

Once Arnold had become the lord of Ardres and a peer and companion of the count of Flanders, he attended the court of Flanders. He honored the nobles of Flanders with as much zeal as he could, so that with their help he might acquire for himself and subjugate the men of Hénin and Ecluse, who disdained him — Alas, the shame and crime of disloyalty! — and who were particularly rebellious and contumacious toward him when they were before the count of Flanders.

And so to clarify and elucidate the obscurity of the following events, to wit, so that I may wholly disclose the nobility of the lordship of Ardres, just as I planned, and so that I will not unwisely leave the genealogy of the family of Bourbourg untouched upon, inasmuch as this matter lies close to my narrative, let me show that the family of Ardres and also the family of Bourbourg took their origins, on one side, from the family of Aalst, as I have been taught and informed by truthful fathers. In this I do not deviate or digress, nor do I wander away from my narrative to these certain other matters, for they are, indeed, not foreign, but related, and as much akin to the family of Ardres as that of Bourbourg.

122. The genealogy of the family of Bourbourg and how the families of Bourbourg and Ardres descended in part from the lineage of Aalst.

So, then, there was a certain noble man in the land of Brabant, Baldwin, surnamed the Fat or the Great,[422] who was the heir and lord of the lordship of Aalst. He had a wife named Matilda,[423] born into a noble lineage, who was called by a similar name, the Fat or the Great, because of the size or bulk of her husband. Now this Baldwin had a brother named Ingelbert of Petegem[424] and a most beautiful sister named Gertrude; she was married at some time to Arnold, the lord of Ardres, who was called the Old or the Old Man, because of his son Arnold, who was called the Young or Junior.[425] By his wife Matilda the Fat, Baldwin the Fat had Baldwin the One-eyed, who was afterward the lord of Aalst (he was also called the Whiskered because of the fullness of his beard), and Ivan, called of Ghent.[426] Then Baldwin the Whiskered had Beatrice by Leutgard, a most noble lady from Grimbergen.

But when Baldwin the Bearded went the way of all flesh and was buried, his brother Ivan did not consider what was just or honest, that his brother's daughter Beatrice was alive and survived and was the heir. He violently broke out and obtained Aalst, for Count Thierry of Flanders gave his consent in some manner, or rather his permission. And he also married his niece Beatrice (his brother Baldwin's daughter) to Castellan Henry of Bourbourg, Thein-ard's son;[427] he left to her the smallest of the allods in the land of Brabant that belonged to her on her mother Leutgard's side, namely Weert-Saint-Georges and Meinthia.[428] She was still tender in years and very young and ignorant of the outcome of the business, and she knew little and was not wisely fore-sighted about what was done concerning her.

This Henry, castellan of Bourbourg, had earlier married the only daugh-ter of Count Manasses of Guines, properly named Sybil, but called Rose, who died in giving birth;[429] his father, Theinard, the earlier castellan of Bour-bourg, was slain in the church of St. Donatian in Bruges. Theinard was with Count Charles of Flanders when he was murdered with an unexpectedly mor-tal blade by the treacherous people of Bruges, while he was kneeling in prayer in front of the altar of the holy father Basil; when Theinard did not wish to or was unable to help the count, he was also slain.[430] Then this Castellan Henry of Bourbourg had seven sons by Beatrice of Aalst, namely Baldwin, Walter and Henry, Gilbert and Ralph, Siger and Walter, and five daughters, namely Mabel, Matilda, Leutgard, Adelaide, and Beatrice.

And so Baldwin, the firstborn, when he had become the castellan of Bourbourg after his father Henry died and was buried at Saint-Bertin,[431] asked Count Philip of Flanders for Kortenhoek and Lang-Mark and Bixscote in ex-pectation of his favor and of the recovery of more.[432] These lands were from the lands of the family of Aalst, and, as I have shown here, they belonged to him by hereditary right on his mother's side. And he postponed and put off seeking greater things for the time being. He married Countess Juliana of Duras.[433] But she neither conceived nor bore children by him, but died and was buried without any. And although this same Baldwin afterward married Elizabeth, the daughter of the advocate Robert of Béthune,[434] he died without children and was honorably buried in the church of St. Mary of Bourbourg where all the castellans of Bourbourg are buried except the first Henry, who is buried at Saint-Bertin.

Then the first Walter died as an adolescent. Then Henry died when he had already become a knight.[435] Gilbert, in fact, refused to become the castel-lan, because he lost the acuity of his eyes fighting in tournaments. But Ralph and Siger, who had become clerics, got many livings and ecclesiastical dig-nities. Of these sons, Ralph became the dean of the church of Noyon, and although he had already been seized and elected bishop of Noyon, he died and was buried with great veneration at Péronne under the choir of the church of St. Fursey.[436] Siger also died not much later and was buried in the church of St. Mary at Bourbourg.

And so the seventh child, Walter, the youngest of all the brothers, at length became the castellan of Bourbourg and married Matilda, the daughter of the advocate Robert of Béthune,[437] the sister of the Elizabeth whom Baldwin, his brother, had once married. He had by her Henry and Beatrice. But when Walter died, his son, while still a boy, became castellan of Bourbourg.[438] Then Henry's sister Beatrice was handed over to the cloister of nuns at Bourbourg, not so much to be taken care of, as to be educated in morals and imbued with liberal studies.[439]

Now then, to continue the story of truth in proper order of enumeration concerning the five daughters of Castellan Henry I of Bourbourg: the first, namely Mabel, was married to Baldwin of Bailleul and became the viscountess of Ypres.[440] The second, namely Matilda, was first given to liberal studies, and then was seized and seduced, or rather elected,[441] by the nuns because of the honesty of her life and the sanctity of her merit as a nun among the daughters and nuns of the church of Bourbourg; she received the symbol of the abbess and the dignity of that office.[442] The third, Leutgard, was coupled as a wife and wed to a noble man across the Rhine, Arnold of Cuerthedra.[443] The fourth, Adelaide, was bound in legitimate marriage to the noble man Stephen of Seninghem.[444] The fifth, namely Beatrice, was more beautiful than the rest. Hearing and understanding that the conjugal life is good, the continence of the widow is better, and the best is virginal perfection, she

Remained for all eternity a maid;
To her forever fame and accolade!

This woman, then, was dear to the clergy, commended to God, and praised by the world because of the purity of her character, the sanctity of her life, her generosity with her possessions, her innate goodness, and her divine charity. Having imitated the saints, she married Christ, a nun without a habit. She was an abbess without the name and dignity, although in her dutiful zeal she was not so much like a ruler as a servant in all the sanctity and religion of the nuns. She lived in her own home, content with her own possessions and rents.[445] After the death of her sister, the venerable matron and abbess Matilda, she worked diligently and appropriately in the place of the abbess; when the abbess was alive, however, she acted as the vice-abbess. All the nuns' actions and business were carried out according to her wish and desire and disposition. And also all of the monastics in that place, both the servants and the nuns, were protected, governed, and supplied by her foresight.

Let these reports, which I have touched on briefly and succinctly and succinctly laid out on account of certain incidents of my narrative, suffice to clarify the following matters concerning the lineage of Aalst and the lineage of Bourbourg and the lineage of Béthune. But now, let us return to the lineage of Ardres, so that I may bring the narrative I have undertaken to its conclusion.

123. How Arnold the Old married Gertrude.

And so, since my grandfather,[446] the lord of Ardres, who was called the Old, attended the court of Flanders, and fame of his greatness reached all the nobles of the kingdom of France and resounded and with truthful voice spoke well of him, his reputation, magnificence, and knightly splendor came to the ears of Baldwin, the lord of Aalst. For that reason, Baldwin the Fat of Aalst invited him to be his guest one day at a certain tournament that was glorious and famous within the boundaries of Tournai, when Arnold had won and gotten for himself there the preponderance and glory of the day of battle and the tournament, and even the envious agreed. And Baldwin solemnly provided him and his followers with very refined food and drink. When the next day came, the two talked things over in many words, and Arnold married and wed Gertrude, the noble man's sister, in legitimate marriage.[447] At the same time that he took his wife, he accepted the allods she possessed in the castellany of Bergues, at Aardenbourg and Oostbourg, and around Yzendijke and Vulendick and Gaternesse.[448]

Then, Arnold, coming with his wife Gertrude to his Ardres, was received by the clergy and people in his church with the bells solemnly ringing; having made a brief prayer there, they were received together with joy into the castle of his house. For three days, as though they were celebrating the triennial feast of Bacchus there, they celebrated their solemn nuptials, abandoning themselves to food and drink, in games and amusements, with pleasure and rejoicing. At these nuptials, Arnold performed this memorable feat, or rather one marvelous to relate.

124. How Arnold hanged a rogue on a gibbet.

Now, among the many folk coming together from many regions to attend the nuptials, there was a certain rogue, a beer-drinker—as the custom of that time was. When he dined in the house with the other feasters, he proclaimed and boasted amongst them that he was such a great drinker that if the lord bridegroom would give him some sort of nag or horse, he would drink up a great keg, completely full of beer, that Arnold had in his cellar. When the bung had been pulled, he would place his mouth at the opening and not remove it until the keg was empty. And he would void his waste at the same time, as he had just prepared and arranged a place where he might pour out or release the urine from his manly rod. When the bridegroom took the bet, the rogue matched his deeds to the words and emptied the keg — Oh, the gluttony of drinkers! Oh, the indiscreet prodigality of princes! — just as he had predicted and accepted in the bet: he drained, chugged, drank, and, at the same time, urinated.

When it was empty, the wretch jumped amongst them and placed the bung of the keg in his mouth as a sign of jocularity, or rather of gluttony. He began boldly and repeatedly to demand in a clamorous and victorious voice the horse that he won in the agreement and by drinking. But the bridegroom looked at him with burning eyes and ordered that the horse be saddled for him and be given to him as quickly as possible according to the agreement. But Arnold's cronies had cut trees into a gibbet, as they were well-informed of the intention of their lord; they jumped up at once and hanged the rogue from the gibbet.[449]

Then Arnold knew his wife Gertrude and by her he had Arnold, called the Young or the Younger; Manasses and Baldwin and Hugh the monk; Adeline; Agnes; and Alice.

125. How peace was made between Ardres and Fiennes.

At the time my grandfather Arnold, the lord of Ardres (called the Old to distinguish him, as I have said above, from his son Arnold the Younger), was living in peaceful tranquility and in prosperity, he enclosed and stilled the waters of the living springs at Brêmes and made a fish pond, and built and constructed a mill over the fish pond, much to the indignation of the count of Guines, the people of Balinghem, and many others. Then the family of Fiennes rose up again with great force and strength and asked again for the hereditary allods in Ardres which they alleged belonged to them and were theirs.[450] But since the family of Ardres responded with indignation that they would provide no allods or holdings to the family of Fiennes, the family of Fiennes retreated, driven to rage. Returning again and making an assault on Ardres, they began to attack and trouble them greatly. But the men of Ardres provoked and harassed the men of Fiennes in battle in a not dissimilar way and often carried off their possessions. But when they had gathered their troops, the men of Fiennes carried off with them not just their own possessions—how, indeed, does it help to cover up the truth?—but also they often carried off the goods of the men of Ardres along with their own. And for this reason, the lord of Ardres, my grandfather Arnold, enclosed the courtyard belonging to the men of Ferlinghem with a solid earthwork, the better to protect their animals. (This earthwork was later razed to the ground in the dedication of the little church established in that same courtyard.) Then when they had fought each other in this way for a long time and had provoked each other, and each side had wounded some of the other side, the opposing sides gnashed their teeth at each other.

But after a long struggle between this side and that and many attacks by warriors of both parties, in the end, those who were equally friendly to both sides mediated. Peace was established between them and they became friends and allies in the love that comes from kinship. Then the estates at Fiennes belonging to the family of Ardres, along with the serfs living there, fell to the family of Fiennes as part of their inheritance and remained as such; they ran from the enclosure of the cemetery through the middle of the market all around unbroken up to the castle. But the estates of the family of Fiennes at Ardres, if they held any, remained an inheritance for the family of Ardres forever.

126. The war between Ardres and Guines and how Arnold the Old fortified the town and the wood of Ardres with a great and long earthwork.

Then after these things had happened, Arnold's sons, both those who had been conceived in the love of pleasure and those born of his noble wife Gertrude, became knights and were in the flower of youth and grew great amidst the nobility of the Flemish court. And since Arnold failed to serve Count Manasses of Guines and not only was not loyal to him according to the tenor of homage, but was also a rebel and a contumacious man, Arnold refused to appear before him and respect him. So the count greatly molested him in many ways to the point that the count often put him to flight in his Ardres—indeed, I must not hide the truth—whether Arnold wished it or not. The count besieged and encircled Ardres, not without much bloodshed on either side, and turned the houses and similarly the village church to em-

bers and reduced them to ash. (Oh, the blasphemous rage of persecuting enemies!) When Manasses drove the fleeing man into the stronghold of the castle,
however, and could neither conquer it himself nor force it to surrender, the
count heard that knights were gathering all around in aid of the family of
Ardres, and for this reason he retreated from Ardres. Then the family of Ardres emerged enraged and ardent with fury,[451] and when the knights allied to
them arrived in aid, after many enemies had fallen on either side, they put
the count to flight into Guines.

Nevertheless, truces were granted and accepted at the desire of both
parties, and good faith in peace was given and accepted by both for a time.
The earthwork of the exterior wall of the fortress of Ardres was repaired and
enlarged and surrounded and penned in with fences and military hedgehogs,[452] and towers and war machines were built on top and prepared in defense against the attack of enemies. Then Arnold extended the great and deep
and wide earthwork outside the village and cemetery, from the upper side
of the fish pond as far as Fulbert's wood or grove. It enclosed and fortified
both the communal lands of his people and the plain of the fields as well as
the houses of the whole village of Ardres. And he ordered and had oaks and
other trees planted together on top of the earthwork, as can be seen today.
Then around the same time, he made his son Hugh a monk in the church of
Saint-Bertin and, along with his son, he gave whatever the church of Saint-
Bertin possesses to this day at Rodelinghem to the abbot and monks of that
place in free alms.[453]

There is one thing, however, that I include in the course of these words,
that is as marvelous as it is memorable, to wit: when war's contest between
the lords of Ardres and Guines was very great, while the men of Ardres were
within the land of Guines, they were always rebellious and contumacious
toward the count of Guines and his men. They not only refused to show him
the respect they owed him, but also persecuted and attacked him and his followers with indignation. And the count of Guines and his followers, when
they stayed in the land of Guines, did no less; they plotted against and attacked the men of Ardres with similar persecution and harassment. Nevertheless, the more rebellious and contumacious the lords of Ardres had been
toward the count of Guines and his men within the territory, when the former
and the latter came together any place outside Guines, in foreign lands, in any
court or hall, or even in any tournament or inn, the more prompt they were
in service and the more they were devoted with an unfeigned fidelity to the
count and his men of Guines. And the men of Guines, no matter how greatly
and with what justice and merit they were hostile toward the men of Ardres in

their own country, were just as mild and totally benign to them abroad whenever they came together, and they showed them a calm and almost peaceable countenance. Therefore, *forestalling each other in honor* [Rom. 12:10], each showed the other the voluntary benefit of the loyalty they owed each other.

127. How Arnold built a great and tall house in the castle of Ardres and this is its description.

Then afterward, when peace had been made and confirmed between Count Manasses of Guines and Lord Arnold of Ardres, using the marvelous skill of carpenters, Arnold constructed a wooden house above the keep of Ardres that surpassed the houses built of the same material in all of Flanders at that time. A certain architect or carpenter from Bourbourg named Louis, who differed little from Daedalus in the genius of this art, forged and constructed it.[454] And he made and created an inescapable labyrinth of it; he attached room to room, chamber to chamber, and compartment to compartment, and joined the granaries or storerooms to the cellars; he built the chapel above in a very suitable place on high in the eastern part of the house.

Then he built a three-storey structure in it and suspended storey upon storey a long way from the ground,[455] as if in the air. The first storey, where there were cellars and granaries, also great chests, kegs, and vats, and other implements of the house, was on ground level. Then the common living and work spaces of the inhabitants were on the second floor, where there were workrooms, on one side the room of the bakers, on the other, that of the butlers. Over here was the great chamber of the lord and his wife, in which they slept; the side chamber was contiguous to this, that is, the chamber or dormitory of the attendants and children. Here in a more private part of the great chamber there was a private alcove, where they used to make a fire at full dawn or at dusk or during an illness, or for letting blood or for warming the attendants or the weaned children.[456] Then on this floor was the house kitchen, which was divided into two levels. On the lower level, they put pigs that were to be fattened up over here, over there the geese to be fed, and over there capons and other fowl that were being prepared to be killed and eaten. On the second level of the kitchen, however, the cooks and those who supplied the kitchen stayed; on this level, the lord's very refined food was processed[457] and prepared to be eaten with varied sorts of preparation and labor on the part of the cooks. The food of household members and domestics was also prepared there through daily provisioning and dutiful labor.

On the top storey of the house, the rooms of the uppermost chambers[458] were constructed, in which the sons might lie when they wished over here, while the daughters of the lord of the house might lie down over there, as was suitable; vigilant servants, positioned and appointed to take care of the house, and the always ready guards might catch some sleep over yonder.

There were flights of stairs and passages from storey to storey, from the house into the kitchen, from room to room, and from the house into the loggia, and again from the loggia into the oratory or the chapel, which resembled the tabernacle of Solomon in its painting and carving. (The loggia is well named, for the following reason; the word is derived from *logos*, which means "word," and, indeed, they were accustomed to sit there amidst delights to converse.)

Now I have reminded you, fathers and lords, of these things concerning this house which you see and in which you live, not so much for you as for the people from foreign places who stay here with us. It is no wonder that guests and outsiders do not know all the rooms of this house, since many who have been raised from infancy and brought to man's estate in this house cannot know and comprehend the number of doors, gates, little entries, and windows.

128. Why the oven dues were granted at Ardres.

When this house of Solomonic glory had been built, Arnold went to England, where

With the king for some days he did rest,
And did a bear of wondrous size request

from this same king. After his business throughout his land in England had been attended to and well organized, he took the bear back with him to Ardres. When it had been brought out and shown before the people and it had been baited by dogs and mangled almost to death and its hair had been torn out, everyone marvelled and was happy and pleased at the spectacle. But later on, when the people would gladly have seen it baited by dogs during the feast days and requested this, the bear-keeper refused for some time at the prompting of the lord. He demanded bread from the people to feed the bear — Oh, the foolishness of the simple people! Oh, the lamentable avarice of the lord, hardened by the melody of Scylla!! The foolish people (but not the rear-vassals and clergy) swore and promised the lord of their own free will that they would give the bear-keeper one loaf of bread from any oven in the citadel for any provisioning whatsoever to provide for and feed the bear; thus they might have and see the bear-baiting and spectacle every feast day for their pleasure. But alas for the bear-baiting! Through it the populace of Ardres were made sport of and seduced and corrupted into a bad usage and evil custom! For the exaction of oven dues for this bear grew into such an execrable custom, that this bear's bread may be extorted and demanded forever by the lords from the people's descendants, whether the wretched populace wills it or not, by right of custom, without any bear-baiting, unless the mercy of God and yours, most merciful father and lord, should come to their aid. Thus this bread is held to be the bread of affliction, which the lord possesses as if by right. On account of this right, he demands and extorts oven dues to this day as a right in certain places in Ardres which are recorded and held of old to be responsible for this.

129. Of Gertrude's severity.

Now, Gertrude, the wife of Lord Arnold of Ardres, could glory that because of the nobility of her family she arose from noble origins and that she was ennobled by the proud chastity of her words and deeds, and could extol and exalt herself, but she was ambitious for possessions and famous for the vice of cupidity and for notorious avarice. Consequently one day (I shall be silent about other events and matters concerning her), she ordered sheep to be exacted and collected throughout Ardres's jurisdiction to establish a sheep-farm. When her officials had already gathered some, or rather many, sheep, they came to the little tiny house of a very poor humble woman, in which the little woman of that domicile lived with her seven little children. She was crying and lamenting that she had nothing to give the children, who were also crying, to eat. And when these domestic ministers, worse than any serf, mocked the humble woman as if they were demanding a lamb from her, the woman answered simply that she had neither a sheep or cow, but that if they wished to take one of her little children to their lady, she would freely present it to be raised or fed. These most evil serfs went away and came to the lady and spoke ill of the little woman to her; they not only mocked the humble woman, but also basely accused her before the lady; hirelings were sent, who demanded the child promised to them. And in the end, the lady obtained the child she demanded, whether the humble woman liked it or not.

The lady had it fed and adopted as her own in place of a sheep. But when the little girl (the child that had been exacted was of the feminine sex) then came to nubile years, the lady — for shame! — married her off to a man; she had now been turned into a bondmaid and was called a bondmaid, or rather she had been recorded as being one. The lady condemned her to servility and thrust her down and submerged her and her heirs in it forever.

This same Gertrude had brought some free people, as they say, with her from her land, to wit, from Oostbourg, to serve and minister to her at Ardres. She sometimes attacked them in rage and in a fury of words and called them — Oh, cruel mother and matron! — ungrateful, unfaithful, and serfs. And consequently, their posterity was reputed to be unfree by some of those who came later.

Now, a rather pretty young woman named Eremberg was repudiated[459] by a compatriot, who was the lady's servant, whom the lady had similarly brought with her from Flanders, so that Eremberg was rejected by many men. She wanted to have him as a husband and he refused and rejected her as unworthy. So she ran to her lady and offered her hands to the lady in servitude so that she might manage to get and have as her husband the servant who was refusing to marry her. Although he completely rejected her as a wife, nevertheless, she was married by him whether he was willing or not, and this same Gertrude made each of them a serf, with their descendants forever.[460]

However, when my father Baldwin, the son of Arnold, lord of Ardres, and Gertrude, became the lord of Ardres after some years and went to Jerusalem, he freed these people, the others mentioned above, and the descendants of their lineage from this shameful servile condition, no matter for what reason they had formerly been recorded as such. Before God and all his populace, he manumitted and surrendered them as free men into the hands of Thierry, the abbot of blessed Mary of Capella. These same people and their children and their posterity and descendants were to pay the aforementioned abbot and his successors a single penny as an annual payment and four when they married or upon their deaths.[461]

130. How Arnold, who was devoted to the church of God, at length taking the Lord's cross upon himself, went to Antioch.

Now Arnold, although he was seen somewhat by worldly people as a secular man of the world, was very devout toward God and swift in his service. Consequently, although he had a chapel in his castle, as if to supplement the church of Ardres, nevertheless, no chaplain was to serve or minister there except with the assent of the canons of the church of Ardres. And although he always had his own chaplain in the house, on whose behalf he sent vestments to those people in England who are now assigned revenues in the vestiary of the church of St. Mary of Capella, nevertheless, to the degree that his secular activities permitted him, he always heard the divine service in the church of the canons, and not just during the day but also at night. And when he knew that some canon or his vicar had been absent from Matins or even some of the other canonical hours, as he was the provost, he corrected him either leniently or harshly like a good shepherd. And so in this manner he showed himself to be as devout and dutiful toward the church of God and churchmen as the condition of human frailty permitted.

Consequently, when the council sat at Clermont in 1096 a. d. on the 18th of November,[462] just as I heard at some time in the chronicle writings of Flanders, and in that council Pope Urban through his apostolic authority invited the people of the whole world to go with war gear to free Jerusalem from the hands of the Muslims and Turks, this same Arnold, namely the Old, no deaf auditor of this evangelical truth, that *"He who wishes to come after me should deny himself and take up his cross and follow me"* [Mt. 61:24], affixed the sign of the cross to his shoulders. He set forth and went abroad toward Jerusalem very quickly and devoutly with arms, horses, and companions, as well as sufficient funds, along with King Philip of France and Count Robert of Flanders, the son of Robert the Frisian.[463] He came to and reached Antioch, where the wisdom and strength of his knighthood were known and attested by all. Although one bean, as they say, in this same Antiochian army cost a gold bezant and an ass's head sold for five shillings of Byzantine gold,[464] nevertheless he always remained strong and robust. When Antioch was captured by the Christians and Jerusalem liberated from the hands of the Turks and Godfrey ruled, Arnold, having acquitted his vow with the help of the venerable lord and his kinsman from Puy,[465] returned happily and with a swift step and brought back the only thing he wanted to his church at Ardres. He brought, indeed, a sign of the holy victory from Jerusalem, a reliquary more precious than gold and precious stones, namely some of the Lord's beard, some of the Lord's cross, and some of the stone from which the Lord ascended to heaven. But from Antioch he brought a piece of the Holy Lance[466] and relics of St. George the martyr[467] and many other relics of other saints.

It ought to be known, however, that in this fight at Antioch, Arnold the Old was reputed to be the best of the best among the many nobles of many

nations and peoples, because of the strength of his spirit as much as the skill
in knighthood of his outstanding body. He fought so that in his strength he
might please God's gaze. But while he pleased the Divine Majesty when he
was fighting in the company of the knights fighting for Christ, he also pleased
the knights, or rather all the people who were gathered there, whether they
had come out of ambition for human praise or even for temporal gain. But
since he did not dedicate his innumerable acts of skill to men but to God, he
hid the praiseworthy acts of his skill and knighthood as much as he could,
lest in being praised by worldly and secular men in time, he should at some
time be cheated of the reward of divine recompense and praise at the end of
the world. He either attributed or ascribed the glory of his deeds and actions
to others, in fact, or he glorified and magnified God by disguising himself.
But since "*a city on a mountain cannot be hidden*" [Mt. 5:14], the more care he
took to hide and cover up his glorious knighthood, the more widely the fame
of his praiseworthy skill proclaimed him and resounded among the people.
For as it is said,

> The fire that's more hidden, grows more hot.

And yet the singer of the *Song of Antioch*,[468] who was led by avaricious zeal
and was more desirous of the reward of temporal gain than Arnold was of
human praise, suppressed the glory and tribute of praise he deserved. (Oh,
the always injurious praise of hirelings and minstrels, or rather of sycophants!
Oh, the unworthy and foolish exaltation of sluggish princes!) For Arnold,

> Who was in strength and skill in every way,
> A noble hero

refused to give two scarlet stockings to this same wretch, who deserves to be
known by no name. So he made no mention of Arnold in his song; in this
song he mixed false things with true ones, but nevertheless left many deeds
of many praiseworthy men untouched under a blanket of silence. But oh, the
praiseworthy knighthood of Arnold! It ought to be made public everywhere
on earth! Oh, the memorable vigor and glory of his skill in all worldly matters! Oh the constancy of his humility in the works of virtue! It is not to be
despised, but cannot be expressed! He by no means sought human glory, although he was held to be worthy of all praise, and he preferred to deny a rogue
some little present than to be carried around the sphere of the world in the
mouth and name of an unworthy wretch and to be sung about and declaimed

with an instrument. But although that most ignominious minstrel took care to extinguish the name of Arnold, once the lamp of his virtues had been lit by fame, fame proclaimed and glorified him. For the name the avaricious and greedy man took from him through envy, or rather though greed and avarice, reverberated throughout the earth and was attributed to him in virtuous and praiseworthy magnificence, once the glory of his skill was known.

131. How Arnold the Young challenged Eustace of Hénin to single combat over his treachery.

Now his son Arnold, who called the Youth or the Younger for the reason mentioned above, was as much more well known and notable throughout all the provinces of France as he was more glorious and outstanding in knighthood than all the knights living in the whole of Guines. One day, he saw Eustace of Hénin in the court of Flanders before Count Thierry; he gazed at Eustace with burning eyes and challenged him to single combat because of his treachery. For Eustace had defrauded Arnold's father and Arnold himself when, with unwarranted insolence toward custom, he had received Hénin from the count of Flanders and had refused to do homage to the domain of Ardres. Eustace was supported by the count, but nevertheless, he sought refuge and basely left like a traitor without answering. But afterward Arnold challenged Eustace before the count of Boulogne at Boulogne in a similar manner and for the same reason, his treachery. Since Eustace (for shame!) said nothing to him, however, Arnold girded himself and prepared to lay hands on him. So in the end Eustace left the house by the little gate and, by fleeing and not looking back, he escaped from his hands by a whisker.

132. How Arnold the Old, when he returned from Antioch, married off his daughters.

Then after these things, Arnold the Old married his daughter Agnes to Franco, the lord of Vinnezeele and Harzeele. She conceived and bore Baldwin and other sons and daughters for him.[469] Now this Baldwin wished to have the land of the lordship of Ardres, when his mother Agnes had already died, and also after her brothers Arnold, Manasses, and Baldwin had died and her other brother Hugh had become a monk, although Adeline, the sister of the already dead Agnes, was still alive. But since the sister was judged a nearer heir than the nephew, he got some money from his maternal aunt, that is, Adeline, and left her and the land in peace without further false accusation. Then this Arnold the Old married his other daughter, Adeline, to the viscount of Merck.

133. The genealogy of the lords of Merck and the death of Gertrude.

Now there was once a certain viscount at Merck named Elembert. He was the viscount, to wit, of the count of Guines; he acted in the absence of the count in his stead and hence had this title.[470] This Elembert married a wife in England; she was named Matilda, and was a woman of most holy merit and of a life pleasing to God. Afterward she was both called and truly became a saint. By her, this Elembert had Eustace and Pagan[471] and Adelaide, who was the mother of Henry, William, and Geoffrey of Beaulieu or Belle. But when Matilda died and was honorably buried at the foot of the tower of the church of Merck, as she should have been and deserved to be, innumerable miracles occurred more and more frequently at her venerable tomb through the merits and pious intercession of St. Matilda, the matron dear to God. So her sons and the people appropriately built a certain small chapel onto the tomb, which can still be seen, in which she might stop and rest while greater miracles happened and appeared through her and in her name. Still, whether, as some people say, the bones of this most holy woman were carried off and placed elsewhere by her relatives, specifically the English, or the Scots, it is better in a dubious situation not to know, as it were, than to dare to pronounce as if for sure, when one is in doubt.

Afterward, this Elembert married Adelaide, the sister of Eustace the Old of Licques. By her he had Arnold, who became the viscount of Merck[472] when his father Elembert had died at some time, and when his brothers, Eustace and Pagan, had succeeded one another in the vicecomital office and died without heirs of the body. He also had Simon of Merck, the father of Eustace, William, and Ivan of Cauquelle. And he had Natalie, who was given as a wife to Henry of Guines, the father of Baron Geoffrey; and Windesmode, who was married in legitimate wedlock to Pagan of Northout; and Clarice, who was married to Rainier the Potter of Tornehem; and Eila, who was married to Baldwin Hascard of Inxent;[473] and Beatrice, who was first married to Roger of Basinghem; and Belle or Elizabeth, who was married to William of Herlin; and Sara, who was married to Fulk of Merck, the father of Simon of La Chaussée.

Then Gertrude grew old in her days. She was crushed, broken, and weighed down, not least by the sorrow she had conceived from the death of her son Manasses, who died in the land of Jerusalem, and no less by age. She sank into death[474] and was lamented, indeed, by her children, but eulogized by the populace with dry eyes and lips barely parted. She was buried honorably in the cemetery church of Saint-Omer at Ardres.

134. How Arnold the Old died and Arnold the Young became lord of Ardres.

But not long afterward, Arnold the Old was afflicted and impaired by long-term illness. Although he desired death more than life, but nevertheless could not die as quickly as he wished, he had the little cross he had brought back from the Lord's tomb brought to him and hung around his neck on a slender silver chain. He truly believed that in it was hidden one hair from the beard of the Lord. When it had been brought and hung around his neck by the slender chain, after he was anointed with oil, he was barely able to say and finish the Lord's Prayer. With his sons and friends and people standing around him, he clasped the little cross in his hands. Giving it veneration with the kiss of peace and saying farewell to all, he fell asleep in the Lord and left the world. And he was buried in the cemetery church at Ardres near the tomb of his wife Gertrude, while his sons and all the people and clergy lamented. Then his son Arnold the Young or the Younger (who was sometimes even called the Red) became lord of Ardres and provost. Since he was full-bodied, noble in height even among the nobles, handsome of face, a very notable knight, very rich in goods, and illustrious in family, he married the niece of Thierry, the count of Flanders, who was named Petronilla of Bouchain. She was a virgin quite as beautiful as she was noble and was born of distinguished and very rich parents.[475]

At the same time, his brother Baldwin, who was also my father, had an affair with a virgin (one is ashamed, and yet behold! it is no shame to say it), a girl by the name of Adele, who was the daughter of his paternal uncle, that is, Ralph the canon. She conceived and bore him a son, the person telling you these things, me, Walter of Le Clud.[476] And later on my father Baldwin deflowered another girl named Natalie; she was of great or rather surpassing beauty and a young woman of exalted nobility, the daughter of Robert the canon and his noble wife Adelaide. By her he had Simon, who died as a youth when he was already full-grown,[477] and a girl of most famous reputation named Margaret. Baldwin the Bastard, the son of William, the brother of Count Baldwin of Guines,[478] was born of her and so was Warren, the son of Warren, a canon of Thérouanne.

Now before he married the noble Petronilla, my paternal uncle Arnold the Young had an affair with a girl named Heloise, who was born in Herchem, and by her he had Robert, who was called, using an appropriated name, the nephew of Lady Adeline.[479] He married a noble and rich wife named Matilda at Colembert; by her he had Arnold and his brothers. He, that is, Arnold, afterward married Christine, the daughter of Master Lambert of the church of Ardres;[480] by her he had Baldwin and his brothers. Again, my paternal uncle Arnold the Young had an affair with a certain girl at Ardres and by her he had Mabel the Red, who was married to a certain John of Oudeland near Licques; John had many sons by her.

Now after he married the noble Petronilla, although this Arnold the Young, my paternal uncle, was said to be munificent, liberal, and a spendthrift when he was outside the country, and when it came to knighthood, he spent almost prodigally whatever the custom and rationale of those tourneying and fighting demanded, nevertheless, when he was in his county he was not so much a miser as financially cautious. Consequently he was said to have a great treasury of both gold and silver. Although he asked little or nothing, in fact, from his subjects except what they owed him by duty and custom, still he demanded his rents and other debts and rights so boldly and inhumanely that his subjects and many others thought he was hateful and abhorrent.

His wife Petronilla, however, was a young woman pleasing to God. She was simple and God-fearing, and either did her meticulous duty toward God in church or frequently turned her youthful spirit to childish jokes and songs among her maidens and to entertainments and frivolities similar to these.[481] In the summer, often impelled by her great simplicity of soul and bodily foolishness, she stripped off her clothes down to only her undershirt or shift and lowered herself and descended into the fish pond, not so much to wash or bathe as to cool off and gad about. Swimming here and there through the currents and channels of the waters, at one time she appeared prone, then on her back; then she was hidden in the water, then she was displayed whiter than snow above the waters (or her very white dry shift was displayed) before the knights no less than her attendants. So expressing in these behaviors and in things similar to these the forms and qualities of her benevolence, she showed how gracious and rightly lovable she was to her husband, the knights, and the populace.

135. How Arnold the Younger was killed by his very evil servants and grooms.[482]

The more gracious and welcome Arnold the Young, Petronilla's husband, was to knights, however, and the less prompt and careful he was in service to the princes of the superior lordship of Guines, the more truculent and proud he was to his inferiors and subjects, and he acted with a certain harsh monstrosity. And consequently his serfs and subjects, and even his intimates and cooks and other spawn of their wicked and noxious circle, having sworn to bring about his death, conspired to kill him. And so one day, Arnold went out in the morning and left Ardres for Brêmes on the feast of the Holy Innocents, as if he would hear the mass anyhow standing outside the church. (The canons or priests of Ardres were not, in fact, permitted to celebrate the divine mystery in his presence nor as long as he was in Ardres, because he had been legally summoned to stand judgment in the presence of the bishop of Thérouanne. Being a rebellious and defiant man, he refused to obey, and for this reason he had been struck by a sentence of ecclesiastical rigor and excommunication.) One of the very evil and depraved traitors, one of the number of those who had sworn to kill him, hurried and hastened to him and, lying like that most perfidious and most damned traitor Judas, said that he had heard and seen a certain rich countryman cutting down the tallest oak in the whole forest in Fulbert's Wood, near the road that led to Northout.

Now as that man was avaricious and grasping with regard to land and harsh and tyrannical toward his subjects, as I have already said, he hoped and thought with respect to this countryman, that he might get a lot of money from this rustic (who nevertheless didn't exist). So he went alone into Fulbert's Wood with only the betrayer, so that he would not, perchance, be discovered by the countryman. But as he hurried by himself with this man alone along the very narrow path toward the sound made by the traitors, who were hammering on an oak to imitate the sound of a peasant's adze cutting down the oak, the traitor and hireling followed him. Taking out a club, which he had hidden in the wood to carry out the crime he had already conceived of, he struck down (alas!) the lord (alas!) the warlike knight or rather the glory of knighthood (alas!), the man *more beautiful in body than the sons of* Flanders [Ps. 45:2] from his horse and laid him out on the ground with the first blow to the head. And the other accomplices to this betrayal and those who were privy to the plot hastened and laid hands on him; they took out swords or rather most unmerciful daggers and slit his throat without mercy.[483] His horse, however, fled terrified and ran back to Ardres, as though it feared the savage murderers.

The hireling who killed him also returned to his kitchen as fast as he could, still stained with the blood of his lord—he was one of the cooks—as though he were ignorant of the business. (The others implicated in the lord's death were fleeing to one place or another.) Arnold's entourage and squire, seeing his horse still saddled and fleeing to them as though terrified, feared that the lord had fallen from his horse by some misadventure, although they did not fear such an evil one. While they were looking for him, however, behold, some travelers and other people came running mixed together. They did not proceed cautiously but rushed as quickly as they could; they groaned with a great clamor and raised their voices, the voices of men full of fear or in an uproar, and said that they had seen the lord lying slaughtered, done to death, and with his throat slit in Fulbert's Wood. Then, truly, all of them lamented and mourned; they beat their hands and said, "Oh, this misfortune of the place of Ardres will be made public everywhere! Oh, the shame of Ardres and the scandal before all the world, although it is unmerited!" [484]

136. How his brother Baldwin became the lord of Ardres.[485]

Then Baldwin, his brother (who was also my father), heard the news of this misfortune while he was staying at Guines to eat with Arnold of Ghent, and he flew swiftly to Ardres, bringing Arnold of Ghent with him (he had allied himself with Arnold in friendship against Albert the Boar) and other knights. And he brought his brother from the wood to his house at Ardres on a bier, accompanied by the weeping and lamentation of Arnold's wife, brothers, sisters, knights, and people. Since, indeed, Baldwin could not offer him church burial, because Arnold was bound by the chain of excommunication, when Arnold had been kept and waked there in sadness and tears for one night, Baldwin, nevertheless, did what he could and with much lamentation, plaint, and tears placed him outside the courtyard of the old church of Ardres near the great earthwork which his father had once made on the south side of the temple.

Soon he hunted down the murderers and traitors, along with those who knew about the murder and those who counseled it. Having found many, he broke some on the wheel, quartered some, had others hung on the tails of asses and torn apart, locked some in their own houses and burned them with fire, tormented some others and even more yet with various sorts of diverse tortures. Many of the relatives of those punished, in fact, did not dare to appear openly before men in the country for fear and shame and underwent perpetual exile hither and yon. But afterward my father completely satisfied his brother's wife, the noble matron Petronilla, concerning her dower, as was proper, and brought her back to her family at Bouchain with as much honor as he could. When he had done homage to Arnold of Ghent as well as Count Thierry of Flanders, he became the lord of Ardres and provost.

137. How Abbot Thierry of Capella came to Baldwin when he was wounded, and how Baldwin granted the church of Ardres to that same abbot.[486]

Just around this time, Baldwin, my father, was at Audruick with Arnold of Ghent, who then violently went against what was right and proper and pious, while Beatrice, the wife of Albert the Boar, the heir of the county of Guines by due succession, was still alive. Baldwin hastened without delay to Amaurival, which the people of Bourbourg called The Flower; there Castellan Henry and his supporters, as though they were hermits, hid in a little castle that had been unwisely prepared to defend Guines against Arnold of Ghent and his men. Both those attacking on one side and those defending themselves on the other had entered into a great contest of war against each other in that place, when see! the archers of the people of Bourbourg grew stronger against Arnold and his men and gravely wounded the lord of Ardres, my father Baldwin, with an arrow-shot to the head, that penetrated as far as the brain.

When my father had been wounded nearly to death and at length was carried back to his place at Ardres, many nobles, many religious men and clerics came to him to see him and console him. Among them also came Thierry, the venerable abbot of that most well-known place, St. Mary of Capella. While he was talking over many things with him, and consoling and also warning him, Thierry spoke in honied and salutary words and offered him this advice of his, which was most salubrious to the soul. And exhorting him, he suggested that since Baldwin was completely a layman and did not know letters, it was by no means lawful for him to administer benefices, to hand out livings or altars to clerics, or to obtain or assume any provostship or other dignity in the holy church, since the decrees of the holy fathers and authentic writings forbade and anathematized this. And Thierry announced most beneficially with a word of warning that now that Baldwin had been cautioned, unless he quickly ceased to act in this way, he would be basely polluted with the stains of simoniac depravity, and that he would, in the end, be thrust with Simon Magus among the part of society in Hell.

Then my father, Baldwin, listened willingly and kept it in mind. He feared both temporal death on account of the wound he had received and that he could at some time lapse into the death of eternal damnation, so he was filled morning and evening with the mercy of God and drunk with and infused by the grace of the Holy Spirit, the Paraclete. Upon the wholesome advice of the venerable abbot and confessor, he soon called together the chapter of the canons of the church of Ardres, his knights, his sisters, and the people. In front of all of them (they all assented to this and raised their voices praising God on high), he resigned the provostship of the church of Ardres, or rather the church of Ardres itself, with its associated rights, dependent properties, and dignities, into the hand of the aforementioned abbot and his monks who were present there, and he most freely granted it in free and perpetual alms to them and their successors with the same liberty and under the same right of rule and possession as he and his predecessors had held it up to this time. And he gave it very freely, and he offered it as a privilege most freely of all in this manner[487] — for

If I retain the words themselves in mind,
The meaning will not follow far behind — [488]

I, Baldwin,[489] by the permission of God heir and lord of Ardres and called the provost of the church of Saint-Omer at Ardres give a perpetual greeting to all the sons of the holy Mother Church.

Because it is discerned to be appropriate to the worship of God and the more reverend honor of the holy church of God, I have moved to promote what is necessary and salvific in all my actions as much as I am able. Consequently, since the possession of the office of provost of the church of Ardres fell to me by hereditary right, I considered on the one hand the negligence of the clerics or canons serving in this same church and weighed on the other danger and eternal destruction of punishment. For unless my parents have taught me in vain, the grant and disposition by a lay hand of an ecclesiastical provostship should not by any means accrue to me, for my salvation. So taking more exalted advice, I have planned certain higher things concerning the status of the church of Ardres.

So since a divine response and wise advice concerning the ordering of this same church has been received from Lord Milo, the bishop of the church of Thérouanne, from abbots and many ecclesiastical and lay persons, and from the peers and soldiers of the fortress of Ardres, and since the chapter of the church of Thérouanne as well as that of Ardres give their consent and offer a benevolent assent, I concede and give all rights and all dignities which fell to me by hereditary right in the church of Saint-Omer of Ardres, as well as the whole church with all its possessions, goods, associated rights, and dependent properties to the venerable abbot Thierry and to the monks of St. Mary of Capella (in the village called by the ancient name of Brouckham by those who live there) and to their successors, to be possessed by perpetual right in quiet possession. And I add this: that when a cleric or canon of the said church dies, a monk shall succeed him and thus, when all the canons are dead, the monks shall succeed in place of the canons and freely obtain the church, and however many monks as shall please the abbot shall in the end manage the church and the possessions of the church according to the arrangement of the abbot.

And so that this donation shall suffer no diminution at all with the passage of time and so that it may not be disturbed, troubled, or weakened by anyone's malice or hatred, I have had this present charter written and corroborated by witnesses and strengthened with the application of my seal and have sent it to be confirmed at Thérouanne and Reims and most fruitfully at Rome.

The witnesses of this matter are Lord Milo, the bishop of Thérouanne, a canon of the Premonstratensian order; Philip and Alulf, archdeacons, and the whole chapter of the church of Thérouanne; Lord Leo, the abbot of Saint-Bertin; Lord Geoffrey, the abbot of Andres; Lord Henry, the abbot of Licques; Baldwin Mondolphus, dean; Arnulf, cantor; Master Richard, Eustace and Robert, canons, and the whole chapter of that same church, namely of Ardres; Hugh and Bernard, priests of Wissant, of Brêmes; Thierry, the count of Flanders and Philip and Matthew his sons; Arnulf, indeed, count of Guines, and his son Baldwin; Arnulf the viscount of Merck, my brother-in-law;[490] Drogo Botech; Walo of Ardres; Arnulf Gohel, who is also the castellan of Ardres; Eilbod of Northout and his brother Pagan; Eustace and Baldwin of Balinghem; Baldwin Walameth and many other Christian people. This transaction was carried out in the church of Saint-Omer of Ardres and was solemnly recited and approved in the full synod of Thérouanne in 1144 a. d.[491]

Do not be surprised, fathers and lords, and particularly you chaplains and clerics, if in the recollection of this privilege I shape my words less aptly.

For when words are translated word for word from one language to another, even by a learned or eloquent man, they are presented less properly and less elegantly. Most of all this happens when they are laid out in the vernacular, no matter how well they have been understood or grasped by the clergy.[492]

Then this was set out in this agreement concerning the change from canons to monks: whenever any of the canons of this church died or while he was still alive gave his prebend spontaneously to the monks, as did Simon of Houdinghem, a canon of the church of Ardres, monks would be substituted in place of the canons and as many monks should obtain the prebend and earn it as the abbot of Capella determined.

138. How Abbot Thierry asked those persons whose confirmation was necessary to confirm his possession of the church of Ardres.

Then when the abbot and the monks had delightedly and exultantly accepted this benefit dear to God and themselves with a joyful spirit, upon my father Baldwin's advice, no less that of religious men and of the canons of Ardres, Thierry asked that Bishop Milo I of the church of Thérouanne, the chapter of that place, the archbishop of Reims,[493] and the highest pontiff of the Apostolic See privilege and confirm the church of Ardres, along with its associated rights, to be possessed free and clear in free alms forever. (This church had been conceded to Thierry and given to his church and confirmed by my father, to which Count Arnold of Guines and his son Baldwin and Count Thierry of Flanders and Philip and Matthew [494] had listened and given their assent.) Then as this exchange of love and grace between my father and the abbot and the monks grew and became stronger from day to day, after he had completely recovered from the wound and lesion in his head and from his illness, they became a single matched set out of friendship. They were like a single heart and one soul, to the point that whatever my father asked for when he was in church at Capella, he sensed the monks' easy and propitiatory execution and he perceived the sentiment of good will in the accomplishment and efficiency of the work. And consequently, by a similarly loving exchange, whatever all the things might be, that the abbot, out of pious devotion, either wanted or requested from my father, my father also did not hesitate to fulfill his desire.

139. How Baldwin, the lord of Ardres, sold the mill at Brêmes to the
abbot of Capella, with the adjacent lands, mill, and even the fishery.

But afterward, my father married Beatrice, the daughter of the noble
castellan Henry of Bourbourg and Rose, the daughter of Count Manasses of
Guines, the most rightful heir of the county of Guines and then — it is not
proper to hide the truth — the countess of the land of Guines,[495] and she died
a few days later and was buried in the church of blessed Mary of Capella with
as much pomp as possible. Then he was entangled in much business and was
forced to pay very many debts to very many people. For he was not only liable
to pay his creditors, whether it was the debts he had contracted in fighting
before he was promoted to the honor of the dominion of Ardres, or those he
added to his other debts to satisfy his brother's wife, the noble Petronilla, in
compensation for her dower, or even those he added to the debts of his responsibility in paying relief[496] hither and yon to the princes of the territories,
but he was even forced to do so.[497] And since he also already, as it were, was
tormenting his mind and body, searching with wise solicitude and alert care
for the things he was supposed to bring with him as a crusader on the holy pilgrimage road at some time, he sold for a goodly sum of money both the mill
of Brêmes with certain adjacent lands of his and the marsh and the fishery
to the aforementioned abbot and monks of Capella, as his beloved friends,
and as most religious and holy men. (The fishery is along the branch of the
water flowing from the east mill of Ardres up to Houdledam near Merck.)
And he bestowed these properties and confirmed that they were to be held
in free alms forever. And consequently, since the abbot did not have enough
money to satisfy my father for this sale so useful and necessary to his church,
he denuded and despoiled the bier of St. Mary and certain crosses of both
their gold and silver.

Hence, therefore, after this business was concluded, some people who
were adversarial and envious toward St. Mary of Capella told lies in their
midst and claimed that my father, led and seduced and deceived by depraved
and criminous simoniac zeal, sold the church of Ardres with its associated
rights and dignities to the abbot and monks of the said place, when, nevertheless, he granted and confirmed the church of Ardres to them freely and
entirely in free possession of alms, in that contemplation of divine piety and
reward, which I just now related, almost a year and a half before the purchase
and sale of this mill, this land, this marsh, and this fishery had taken place.
He did not oppress this church, but honored it with more lofty and worthy
people and converted it and led it forward to the higher status and grade of

a higher order. He did not expel or remove the canons from the church of
Ardres, in imitation of some sort of simoniac conspiracy, but introduced into
it holy and religious men and monks of the eremitic and apostolic life in all
sanctity and religion.

140. How the monks remained near the mill at Brêmes.

Then the abbot, as soon as he had obtained the mill at Brêmes and the
adjacent land with the marsh and the fishery, sent the venerable man Caradoc
to Brêmes. (Later on, Caradoc was the abbot of the church of Capella.) [498] And
the abbot built houses near the mill and a chapel and enclosed these with an
earthwork and walls and thus he built a cell of monks there, and Lord Caradoc was appointed the first prior there. Then Caradoc of venerable life, and a
certain other man named Basil, righteously and piously lived a solitary and
almost eremitic life there in all sanctity and religion and strove to please God
and men in every way. Wherefore, so that they might thus please my father in
this as in certain other actions, they took his brother, Lord Arnold the Young
or the Younger, who was buried in a cairn outside the courtyard of Ardres,
to their cell at Brêmes and they placed him thus in a cairn outside the walls
of their chapel. They were able to do this with propriety because there was as
yet no hallowed courtyard nor cemetery there.[499]

141. How Baldwin, the lord of Ardres, set out for Jerusalem.

But after the passage of this time, since my father Baldwin had prepared
all the necessities for the voyage of the holy pilgrimage and was obligated to
take the holy road to seek Jerusalem, the venerable abbot Thierry generously
offered my father an excellent packhorse in helpful support of the holy journey and he presented it as a free, or rather a completely gratuitous gift. He
did this in accordance with the wise man's ethos, not unmindful of the gift he
had received, so that he would not be found ungrateful for the magnificent
gift accepted from Baldwin. Thierry was not forewarned or forearmed, as certain people envious of the monks gossip, by the recollection of any simoniac
malignancy, but he did this at the prompting of divine love alone.

So when all the things necessary for the voyage had been prepared for
him, my father Baldwin took to the road to seek Jerusalem, with the knights
from his land who had joined with him, that is, Baldwin Wallameth, Marsilio

of Bredenarde, and some others.[500] They went with his lord, Count Thierry of Flanders, and many of the barons of Flanders, under the patronage and leadership of the most noble and holy king Louis of France, along with many French barons, also knights, and innumerable thousands of people. And he hurried with as much passion of mind and body as he could, so that he might deserve to see and venerate the Lord's tomb, which he would, nevertheless, never see. This departure occurred in 1146 a. d. in the month of May.[501] First, however, he entrusted and gave his land to Arnold Gohel, the lord of Surques, to be kept safe, because Arnold was called and was the castellan of Ardres and because Baldwin knew him to be a prudent man and faithful to him. Baldwin's brother-in-law, Viscount Arnold of Merck, nevertheless, grumbled and complained about this arrangement, rather than giving good-willed consent.[502]

142. How Baldwin died on the road and, since he was thrown in the sea, he never again was seen by his followers.

Then they went forth across the land and entered Romania; they came at length to Constantinople, where they came to the shore of the sea of Marmora, oppressed by many inconveniences, since they felt that the emperor of Constantinople was faithless and treacherous toward them. Hence, the whole army of the French was spread and stretched out in Satalieh and sustained many evils and misfortunes there. For many died of hunger, many of the inclemency of the air, many from the plots and arrows of their adversaries, many because of bodily weakness, and many were seized by some sort of illness, and my father also. He did not die of hunger among them, as some people lie, but he was weakened by an illness of the body and lacking all bodily strength, he succumbed to death. And just as he had asked earlier, he was thrown into the sea and never again appeared before his men.

143. Of the pseudopilgrim who pretended he was Baldwin of Ardres.

Nevertheless, there were some people who asserted that they had seen him at Planques near Douai in the thirtieth year after my father had taken up the voyage of the holy pilgrimage. In 1176 a. d., there was a certain pseudopilgrim, who wore the habit of religious life. He came to Douai under the guise of religious holiness and sheeplike simplicity, so that perhaps at first he might delude and deceive incautious and simple men and afterward others more easily. He went around the neighborhoods and streets there in clothes of white hide, the clothing of penance, showing the sackcloth and the hair shirt to pious and simple men, as though not of his own will, and he simulated the dirtiness of penance under a full, snowy beard and a venerable hoariness of head. He also added, but as though he wished to hide who he was, that he had once been Baldwin, the heir and lord of the citadel of Ardres, but he asserted with a false and lying tongue that he had preferred to be in exile wearing base clothes and to persist in pious works so that he might earn Christ than to return to his Ardres and take up again his hereditary house and holding.

Then whoever or whatever this Baldwin was, he spoke with the burgers of the aforementioned place and also with the princes of the adjacent province at the appropriate time and place and, following their advice, he decided to make the road that led from Douai to Planques more passable and easier for travelers and to make it into a causeway by piling up earth and stones, because it was up to this point difficult to travel along and prone to flood. And he built a little house or domicile along the road and procured necessities for those workers working on the road. But he rode astride a donkey and asked the princes of the territories, the abbots, and the burgers and people of the adjoining lands for many things to further the road and he got many things. And so that he might be respected and acquire the favor of the people for himself, in the sight of the people he scattered, as it were, and gave away many things to the poor — Oh, cunning man and hypocrite!! But he kept many things for himself and his accomplices. At length, when he was well known, or rather, as it were, he had been made well known, he named himself as Baldwin of Ardres before the abbot and canons of Hénin.

So the prior of the house, a man named Geoffrey, as he heard him calling himself Baldwin, flew quickly to Ardres, because that prior himself came from the regions of the land of Ardres. He told Baldwin, the count of Guines and the lord of Ardres, and his wife Christine, that his wife's maternal uncle, Baldwin, the lord of Ardres, was still alive and was living like a pilgrim at Planques near Douai. He also added many other things that he had learned from him and heard and seen. But Count Baldwin listened to this as though it were an hallucination and repeatedly affirmed and said, as he truthfully could, that Baldwin, formerly the lord of Ardres, had died on pilgrimage to Jerusalem and had been thrown in the sea. He did not mince words, but said that this Baldwin, who had recently emerged among those people, was a tramp and a seducer of the people and a pseudomonk. Consequently, he took care neither to go nor send to him.

When I heard that my father was alive, however, I did not believe it with any certainty, but nevertheless, I took with me some of my older friends who had once known my father well and went to him, as if the count and countess didn't know. And when I had spoken extensively with him, sometimes when I was alone with him and sometimes when others were also present, I could perceive nothing in him, nor could the companions who came with me, whereby we could be more certain of his identity. Nevertheless, I was thought badly of and rebuked by many people, because he and I each greeted each other and because he gave me many presents, so that I would declare I was his son. But in the end, after we left him, we had just come to the count in the county, when we heard and knew for certain that he had left Planques and carried off a great treasure and that he truly was a tramp.[503]

144. Next, how the viscount of Merck, who was named Arnold of Colvida, became the lord of Ardres.

Then, when my father Baldwin had most truly died at Satalieh and been thrown into the sea, fame flew and announced his death to Arnold of Colvida, his brother-in-law, the viscount of Merck. Then Arnold, the tireless viscount of Merck, won himself the good will of Count Arnold of Guines, and when he had done him homage, he hastened to Sybil,[504] the countess of Flanders, for Count Thierry of Flanders, who had gone abroad to Jerusalem, had not yet returned.[505] Then Arnold of Merck asked the aforementioned countess of Flanders for the land in his jurisdiction or in the castellany of Bruges and other things in Ardres that came and fell to him from his wife Adeline's side, from his brother-in-law Baldwin, who was now dead. And when he wished to pay the relief,[506] as is to this day the usage of custom and tradition, Baldwin, the lord of Vinnezeele and Harzeele, stood up saying that he was a nearer heir to the lordship and honor of Ardres than Arnold of Merck.[507]

But when at length the truth of the case was known, Adeline, the sister of Baldwin, the former lord of Ardres, was judged the nearer heir than Baldwin of Vinnezeele, the son of her sister Agnes, as was proper and just, for the mother of Baldwin of Vinnezeele, Agnes, who was indeed the sister of Baldwin, the former lord of Ardres, had been dead for a while, and she was also the sister of Adeline, the wife of Arnold of Merck, who was still alive and surviving.[508] Nevertheless, following the advice of his friends, Baldwin of Vinnezeele was given 100 marks and peace was confirmed between Baldwin and Arnold; when he had done homage to the countess of Flanders as custom demands and requires, Arnold of Merck became the heir and lord of the honor of Ardres.

So the peers of the citadel of Ardres and the barons of all of Guines congratulated him, and the other knights and the people of the whole land also congratulated him. He did service to the higher-status princes in the lordships of the earth outside the country with reverence, in magnificence and glory, just as he knew through discreet consideration suited their authority and just as he was liable to do. He showed himself to the peers to be a companion, and to the knights he was a mild and affable fellow-knight, but he respected knights with marvelous affection.[509] Consequently, when he was living in his land, he supported with full liberality and generous sufficiency ten knights, never fewer, as his intimates and constant companions, and also a chaplain and clerics and a most decent entourage. So he showed himself, not only in his own land but also outside his land, to be a man of such quality through his generosity with his property and the continence of his worthy rulership that he seemed more like a count than the lord of any lesser domain and he was often called that.

145. How Arnold moved the monks from Brêmes and a little while after they had been expelled from Ardres, he called them back to Ardres.

At first, then, he moved the monks who were staying at Brêmes and all their buildings to Ardres and had them stay next to the church which is positioned in the cemetery of that place, where they have a house and congress to this day. Then following the request of his wife Adeline, he had Alice, his wife Adeline's sister, stay at Welles near Tornehem and he granted her the rents of that village to sustain and provide for her as long as she lived. She was still a girl, but unmarried, and, as they say, a virgin to the end of her days.

Then Caradoc, the first prior of Ardres, who was a monk of worthy name and life, as soon as he began to stay at Ardres, upon the advice of his venerable abbot Thierry, completely satisfied the reverend father and lord bishop Milo I of the church of Thérouanne concerning the fault for which the former lord of Ardres, Arnold the Young or the Younger was held accountable to him. Because of this fault Arnold had been buried thus far without honor in a cairn above ground. Caradoc translated the same Arnold from Brêmes to Ardres and brought him into the cloister in the cemetery and honorably buried him at the foot of the wall in the southern part of the shrine. But later on, when the venerable father Thierry was called back to rule over the church of Bergues, from whence he had been brought, and was appointed and made abbot in that same monastery, that is Bergues, Caradoc of venerable memory was appointed abbot in the church of St. Mary of Capella and Lord Basil of Ardres became the second prior of Ardres.[510]

In Basil's time, Arnold of Colvida, the lord of Ardres, violently seized and extorted the rents of the church of Ardres, because the church tower that is situated in the market of Ardres fell down, and he drove out and put all the monks to flight (except for Henry Butler of Bredenarde, who alone during this persecution hid as best he could and stayed) and had the tower repaired. But the monks held that this Lord Arnold was an excommunicate, because he had attacked them without cause and driven them basely from the church that had been given and granted to them, so Arnold could not bear it any longer. At length, he reinstated the monks, as he was liable to have done and should have done (they were recalled after being exiled for almost three years), and he restored to their control the things he had taken away. After these things happened, when Basil left Ardres, William of Leda became the third prior of Ardres. The fourth after him was Boldekin of Rodelinghem, a liberal monk, indeed, and one beloved by men and princes of the earth and pleasing and praiseworthy to the prelates of the church in everything.

146. How Baldwin of Hondschote asked for the parsonage of Hondschote at that time.

Then, in that time in which Boldekin the Monk had procured the office of prior of Ardres,[511] William Morannus of Hondschote died, and Baldwin, the son of this same William Morannus, came to Prior Boldekin. And he asked for the parsonage of the church of Hondschote that his father William Morannus had earlier held for one or two years from the canons and monks of Ardres for the assessment of an annual payment. And he called it to his memory and recalled that

It costs one dear to put off what's arranged[512]

and gave them on the spot one hundred shillings for the restoration of the tower. He received the parsonage from Prior Boldekin under the same terms as his father himself had earlier held it and he holds the parsonage up to this day, or rather he withholds it, as if it were his by inheritance. The abbot and monks of Capella were not been consulted, although the monks of the church of Ardres and the canons who were still alive were present and protested.[513] And no matter what the monks who possess the church of Ardres might say as they attacked him and complained about the injury or the violence brought against them by him,

> With wagging head and hand he made a threat.
> He discoursed with himself. "I hold it yet!
> And long will I! Except in death, I'll not
> Let go of anything my father got!"[514]

147. How when Arnold of Guines had heard the history of Ardres, and the rains had ceased, he went a short way outside of Guines on a walk and heard that Mark du Bois had been killed.

> And to this point old Walter does relate
> The deeds of Ardres's men, so noble and great,
> They praise the old man, and the root is praised,
> The seed from whom the family of Ardres is raised,
> And most this lord on whose grace they rely.
> The rains now cease, now calm and clear the sky.
> The lord now calls Raulin and Simonet;
> They go outside, while all the others stay.
> He walks with them and ponders deeds of youth,
> And says, "Old men admire old men, in truth,
> And our grandsires. But we, the youths today
> Who bear the arms of youth, now let us pay
> Respect to young men and those of our years
> And our companions. For all that one hears
> Is old men praised, for Hugh is silent and
> So Eustace too, our brothers, and our band
> Of comrades. But the men today are due
> More praise, and let that person lack praise too,
> Who judges ill the people of our days!"
> The brothers hail these comments and they praise
> The voice so speaking, and their voice they raise,
> And thus applause for all about they bruit,
> Young men and old each other thus salute.

Now then, since I have interpolated and continued the history of Ardres in Melibœian fashion [515] with as much studious assiduousness as I appropriately could, let me return, as I proposed from the first inception of this work, to those remaining deeds of the people of Guines, in whom both the beginning and the end of my work lies.

Then Arnold of Guines, who had been kept for a long time in his house with his companions by torrential rains, jumped up as the fluctuations of the Hyades were just ceasing and the air was becoming calm, although he had gladly heard the history of Ardres, in which he saw himself, from the mouth of his maternal kinsman, Walter of Le Clud. Going out as though he were leaving a prison cell with his chains unlocked and made rather joyful by the serenity of the air, he went away from the house through the village with his companions and fellow-knights. And lo! A messenger came flying to his side who announced that Mark of Nemours or du Bois, a servant of his father, was slain and dead. He had unexpectedly received the barbed arrow of William Pragot of Nielles in his heart, while he was residing at the count's table at La Montoire and eating from the bowl of the count's son Manasses.[516]

148. The litigation concerning the church of Ardres between Arnold and the monks.

Then when a little time had passed, Arnold of Guines, following the advice of his father, Count Baldwin of Guines, and certain other people, namely clerics who attended the Roman curia, provoked Abbot Hugh and the monks of St. Mary of Capella to sue and litigate at last before judges sent by the highest Pontiff Clement: Hugh of Cambrai and John of Arras, deans, and Master Gerard of Cambrai, a canon. This matter concerned the prebends of the church of Ardres and the removal of the monks from Ardres and the restoration of canons in that place. They got and entreated such letters as they could from Alexander, Lucius, and Clement,[517] the rectors of the highest pontificate and the Apostolic See, through Master Philip of Nemours, Master Adam, a former canon of the church of Thérouanne, and through other messengers, clerics, and masters known in the Roman court.[518] But when some sort of peace was restored and fashioned by some means before the aforementioned judges, the monks remained as before in their place at Ardres, and do to this day. The litigation of this quarrel between Baldwin, the count of Guines, and Arnold, his son, on one side, and Abbot Hugh and the monks of St. Mary of Capella on the other, which concerned the return of the church of Ardres to its earlier state, was nevertheless heard in 1190 a. d. on the 31st of October, in the house of the bishop at Cambrai, before the aforementioned judges and many archdeacons, deans, canons, clerics, abbots and priors and provosts and also monks and as many other ecclesiastical persons, both of the church of Cambrai and of Arras and of other episcopal churches.

149. How Arnold married Beatrice, the châtelaine of Bourbourg.

Then with the passage of time, after the span of almost four years had passed, the boy castellan of Bourbourg, Henry, the son of the noble Walter, died without an heir of the body around the feast of St. Michael, having not yet attained young adulthood, and he was honorably buried in the church of St. Mary of Bourbourg, as was proper. Then Arnold of Guines cast aside Eustochia or Eustacia, the daughter of Hugh, the count of Saint-Pol, called Candavène, to whom he had first been engaged,[519] and following the advice of his father, Count Baldwin of Guines, who was still alive and well, joined to himself as a legal wife and married in legitimate wedlock a young woman of vigorous nobility. She was a virgin of a most noble lineage and descent, most learned and adept in liberal disciplines, as glorious in her character and life as her still tender little age demanded, enviable by Cassandra or even Helen for the outstanding beauty of her remarkable body, similar in all wisdom to Minerva, equal to Juno in the plenitude of her possessions. She was the sole and most rightful heir of the castellany of Bourbourg, the sister of that most noble boy, Castellan Henry of Bourbourg (now dead and buried), indeed, the châtelaine of Bourbourg. The noble advocate William of Béthune and his brothers, Lord Cano, Count Baldwin of Aumale, and John, who afterward became the venerable bishop of Cambrai, gave their assistance,[520] and also Henry of Bailleul,[521] at whose pleasure the castellany of Bourbourg was at that time to be disposed. The venerable rectors of holy mother church, Archbishop William of Reims and Bishop Lambert of Thérouanne, gave their consent.[522] Arnold gave her Ardres and Colvida, with all the associated rights and dependent properties in Ardres and Colvida, as her dower.[523]

Although these aforementioned noble and discreet men had come together to contract this marriage of such great nobility, Arnold of Guines had been for some time bound and tied by ecclesiastical censure and a sentence of excommunication upon the authority of Archbishop William of Reims, because of a certain mill near Peupelingue belonging to a certain widow Agnes, namely of Skibborna, that had been destroyed and torn down. Nevertheless, his father, Count Baldwin of Guines, sent a message through messengers who were certainly inadequate and without authentic validation, or rather I, who at that time carried out the office of priest in the church of Ardres, although unworthy, did not know them. He said that just as the tenor and reasoning of ecclesiastical order prescribes, Arnold had satisfied the widow and the holy church and had been completely absolved through the agency of Stephen Roman, a canon of Saint-Omer and an official of Archbishop William of Reims, as ecclesiastical order prescribes. Wherefore as a sign of the absolution of his son Arnold, the lord of Ardres, who was also living at Ardres, I, the parish priest, should by no means delay ringing the bells of the church.

But I had not yet learned or did not know for certain through the authority of any authorized men that he had been absolved, as I have just said, and because of this, in the grip of a presumptuous boldness, I put off ringing the bells and obeying his wish longer than pleased him, but not, however, for the span of two hours, that is, until I had presented myself at his council to make a full account to him. So in front of the gate of the venerable and rich man Matthew of Zudkerque, in front of his sons, Arnold, and also many other knights and people, he cried out and thundered forth against me, as a rebel and one who disdained and scorned to obey and heed his wish. He raged to the point that I was stupefied and astounded by the thunder of his words as they called out reproaches and terrors, rebukes and taunts, and by the lightning of his eyes, as they flamed and sparkled like coals against my innocent person and I fell and collapsed from my horse at his feet in terror, while his son Arnold and his brothers and all those who heard and saw groaned and took pity on me. But the knights seized the count and put me—a despised man, a *man of sorrow* [Is. 53: 3] and nearly dead, a man scarcely hanging on to the spirit—back on my horse, as best they could. And they spoke amongst themselves on the road and in turns alone with the count until at Audruick the count showed me a mollified countenance. But never afterward, except when he was carrying out his business, did he ever show me as friendly or joyful a face as he had before, but indeed only a face about as mollified as this. This is a great reason, then, but not the primary one, why I decided to strive at this work, namely to recover his grace and love.

And so after he had become affianced to his noble wife, Beatrice, the châtelaine of Bourbourg, Arnold of Guines made solemn nuptials at Guines such as we never saw or heard to have been made before or after in all Guines. On the first evening, when the bride and groom were put in one bed, the count, full of the zeal of the divine spirit, called me and my sons Baldwin, William, and Robert, the priest of Audruick. He indicated to us and desired us to asperge the bride and groom with holy water, and also to go around and cense their bed with thuribles and aromatic gums and unguents prepared for this purpose and to bless them and commend them to God.[524] We carried this out according to the most devout desire of the count in all things and in every detail, with as much care and careful devotion as we might. When we stepped back, the count, continuing in the devotion of divine love and grace of spiritual virtue, raised his eyes and hands to heaven and spoke, adding this: "Holy Lord, Omnipotent Father, eternal God, you who blessed Abraham and his seed and conferred the grace of benediction upon them, pour out your mercy upon us and deign to bless these your servants, joined by the law of holy intercourse and by the rite of marriage, so that they may live in your divine love and persevere in concord and their seed may be multiplied in the length of days and for unending eternity." And when we responded, "Amen," he added, "To you, however, my most dear and firstborn son Arnold, beloved to me above all my sons, if there is any grace in a father's blessing upon his son, if any bounty and grace of benediction has been left to me by the ancient fathers, I give to you the same grace of benediction that God the Father once granted our father Abraham, Abraham gave his son Isaac, Isaac then conferred upon his son Jacob and his seed, to the extent this devotion pertains to our faith." And when Arnold had joined his hands and bent his head toward his father and invoked God the Father in a pious murmur, the count added, speaking expressly and confirming his benediction, "I bless you, except for what belongs by right to your brothers, and I leave you my benediction, if I have any power of benediction, here and forever." And everyone answered, "Amen," and left the chamber, each one going to his own home.

150. How the châtelaine bore him daughters and Baldwin, and of the siege of Saint-Omer.

Then the truly blessed Beatrice, the noble châtelaine of Bourbourg and the lady of Ardres, conceived by her noble husband, Arnold of Guines, in the unrolling passage of time, and bore Beatrice, Christine, and Matilda.[525]

But later on, Baldwin, the count of Flanders and Hainaut, the nephew of the noble Philip, former count of Flanders, besieged the town of Saint-Omer in 1198 a. d.,[526] and Count Baldwin of Guines took up the side of the count of Flanders against the power of King Philip of France and against the people of Saint-Omer, who were completely enclosed in their walls. Then Arnold of Guines stayed with the people of Bourbourg and his people of

Ardres in his pavilion or glorious tent about a catapult's throw outside the walls of Saint-Omer, not far from the gate leading to Boulogne (consequently called the Boulogne gate). He built the tower of a war machine, equal to the tower of Babylon in height, much taller than the siege towers at the assault on Saint-Omer, with turrets and cross-beams and shelters of wicker, and with all the equipment necessary for such assaults. By means of this tower and from it, Arnold wonderfully assailed, attacked, and assaulted the walls of Saint-Omer with as many troops as he could (although truly he knew that his most beloved kinsman, Castellan William of Saint-Omer,[527] was the provost appointed in these matters under King Philip of France to defend and protect the people of Saint-Omer.[528] At the same time, Count Reynold of Boulogne was devastating Fauquemberg and all of the adjacent land of this same Castellan William.[529]) As a result, Arnold so greatly won the grace of the count of Flanders that this count of Flanders gave him to redeem his pledges an infinite number of sterling pennies from casks, full of gold and silver, which had been collected by King Richard of England for the count of Flanders, so that the count would fight the king of France for him.[530] Then after this, when the people of Saint-Omer had been forced and compelled to surrender, he remained a great intimate of Count Baldwin of Flanders and a notable friend. Consequently, when this same Count Baldwin of Flanders went abroad to Jerusalem,[531] as a token of his perpetual love, he liberally gave and granted Arnold two hundred marks to redeem his pledges and pay his debts. And with reference to Aalst, which belonged to him from his noble wife Beatrice's side, as all the barons of Flanders knew,[532] Baldwin also gave him the land of Moorsel and Jabbeke to be possessed in perpetuity, in expectation of more grace and the recovery of more land.

Then around this time, Beatrice, the noble heroine and powerful matron, the châtelaine of Bourbourg and the lady of Ardres, who was most blessed among the blessed,[533] conceived and bore a sweet boy, Baldwin, at Ardres, whom I baptized in the sacred font, so that he might receive the grace of the new law and holy baptism and the sacrament of new regeneration, and whom I catechized. She also bore Adelaide and another Beatrice at Ardres, whom I similarly confirmed and baptized to drive out the old man through the purification of the new man; Christ mediated and confirmed the grace and sacrament of baptism.

151. How certain knights fought first against the count of Boulogne, then against the count of Guines.

Far and wide the princes of the earth were growing proud and wars were increasing to the point that certain knights on this side and that did not fear to attack and harass the princes and counts of the territories. Then Eustace of Hames, a man very confident in his skill and the strength of his body, and very much in the nobility of his family, attacked Count Reynold of Boulogne in many ways. He inflicted many injuries on Reynold and carried off booty and captured men and he forced great shame upon him and the sign of perpetual dishonor. But in the end Eustace was reconciled with Reynold by virtue of his family and knighthood—who may speak *of his begetting* [Is. 53:8] or rather his military ability?—and he began to harass Count Baldwin of Guines, although not in the same frame of mind or manner. But at length peace was made and confirmed between them, and the count offered him a bond of perpetual peace and an aid to enduring love; he married him to Matilda, the daughter of the count's sister Giselle and Walter of Pollaer.

Now then, who does not know that Guy des Champs often attacked Count Baldwin of Guines and carried off his men as captives and booty from Escales and Hervelinghem, and also that Eustace of Rinquesen came into Guines secretly and at night, like a thief in the territory, and preyed—for shame!—upon the land as much as he could? In return, Hugh of Le Vale-en-Surques attacked Count Reynold of Boulogne at Mentque-Nortbécourt and Simon of La Chaussée attacked him near La Chaussée at Le Nieulet and other places in Boulogne, and they inflicted injuries on him; nevertheless, they did less than they could have.[534]

At this time, Manasses, the son of Count Baldwin II of Guines, took some marsh and pasture, which had been granted and given and conferred long ago as common land to all of those living in the parish of Andres by the former Count Baldwin I of Guines (who was the founder of the monastery of Andres) and had it dug up and cut into turfs, and in the same way a certain marsh that was the property of the monks of that place, as they say. When Ralph of Fiennes[535] reproached him and protested the injury to God and to himself and to his people and to all those living and residing in the parish, Manasses didn't take it at all well. And consequently moved to anger, he withdrew for the time being from Andres and talked it over for a while with the men of Fiennes and other of his relatives. But the abbot and the monks of Andres, or rather also the priests of the whole deanery of Guines, bound all those who violently dug up or cut turfs in the aforementioned marsh or pasture—the reapers, the workers, and their defenders — with the chain of anathema on the authority of Bishop Lambert of Thérouanne.

152. How Arnold of Guines enclosed Ardres with a great earthwork.

Then, when Count Baldwin and his men were rising up, as I have said, on one side and on the other, Count Reynold and his men, and each set snares against the other as much as he could, Arnold of Guines saw his father, Count Baldwin of Guines, fortifying and strengthening all his castles and fortresses, although they were strong and well-armed. So following his father's advice and also that of the peers and burgers of the citadel of Ardres, he surrounded and enclosed his Ardres with an earthwork as strong as the earthwork at Saint-Omer, such as hands had never undertaken nor eyes seen before in Guines. He did so, because Ardres, located at the navel and in the middle of the land of Guines, had now begun to become richer than the other castles and citadels of the land of Guines and was coveted by angry adversaries, and for this reason he intended to keep it with the greatest of care. Then there was no small number of workers to make and dig the aforesaid earthwork, although they were more afflicted by the bitterness of the time and the great hunger of famine than the work and the heat of the day. Nevertheless, the workmen told each other stories and often lightened the work with joking words and so tempered their hunger.[536]

And so many people came for many reasons to the spectacle of such a great earthwork. Poor people, indeed, who were not workers did not feel the penury of their possessions in their enjoyment of the work they beheld. But rich knights and burgers and often priests and monks came together not only once a day, but many times daily, in the physical enjoyment of such a marvelous spectacle. Who, indeed, unless he were lazy or nearly dead of old age and care, would not have delighted to see the ever so learned Simon the builder, the master of the geometrical work, proceed hither and yon with his stick in a magisterial way, as he measured, not so much with his stick as with the ruler of his eyes, the progress of the work he had conceived in his mind? And as he tore up houses and granges and cut down flowering orchards and fruit-bearing trees and gazed at flat paths prepared with the greatest labor and care for the complete ease of all those who passed by not so much on feast days as working days? And as he dug up gardens full of vegetables and flax, destroying and treading underfoot what had been sown, so that he could restore the roads, although some people raged and groaned and cursed him in silence?

Over here, countrymen were carrying stones in marl carts and farm carts to strew on the road, and dressed in work-gloves and work-aprons, they egged each other on in the work. And over there, trenchers labored with trenching tools, diggers with spades, pickaxe-men with pickaxes, hammerers with hammers, clearers or scrapers with clearing tools. There were also preparers and wall-builders and removers and pavers, all with the appropriate and necessary tools and instruments,[537] and loaders and woodcutters with hooks, turfers with rectangular turfs on their shoulders, cut in whatever fields they could find them at the pleasure of the masters. There were also servants and bailiffs with rods and harsh switches, and the workers prodded each other and urged each other to work under the supervision of the measurers and masters of the work, who were always presiding and taking pains. For a work can never be finished unless the workers are driven and oppressed in labor and hardship, in horror and sorrow.

153. How the queen of Portugal, Matilda of Flanders, wished to rule the people of Furnes, but was conquered by the people of Furnes and the Blauwvoets.

Then, in the meantime, the wife of the former count Philip of Flanders, and the countess, who was called Theresia by her Portuguese people but Queen Matilda among us,[538] was living in her dower land at the castle or town in Flemish jurisdiction called Lille, and she held the people of Bourbourg, who were faithful to her in every way, to be detestable and obnoxious, because she demanded many things from them which neither they nor their ancestors were ever wont to give. And she also viewed the people of Furnes this way, most of all because she could never subjugate or master the Blauwvoets.[539] So she gathered her armies and all the knights of her dower lands, having mustered not only people in her land but also people from outside, and crossed with her whole army through Poperingues *with a strong hand and arm outstretched* [Dt. 5:15; Ezek 20:33, 34] to conquer the people of Bourbourg and the people of Furnes. Then around the feast of St. John,[540] the proud woman occupied a village called Alveringhem, which belonged to the provost of Saint-Omer; she dropped the reins of license far too much and destroyed it by foraging, preying on it, exceeding moderation. But Arnold of Guines, the castellan of Bourbourg, remained in the territory of Bourbourg with his people from Bourbourg and also Ardres and Guines and awaited his lady the queen at the borders of the land of Bourbourg, not so that he could rise up against her, but so that if the queen began to attempt something by violent depredation or devastation in the land of Bourbourg, he would show himself completely prepared to defend himself and the land of Bourbourg with his men and forces.

But when the queen moved heedlessly against the people of Furnes in a barbaric attack with all her might, a certain duke and prince of the Blauw-voets, named Hebben or Herbert, and Walter of Hondschote rose up against the queen and her men, along with certain others and their supporters and followers from the Blauwvoets and other people similarly all mixed together. They put the infinite multitude of the queen's army to flight and destroyed them with war, conquered, and exterminated them. They wounded some, cut off the limbs of others, slit some people's throats in their usual way, put yet others to some other sort of death, took some captive, and imprisoned others, leaving some half-alive in the fields and ditches. They put others to flight before them in the face of their swords, and seized from others the booty that they had stolen from the innocent common folk. The queen fled with a few men to her castle at Furnes and from there by night to Dunkirk and barely escaped.

Then Arnold of Guines, the castellan of Bourbourg, did not so much rejoice and exult, as carefully ponder what he should do concerning this event. Since he had always been faithful to his lady the queen and submissive to her and was always determined to persevere in loyalty, following his father's advice, he provided this same queen and certain men she had with her, at the queen's request and prayers, a safe escort by knights to her own lands.

154. How Count Baldwin of Guines drove the people of Merck from the causeway and ditch between Axles and Le Nieulet.

Count Reynold of Boulogne had always envied the land and people of Guines, because he asserted that Count Baldwin of Guines had presumed to do many things against him and to take many things from him around the borders of both lands, near their boundary marks, in the fortification of Sangatte, and in the great and spacious marsh called the royal marsh, which indeed they say is supposed to divide the two lands, namely Guines and Boulogne, by its borders. So approximately around this time, upon the order of this Count Reynold of Boulogne, who was staying in Normandy at Radepont while in the expedition of King Philip of France against King John of England, Eustace the Monk from Course, who was then the seneschal of Boulogne,[541] called upon the people of Merck, both the knights and the foot-soldiers, and told and ordered them by authority of his lord, Count Reynold of Boulogne, upon threat and danger to their honor and life and all they had, to come together on the appointed day at Axles, near the causeway that led to Le Nieulet. From there they were to go to Calais with their arms and arma-ments, spades and other necessary instruments, and sufficient supplies for thirty days, and there they should dig on either side of the causeway and en-close Merck with a great earthwork and strengthen it against the people of Guines. According to what had been told and indicated to them by the afore-mentioned seneschal, they came together on the appointed day in the afore-mentioned place with their arms (truly, they always feared lest the count of Guines should perhaps come in strength with a band of strong men and re-move them from the work) and other necessary instruments. They first began to cut down trees (just so does the truth offer the testimony of those living nearby) that were planted in Guines. Then they began to dig in the land that extended into this county, that is, the land belonging to the count of Guines, and to insult the people of Guines, who were neither present nor indeed lis-tening. And they began to run and race back and forth here and there like bees or even ants, and dig and strip the ground where there was ground and the marsh where there was marsh into a ditch with their spades. And they cried out "Huh!" loudly with the proud voice of indignation, urging each other on in derision and disrespect for the people of Guines.

Hearing, however, that such a great shame and such a great outrage had been so basely and unexpectedly done to him, Count Baldwin of Guines sent to them, warning and telling them that they should desist from the evil and unjust thing they had begun and planned and that they should depart as quickly as they could. But since they did not wish to go away, but grew more and more feverish in the work they had begun, Arnold of Planques, the bai-liff of Mary, the countess of Flanders, the wife of Baldwin, forbade this same thing on the part of the countess of Flanders (Baldwin was dwelling in the Holy Land):[542] namely that they should stop work and cease to dig until Count Reynold of Boulogne came back into the territory.

But they did not obey Arnold of Planques, the countess of Flanders's bailiff, but made fun of him and insulted the people of Guines, yelling "Huh!" with the voices of angry men egging each other on, so Count Baldwin of Guines gathered the men and forces of all of Guines, stopping near the region of Sclive with his armed band, and ordered them over and over again to go away now, or else. (His son Arnold of Guines was litigating and pleading in the land of Brabant at Louvain in the presence of Duke Baldwin of Lorraine[543] concerning a certain piece of land, which Beatrice,[544] the paternal aunt of his wife, the châtelaine Beatrice of Bourbourg, intended and wished to sell to some monks without consulting him and without his consent.) But since they by no means wished to withdraw from the place, but most constantly persisted and persevered in their stupid project, William of Colvida and Daniel of Ghent,[545] who was at that time the leader and lord of the people of Balinghem, together fell upon them with crowds from Ardres and a few others and attacked their enemies, with the assent of the count, who was standing by on the mountain. But these men were basely turned to flight and confused; they were conquered without war and overcome without blood. They left work behind and hid where they could. But the people of Ardres pursued and followed the people of Merck, who were now wretched and fleeing, step by step with an ardent spirit.[546] They took some of them captive on the road, some in the ditch, others while they were dispersed here and there in the marsh, others as they hastened and headed to their homes around Le Nieulet for safety with their tokens and arms and banners, which are still hanging in the church of Ardres as a sign of victory. Or else they permitted the wretches to flee, once they had turned out their pockets and all their booty and armaments had been taken away. But Count Baldwin of Guines, who stayed up on the mountain and looked down at the outcome of the business from on high, could not restrain his people's attack. And so the whole populace of the army of Guines rose up as one man against the wretched people of Merck and if there was anything in these same and. . . .[547]

Notes

1. *Lamberti Ardensis historia comitum Ghisnensium*, ed. J. Heller, in *Monumenta Germaniae historica inde ab anno Christi quingentesimo usque ad annum millesimum et quingentesimum. Scriptorum*, 24: 550–642, hereafter cited as "Heller." (References to this series will hereafter be cited as *MGH Scriptores*.) The *MGH* edition depended on the earlier edition of D. C. Godefroy de Menilglaise, *Chronique de Guines et d'Ardre* (Paris, 1855), hereafter cited as "Godefroy," which also contained an edition of the Renaissance French translation. References to Lambert's text itself (as distinct from the notes and comments of the various editors) will be cited as "Lambert, 123," where the number is the chapter number.

2. E. A. Freeman, "The Lords of Ardres," *British Quarterly Review* 71 (1880): 2.

3. For the authenticity debate, see, for example, F. L. Ganshof, "A Propos de la chronique de Lambert d'Ardres," in *Mélanges d'histoire du moyen age offerts à M. Ferdinand Lot* (1925; reprint ed. Geneva, 1976), 205–34, who argues for its authenticity, while W. Erben, "Zur Zeitbestimmung Lamberts von Ardre," *Neues Archiv* 44 (1922): 314–40, argues that the text was a late medieval fabrication. Although I have been unable to consult Marie-Françoise Bourdat's unpublished edition and study of Lambert (see Bourdat, "La Chronique de Lambert d'Ardres: Edition critique" in *Positions des thèses soutenues par les élèves de la promotion de 1970* [Paris, 1970], 41–43 for an abstract), P. D. Stirnemann, "Quelques bibliothèques princières et la production hors scriptorium au XIIe siècle," *Bulletin archéologique* n. s. 17–18A (1981–82): 36 n. 64 reports that Bourdat has reaffirmed the text's thirteenth-century origins. Although nearly all scholars now see Lambert's text as genuine, Stirnemann also reports that R.-H. Bautier argues that while the text has an authentic core, it was partially revised much later.

4. See Georges Duby, *The Chivalrous Society*, trans. C. Postan (Berkeley and Los Angeles, 1980), particularly 143–46; *The Knight, the Lady, and the Priest*, trans. B. Bray (New York, 1983), 253–84; *Medieval Marriage: Two Models from Twelfth-Century France*, trans. E. Forster (Baltimore and London, 1978), and *Women of the Twelfth Century*, vol. 2, *Remembering the Dead*, trans. J. Birrell (Chicago, 1997). The reader should be warned, however, that Duby's reading of this text and many others, with respect both to the history of the family and to the history of feudalism, are currently being vigorously challenged. On the question of feudalism, see T. Evergates, "The Feudal Imaginary of Georges Duby," *Journal of Medieval & Early Modern Studies* 27 (1997): 641–61. Although I have not catalogued most of them here, Duby's reading of Lambert's history is also plagued with factual errors.

5. See E. A. Warlop, *The Flemish Nobility Before 1300*, trans. J. B. Ross and H. Vandermoere, 2 parts in 4 vols. (Courtrai, 1975).

6. On murder, see R. Jacob, "Le Meurtre du seigneur dans la société féodale. La mémoire, le rite, la fonction," *Annales ESC* 45 (1990): 249–63. J. R. E. Bliese, "Rhetoric and Morale: A Study of Battle Orations from the Central Middle Ages," *Journal of Medieval History* 15 (1989): 201–26 uses Lambert's text as only one of many examples. P. Beck, "Lambert d'Ardres: Le meutre du seigneur Arnoul d'Ardres," "Lambert d'Ardres: La construction du donjon de bois du château d'Ardres en Boulonnais, vers 1120," and "Lambert d'Ardres: La construction des fortifications d'Ardres en Boulonnais, vers 1200" in G. Brunel and E. Lalou, *Sources d'histoire médiévale IXe–milieu du XIVe siècle. Textes essentiels* (Paris, 1992), 220–21, 331–35 offers translations and comments on several passages from Lambert's text. M. Keen, *Chivalry* (corrected edition New Haven, 1984): 19–20 discusses the dubbing of Arnold II of Guines. L. Milis, "La Frontière linguistique dans le comté de Guînes: Un problème historique et méthodologique," *Actes du 101e congrès national des sociétés savantes* 1 (Lille, 1976): 249–62 uses river names to discuss the linguistic border between French and Flemish.

7. Lambert, 134. Lambert is mentioned in the third person here, but the ostensible narrator is Walter of Le Clud.

8. Lambert, 85.

9. Lambert, 75.

10. See p. 33, on the linguistic character of the region.

11. Lambert, 149; Ganshof, "Lambert d'Ardres," 208. This rationale, however, may be a pretext; see p. 6, on this subject.

12. Lambert, prologue.

13. Lambert, 7, 10, 11.

14. Ganshof, "Lambert d'Ardres," 210–11 suggests 1198, dating from the death of Arnulf I of Flanders.

15. On the Blauwvoets, see Warlop, *Flemish Nobility*, 1/1:261–64; Lambert, 153.

16. For mentions of Baldwin's "memory," see Lambert, 83, 87, 91. Ganshof, "Lambert d'Ardres," 210, on the contrary, argues that Baldwin must have been alive when the work was completed, because Lambert never refers to Baldwin's son Arnold as the count of Guines. However, he was not the count of Guines in the period Lambert discusses, so this is not a particularly strong argument. Duby, *Medieval Marriage*, 84, follows Ganshof.

17. Lambert, 150. Their children seem all to have been born before 1213.

18. Ganshof, "Lambert d'Ardres," 214ff.

19. Ibid., 218ff.

20. The text ends in mid-sentence (Lambert, 154). Chapter 155 contained "An aside to the envious," while chapter 156 was the conclusion (Lambert, table of contents).

21. Heller translates the place-name, "Clusa," as Ecluse (607 n. 2), while Godefroy (494) refers to it as "Cluse." However, Ganshof, "Lambert d'Ardres," 206 and n. 4, convincingly argues that Le Clud is a better translation. Ecluse was 10 km south of Douai (which is east of the area shown on Map 2). Le Clud was a holding near Blendecques, which was not far from Saint-Omer (both appear on Map 1). This was a region where the lords of Ardres and counts of Guines had many connections (al-

though as the overlords of Ecluse, the lords of Ardres had connections there as well, but no land [see Lambert, 108]). Le Clud was called Clus or Clusa in the Middle Ages, whereas Ecluse was generally called Sclusa.

22. Lambert, 54, 135.

23. Lambert, 19, 97–98.

24. On this view of history, see L. Shopkow, *History and Community: Norman Historical Writing in the Eleventh and Twelfth Centuries* (Washington, D.C., 1997), 122–25.

25. On the issue of literacy and the generation of documents, see M. Clanchy, *From Memory to Written Record: England, 1066–1307* (2nd ed., Cambridge, Mass., 1992).

26. Eusebius of Caesarea, in his *Ecclesiastical History*, written in the early fourth century, had included such documents, and a few other historians, such as the Venerable Bede (d. 735) followed in this tradition, but the practice was uncommon until the end of the eleventh century. Monastic histories sometimes took the form of a collection of charters strung together by an historical narrative. On this, see Shopkow, *History and Community*, 125–26.

27. See R. Morse, *Truth and Convention in the Middle Ages* (Cambridge, 1991).

28. See G. Spiegel, *Romancing the Past: The Rise of Vernacular Prose Historiography in Thirteenth-Century France* (Berkeley, 1993), 55–67, on the rise of vernacular prose.

29. Lambert, prologue.

30. Lambert, prologue.

31. See N. Partner, "The New Cornificius: Medieval History and the Artifice of Words," in *Classical Rhetoric & Medieval History*, ed. E. Breisach (Kalamazoo, 1985), 5–59.

32. Lambert, prologue: "And because I have not feared to omit the writings of certain apocryphal authors, written down and discovered among authentic and divine writings in the margins or ends of books, or noted down here and there on little sheets and particularly on charters . . ."

33. "I, who am made certain and illuminated by the clearer ray of truth" (Lambert, prologue).

34. Walter of Châtillon, *The Alexandreis of Walter of Châtillon: A Twelfth-Century Epic*, trans. D. Townsend (Philadelphia, 1996), xiii–xiv.

35. Above, n. 32.

36. Lambert, 1–2, prologue, 30.

37. Lambert, 116, 137; Heller, 618 n. 3. Lambert is our only source for these donations; the confirmations that the principals reportedly sought are not extant.

38. See Lambert's prologue, which quotes Horace and Ovid, and mentions Virgil, Dares Phrygius, and Priscian; Lambert also quotes Lucan and Statius elsewhere in his text. Even the great scholar John of Salisbury, however, got many of the texts he quotes from *florilegia*; on this point, see J. Martin, "John of Salisbury as Classical Scholar," 184–85 in *The World of John of Salisbury*, ed. M. Wilks (Oxford, 1984).

39. Lambert, 61, 55. The echoes are more general ideas—such as the speeches of Pompey and Caesar to their troops, and the general situation of battle (including that the victory went to the unjust cause) rather than slavish quotation. Lucan was

highly influential upon the histories written in the region: see Spiegel, *Romancing the Past*, passim. Statius's subject matter was less historically significant (the Theban civil war), but clearly appropriate to the battle among kin over Guines.

40. See J. O. Ward, "Gothic Architecture, Universities and the Decline of the Humanities in Twelfth Century Europe" in *Principalities, Powers, and Estates: Studies in Medieval and Early Modern Government and Society* (Adelaide, 1979), 68–69 on these new types of works and their authors and on the issue of truth. Among the writers who belong in this group are John of Salisbury, Walter Map, John of Hauville, and Geoffrey of Monmouth. On the violation of narrative protocols, see D. Townsend, " 'Michi Barbaries Incognita Linguae': Other Voices and Other Visions in Walter of Châtillon's *Alexandreis*," *Allegorica* 13 (1992): 21–37. On narrator self-consciousness, see S. Echard, "Map's Metafiction: Author, Narrator and Reader in *De nugis curialium*," *Exemplaria* 8 (1996): 287–314 (on Walter Map) and M. Stevens, "The Performing Self in Twelfth-Century Culture," *Viator* 9 (1978): 193–212.

41. John of Salisbury may have invented the *Institutio Traiani* (see Martin, "John of Salisbury as Classical Scholar," 194ff), but the most famous medieval invented history was probably Geoffrey of Monmouth's *History of the Kings of Britain*.

42. See Lambert's entire prologue, where these issues arise repeatedly; Lambert predicts he will be attacked, defends his work against detractors, urging them not to judge it hastily; the prologue to the *Alexandreis*, where the same theme appears; see also Walter Map, *De Nugis curialium*, ed. and trans. M. R. James, rev. C. N. L. Brooke and R. A. B. Mynors (Oxford, 1983), 246–63, for the story of Parius and Lausus, a disquisition on envy, and also p. 4, for the envy that characterized court life; John of Hauville, *Architrenius*, ed. and trans. W. Wetherbee (Cambridge, 1994), 69–70, 148–51 (the expectation that his work will be attacked, Plato's comments on envy); John of Salisbury, *Entheticus Maior and Minor*, ed. and trans. J van Laarhoven, 2 vols (Leiden, 1987), 1:216–17.

43. Lambert, 11.

44. Lambert, 93–96.

45. Lambert, 67; Chrétien de Troyes, *Cligès*, ed. W. Foerster (Halle, 1291), 64; translated in Chrétien de Troyes, *Arthurian Romances*, trans. W. W. Kibler, 151. Duby, *Medieval Marriage*, 88–89 uses this text to argue that Christine was only perfunctorily consulted, but he ignores the romance coloration of the story.

46. For courtly story-telling, see, for example, Orderic Vitalis, *The Ecclesiastical History of Orderic Vitalis*, ed. and trans. Margery Chibnall, 6 vols. (Oxford, 1969–80), 3:216, in which Gerald of Avranches tells stories to the knights, and 4:216–18, in which the young knights tell their dreams to Isabel de Montfort; see also Chrétien de Troyes, *Le chevalier au Lion (Yvain)*, ed. M. Roques (Paris, 1971), 2–3, where the queen comes out to listen to the knights talking about their adventures (translated in Chrétien, *Arthurian Romances*, 296).

47. Lambert, 116, 137.

48. Lambert, 81.

49. For example, Procopius's *Secret History* or William Byrd's *Secret History of the Line*.

50. For other accounts of lay religious participation in new foundations and monastic restoration, see Radulph Glaber, *Rodulfus Glaber Opera*, ed. and trans.

J. France, N. Bulst, and P. Reynolds (Oxford, 1989), 114–15 (first third of eleventh century) and Guibert of Nogent, *Autobiographie*, ed. and trans. E.-R. Labande (Paris, 1981), 52ff.; trans. in *Self and Society in Medieval France*, ed. J. F. Benton (Reprint ed. Toronto, 1984), 53ff. (early twelfth century).

51. Lambert, 29–30. Charroux was so well rewarded by its location on the pilgrimage route that it was able to build a new church with a magnificent rotunda in the early twelfth century (K. J. Conant, *Carolingian and Romanesque Architecture: 800–1200* [3rd ed., Harmondsworth, 1973], 157).

52. William of Andres, *Chronicon Andrensis monasterii*, ed. L. d'Achery, *Spicilegium*, vol. 2 (Paris, 1723), 806, mentions that by the 1150s the Flemish and Poitevins in the monastery were at each others' throats; Andres eventually escaped from Charroux's control. (The edition in *MGH Scriptores* 24: 690–733 is not complete.)

53. William of Andres lists many of these gifts, which required the confirmation of the counts of Guines when the givers were donating property in Guines.

54. Lambert, 115–18.

55. Lambert, 51.

56. Lambert, 69–70. On leprosy, see R. I. Moore, *Formation of a Persecuting Society* (Oxford, 1987), 50ff., esp. 53–54, where he mentions leprosaria in Flanders.

57. Lambert, 38–39; on the various movements of regular canons, see R. W. Southern, *Western Society and the Church in the Middle Ages* (Harmondsworth, 1970), 240–50; C. H. Lawrence, *Medieval Monasticism: Forms of Religious Life in Western Europe in the Middle Ages* (2nd ed. London, 1989), 163–72.

58. Lambert, 40. On Arrouaise, see Lawrence, *Medieval Monasticism*, 165, 167–68. Arrouaise had a stricter rule than the Augustinian canons.

59. Lambert, 41.

60. William of Andres, *Chronicon*, 811.

61. On Beatrice, see Lambert, 122, 154; on Alice, 145; on Beguines, see Southern, *Western Society*, 319–20 (who does not say much about the Flemish Beguines); Lawrence, *Medieval Monasticism*, 231–32.

62. Lambert, 137.

63. Lambert, 148.

64. Lambert, 146.

65. Lambert, 40.

66. Lambert, 135, 140, 145. The arrangement seems to have been the result of a quid pro quo in which Arnold IV of Ardres relinquished rights over the church of Ardres and his brother-in-law was then able to be buried in consecrated ground.

67. Lambert, 11. Duby, *Medieval Marriage*, 105ff. suggests that this part of the story was intended to emphasize the independence of the "youths" from paternal authority.

68. Lambert, 110, 114. Through the first marriage to the heiress of Marquise, one of Arnold's sons established the lineage of Marquise. See L.-E. de la Gorgue-Rosny, *Recherches généalogiques sur les comtés de Ponthieu, de Boulogne, de Guines, et pays circonvoisins*, 4 vols. (1874–77; reprint ed. Paris, 1974), 2: 955. The second marriage was childless.

69. Lambert says that the Siger of *Gherminiis* was the chancellor of Flanders, but there was no "chancellor of Flanders" in the eleventh century and the Grammene

family cannot be traced back beyond the beginning of the twelfth century (Warlop, *Flemish Nobility*, 1/1:157–58; 2/1:849). Grammene is on the Leie River southwest of Ghent. *Gherminiis* can also be read as Grimmingen.

70. Lambert, 25; Heller, 574 n. 4.

71. Warlop, *Flemish Nobility*, 1/1:45–46.

72. D. Nicholas, *Medieval Flanders* (London and New York, 1992), 52.

73. Warlop, *Flemish Nobility*, 1/1:113.

74. Nicholas, *Medieval Flanders*, 56, 58. C. Frachette, "Guy de Guines fut-il comte de Forez au XIIᵉ siècle?" in *Les Princes et le pouvoir au moyen age* (Paris, 1993), 163–64, connects the marriage of Guy to a woman in the family of Forez to the marriage of Adelaide in nearby Burgundy.

75. Warlop, *Flemish Nobility*, 1/1:325; Duby, *Medieval Marriage*, 88.

76. Lambert, 65. This suggests that Duby, in *The Knight, the Lady, and the Priest*, 257, is wrong to argue that the betrothal occurred when Christine was a toddler and unable to speak (Lambert, 67, in fact, says she does speak). If Lambert is using the classical scheme of Isidore of Seville, *Etymologiae*, XI.2, adolescence began at 14 and stretched to 28. However, Lambert uses "adolescent" and "youth" as synonymous terms, which they are not in Isidore (youth ended at fifty). There is no external evidence for Christine's age, nor can it be calculated. Lambert names ten children, nine of whom were, it would seem, still alive as he wrote. He never mentions children who died before adolescence and only once mentions an infant who died, this because the mother died also, so Christine may well have had more than ten pregnancies. It is, however, difficult to tell the time period in which she bore her ten children. Russell's work on fertility in the nobility (J. C. Russell, *The Control of Late Ancient and Medieval Population* [Philadelphia, 1985], 142–46) suggests that teenage infertility was not uncommon among women — only one of the royal women he studied had given birth to a child by age seventeen, and most were nineteen or older when they had their first child, although some were married as young as twelve — but that, of course, may not have been the case with Christine. If Baldwin and Christine employed a wet-nurse, she might have had a child as frequently as every year and a half, but if she nursed her own children, the interval would have been closer to three years between children. The very large number of children in this family (in comparison to the data gathered for Anglo-Norman families by J. S. Moore, "The Anglo-Norman Family: Size and Structure," *Anglo-Norman Studies* 14 (1991): 153–96, where ten children are rare and where the average number of children seems to have been three or four) suggests that she may have used wet-nurses, but does not determine the matter one way or another. Thus, we cannot calculate backward to determine the date of Christine's marriage or her age; we are forced to rely on what Lambert tells us in this instance.

77. Lambert, 48. Baldwin may well have been older, for William of Andres, *Chronicon*, 802 gives a charter of Manasses which seems to date from about 1130, in which Arnold of Ghent appears as the first witness. Since his marriage to Matilda of Saint-Omer dates from about the time he received Tornehem (Lambert, 47), which is presumably when he came to be important enough to be the first witness of a charter, Baldwin might have been as old as eighteen or so. Duby, *The Knight, the Lady and the Priest*, 257 is probably again mistaken when he assumes that since Baldwin was only knighted in 1160, he must have been younger than ten in 1150.

78. On "aristocratic marriage," see Duby, *Medieval Marriage*, 4–17. He returned to these ideas in later works, but never substantially revised them.

79. Lambert, 149.

80. Lambert, 71.

81. While both William of Andres and Lambert depict Arnold as an easy-going man, Beatrice seems to have been a forceful person. William of Andres (*Chronicon*, 833) notes wryly that the lady was more feared than the lord, while Lambert, 150 calls her a *virago* (see Heller, 639). Beatrice began to act independently politically, and ultimately Arnold imprisoned her (see p. 32). She was rescued, and a four-year estrangement followed. The family as a whole was troubled. The older daughter Beatrice ran off in 1218 to become a nun, an action her mother may have connived in, because Beatrice later became the abbess of Bonham, which her mother had founded; her secret departure suggests she did not have her father's agreement (William of Andres, *Chronicon*, 858, 863; M. Desmarchelier, "La Maison de Guînes et l'ordre de Citeaux," *Cîteaux* 13 [1961]: 222). After Arnold's death in 1220, Countess Beatrice entered into a prolonged dispute with her son, Count Baldwin III, over her dower. Although the two were reconciled in 1224, Baldwin had the last word, as he buried her at Bourbourg against her wishes, rather than among the nuns of Bonham (William of Andres, *Chronicon*, 863–64).

82. Baldwin II of Guines, for instance, made an effort to settle some property on Manasses, one of his younger sons and apparently his favorite (Lambert, 72).

83. See Warlop, *Flemish Nobility*, 1/1:317–18. Duby, *Medieval Marriage*, 102–3 argues that this represents a change in the second half of the twelfth century, but the earlier the period Lambert writes about, the scantier his information about the siblings of his heroes, so it is difficult to support this argument using only his material.

84. Lambert, 89; William of Andres, *Chronicon*, 833.

85. Lambert, 113.

86. Duby, *Medieval Marriage*, 94ff. treats the female illegitimate daughters of the house simply as the sexual preserve of the sons of the house, but ignores how much they were treated like legitimate younger sons of the house, who often married the daughters of the lesser nobility in the region, as Duby notes.

87. Lambert, 89, 113. The law of bastardy contained in the fifteenth-century *Customs of Guines* notes that "no one is a bastard on his mother's side" (G. Espinas, *Le Droit économique et social d'une petite ville artésienne a la fin du moyen-âge, Guines*, Les origines du capitalism, 4 [Lille and Paris, 1949], 57), suggesting that, at least later on, bastard children retained rights of inheritance in their mother's families. Whether this applied earlier is unknown; however, if it did, it means that the fate of such children depended on the status of their mothers as well as the will of their fathers.

88. For general comments on courtesy and other sorts of refinement, see C. S. Jaeger, *The Origins of Courtliness* (Philadelphia, 1985), passim (Jaeger is mostly concerned with the German nobility, although he draws examples from other areas); on descent and the French nobility's military function, see Duby, *Chivalrous Society*, 94–111 ("The Nobility in Medieval France").

89. Warlop, *Flemish Nobility*, 1/1:276–84 on noble debt in Flanders.

90. Lambert, 76, 127.

91. See Keen, *Chivalry*, 83–86 on eleventh- and twelfth-century tournaments.

92. On costs, see Keen, *Chivalry*, 89.

93. Lambert, 92.

94. N. Elias, *Power and Civility, The Civilizing Process*, vol. 2, trans. E. Jephcott (New York, 1982), 91–92.

95. See H. Grundmann, "Literatus-illiteratus: Der Wandel einer Bildungsnorm vom Altertum zum Mittelalter" in *Ausgewählte Aufsätze*, vol. 3 (Stuttgart, 1978), 1–66.

96. On these issues, see M. Richter, "A Socio-Linguistic Approach to the Latin Middle Ages," in *The Materials, Sources, and Methods of Ecclesiastical History*, ed. D. Baker (Oxford, 1975), 71–72, 75–76 and "Kommunikationsprobleme im lateinischen Mittelalter," *Historische Zeitschrift* 222 (1976): esp. 45–46.

97. R. Turner, "The *Miles Literatus* in Twelfth- and Thirteenth-Century England: How Rare a Phenomenon?" *American Historical Review* 83 (1978): 928–45.

98. For some sense of the broad variety of texts available to a reader of French in the twelfth century, see B. Merrilees, "Anglo-Norman Literature," in *Dictionary of the Middle Ages* (New York, 1982), 1: 259–72.

99. Lambert, 81.

100. Lambert, 113, 130.

101. On tournaments, see Lambert, 90–93, 105, 108, 111, 123. On the denunciation of tournaments see Lambert, 18 (Heller, 570, where he says *execrabiles* rather than *detestabiles*); for the canon, see J. Mansi, *Sacrorum conciliarum nova et amplissima collectio*, vol. 21 (2nd ed., Venice, 1776), 437, caput 9. For the praise of Manasses, Lambert, 33; Arnold II spotted at a tournament by Ida, Lambert, 93.

102. Lambert, 93–95, 11, 86.

103. Lambert, 126.

104. Lambert, 87.

105. See John of Salisbury, *Entheticus*, 1: 190–93 on the consequences of royal corruption. The *Entheticus* did not circulate, so Lambert would not have known it, but these kinds of ideas were in the air.

106. For example, Ralph of Guines so oppresses his people with his avarice that he is cursed by his subjects and struck down by God (Lambert, 18).

107. On Rainier, see Lambert, 20–22.

108. On this theme, see R. Turner, "Old Men, New Men, and Government Service," in *Men Raised from the Dust* (Philadelphia, 1988), 1–19. Nicholas, *Medieval Flanders*, 68 suggests that some of the conspirators in the murder of Charles the Good (1127) participated because the count favored "new men."

109. On this point, see Spiegel, *Romancing the Past*, 53–54 and elsewhere.

110. See Lambert, 114.

111. Lambert, 135, 149.

112. Lambert, 128.

113. Lambert, 129.

114. Lambert, 152.

115. Lambert, 129.

116. Lambert, 36.

117. Lambert, 108, 120.

118. On town freedom, see Nicholas, *Medieval Flanders*, 104–5.

119. Nicholas, *Medieval Flanders*, 105–6.

120. See A. Verhulst, "Les franchises rurales dans le comté de Flandre aux XIe et XIIe siècles" in *Femmes: mariages-lignages, XIIe–XIVe siècles: Mélanges offerts á Georges Duby* (Brussels, 1992), 421–22.

121. Cited in Spiegel, *Romancing the Past*, 86.

122. Warlop, *Flemish Nobility*, 1/1:33–40; 75–78; 255–56; see also, for example, Spiegel, *Romancing the Past*, 109–12.

123. Warlop, *Flemish Nobility*, 1/1:284ff. Warlop concludes (320) that social leveling was underway in the 13th century.

124. Lambert, 6, 98, 107.

125. Anonymous of Bethune, *Histoire des ducs de Normandie et des rois d'Angleterre*, ed. F. Michel, Société de l'histoire de France, Publications in octavo, 18 (Paris, 1840), 166. In contrast, Enguerrand de Coucy brought fifty with him and the count of Nevers one hundred (165).

126. Perhaps the best introductions to different genres of historical writing have been published in the Brepols series, Typologie des sources du moyen age occidental: on annals (#14); on genealogies (#15); on ecclesiastical serial biographies (#37); on legendaries and other hagiographic texts (##24, 25); on universal chronicles (#16); on translations of saints (#33); and on local and regional chronicles (#74).

127. For example, Andrew of Marchiennes in the *Chronicon Marchianense* records being rebuked by his abbot for devoting his energy to writing a chronicle of the French kings rather than the history of his own monastery (cited in K. F. Werner, "Andreas von Marchiennes und die Geschichtsschreibung von Anchin und Marchiennes in der zweiten Hälfte des 12. Jahrhundert," *Deutsches Archiv* 9 [1951–52]:405).

128. Flemish historical writing, with a few exceptions, is not well known, despite its abundance. The histories are sometimes available only in partial editions, and few of them have been translated into modern European languages. I have given editions and translations, where they are available, and indicated where they are less than complete. There are no guides in English to this literature. In French, one may consult L. Genicot and P. Tombeur, *Index scriptorum operumque latino-Belgicorum medii aevi: Nouveau repertoire des oeuvres mediolatines belges*, 3 parts in 4 volumes (Brussels, 1977) and A. Molinier, *Les sources de l'histoire de France, des origines aux guerres d'Italie*, 6 vols. (Paris, 1901–6) (a new edition is currently underway). In Flemish (with some English summaries) one can consult the superb and growing database, *Narrative Sources of the Southern Low Countries* maintained by the history faculty of the university of Ghent. (The database may be accessed at <http://www.lib.rug.ac.be/n-exec.html>; choose "secondaire bronnen" and then "Narrative sources." Much of the information below concerning the Flemish tradition of historical writing comes from these sources.

129. Eusebius began the chronicle in Greek; Jerome translated it and continued it to 378. Sigebert's chronicle with its continuations is edited in *MGH Scriptores* 6:268–374. *On Illustrious Men*: R. Witte, *Catalogus Sigeberti Gemblacensis monachi de Viris illustribus* (Bern & Frankfort, 1974). *Deeds of the Abbots of Gembloux*: *MGH Scriptores* 8:523–57. See the database *Medieval Narratives* (n. 128) for Sigebert's full corpus.

130. On Andrew, see Werner, "Andreas von Marchiennes." *Abbreviated history* (*Historia succincta*): parts of the 3rd book are printed in *MGH Scriptores* 26:205–12; parts of the second book are printed in *Recueil des historiens des Gaules et de la*

France, 10: 289–90; 11: 364–66; 13: 419–23; 18: 555–58. *Chronicle of Marchiennes* (*Chronicon Marchianense*): E. Sackur, "Reise nach Nordfrankreich," *Neues Archiv* 15 (1890), 455–61. Genealogy: *Genealogiae Aquicinctinae, MGH Scriptores* 14: 619–22. *Annals of Marchiennes* (*Annales Marchianenses*): *MGH Scriptores*, 16:609–17. Anchin continuation of Sigebert's *Chronicle* (*Continuatio Aquicinctina Sigeberti Gemblacensis*): *MGH Scriptores* 6:406–38. *History of Anchin* (*Historia monasterii Aquicinctini*): *MGH SS*, 14:584–92.

131. Galbert of Bruges, *The Murder of Charles the Good, Count of Flanders*, ed. and trans. J. B. Ross (New York, 1967), 66–67, and nn. 6–11, which contains a full translation; *De multro, traditione et occisione gloriosi Karoli comitis Flandriarum*, ed. J. Rider (Corpus christianorum, continuatio medievalis, 131) (Turnhout, 1994).

132. *Vita Karoli comitis* in *MGH Scriptores* 12:537–61; a translation by Jeffrey Rider is forthcoming from Catholic University of America Press. The *Life of John of Thérouanne* (*Vita domni Iohannis Morinensis episcopi*) is printed in *MGH Scriptores* 15/2:1136–50.

133. L. Vanderkindere, *La Chronique de Gislebert de Mons* (1904; reprint ed. Brussels, 1950); the chronicle was composed in 1195–96.

134. *Chronicon Andrensis monasterii*. (see n. 52).

135. On the *Royal Frankish Annals*, see B. W. Scholz, *Carolingian Chronicles: Royal Frankish Annals and Nithard's Histories* (Ann Arbor, 1972), 2–8. For a discussion and translation of the Saint-Bertin annals, see Janet Nelson, trans., *The Annals of St-Bertin* (Manchester, 1991). For an edition, see F. Grat, J. Vieillard and S. Clémencet, eds., *Les Annales de Saint-Bertin* (Paris, 1964) for Saint-Bertin, and C. C. A. Deshaines, *Les Annales de Saint-Bertin et de Saint-Vaast* (Paris, 1871) for the Saint-Vaast material.

136. See Molinier, *Les Sources*, 2: 164. There is no complete edition of the cartulary, but portions are printed in *MGH Scriptores* 13:710–15. The *Gesta Lamberti*, also a historicized collection of charters composed around 1095, is printed in Migne, *Patrologia latina*, 162: 627–48. The fragmentary serial biography of the bishops is printed in *Recueil des historiens des Gaules et de la France* 13:533–34. On cartulary histories, see P. Geary, *Phantoms of Remembrance: Memory and Oblivion at the End of the First Millennium* (Princeton, 1994), 87f.; and Jean-Philippe Genet, "Cartulaires, registres et histoire: L'exemple anglais," in *Le Métier d'historien au moyen age: études sur l'historiographie médiévale*, ed. Bernard Guenée (Paris, 1977), 95–129.

137. The cartulary: B. E. C. Guérard, ed., *Cartulaire de l'abbaye de Saint-Bertin* (Paris, 1841) and the "Appendix" by M. F. Morand (Paris, 1867) (reprinted in *PL* 136: 1183–1278); Folcard's *Vita sancti Bertini* in *PL* 147: 1083–98 (composed in the mideleventh century) and *Miracula s. Bertini* in *PL* 147: 1097–1140 (for Folcard's many other works, see *Narrative Sources of the Southern Low Countries*); Erembald, *Libellus de miraculis sancti Bertini, MGH, SS* 15/1:522–24 (11th c). See Molinier, *Les Sources*, 2: 169–70, for more texts from Saint-Bertin.

138. Monastic histories: Herimannus of Tournai, *Liber de restauratione S. Martini Tornacensis, PL* 180 (39–106) and also partially in *MGH Scriptores*, 14:274–327 (1142–46, then continued c. 1160), translated by L. H. Nelson as *The Restoration of the Monastery of Saint Martin of Tournai* (Washington, D.C., 1996); *Versus de abbatibus S. Martini Tornacensis, MGH Scriptores* 13: 384–87 (1160–84). History of Tournai:

Historiae Tornacenses, MGH SS 14: 327–52 (mid-twelfth century, by a canon of the cathedral or monk). For the chronicle of Tournai (first part, between 1160 and 1184), see J.- J. De Smet, *Corpus chronicorum Flandriae*, 4 vols. (1837–1865), 2: 473–580. On works from Tournai in general, of which there are many, see Molinier, *Les Sources*, 2: 173–74.

139. Annals (begun 1098 and continued to the sixteenth century): *Annales Laubienses, Leodienses et Fossenses*, MGH *Scriptores*, 4:9–35; serial biography (c. 980): Folcuin, *Gesta abbatum Lobiensium*, MGH *Scriptores*, 4:52–74, and its continuation (to 1159), MGH *Scriptores*, 21:307–33. For other works, see Molinier, *Les Sources*, 174–75.

140. The annals: *Annales Elnonenses majores*, MGH *Scriptores*, 5:10–17 (begun about 1064 and continued); *Annales Elnonenses minores*, MGH *Scriptores*, 5: 17–20 (eleventh century); the fire and miracles: Gislebert of Saint-Amand, *Carmen de incendio S. Amandi Elnonensis*, MGH *Scriptores*, 11:409–32; also by Gislebert, *Historia miraculorum S. Amandi, corpore per Galliam deportato* (*BHL* 345), in Migne, *Patrologia latina* 150:1435–48 (both eleventh century also). (Saint-Amand had inherited a rich body of hagiographic materials from its ninth-century authors as well.)

141. Vicogne (*Historia monasterii Viconiensis*): MGH *Scriptores*, 24:291–313 (mid 12th century, then continued). Liessies (*Chronicon Laetiense*): MGH *Scriptores* 14:487–502 (1204, but now lost; part preserved in the later chronicle of Jacques de Guise [Molinier, *Les Sources*, 166]). Hasnon (*Historia monasterii Hasnoniensis*, composed by Tomellus of Hasnon in the late eleventh century): MGH *Scriptores*, 14: 149–58. Hautmont (1095–1120): edited by A. Poncelet in *Analecta Bollandiana* 10 (1896): 283–84. Saint-Pierre (one hand to 1060, then continued to 1292, with 5 fourteenth-century notes): *Annales Blandinienses*, MGH *Scriptores* 5:20–34. Watten (probably composed by 1091): *Chronica monasterii Watinensis*, MGH *Scriptores* 14:161–63. Floreffe (to 1139, with continuations): *Annales Floreffienses*, MGH *Scriptores* 16:618–31. Anchin (between 1170 and 1174): *Fundatio monasterii Aquicinctini*, MGH *Scriptores* 14: 579–84. Affligem (after 1122): *Chronicon Affligemense*, MGH *Scriptores* 9:407–17 (after 1122).

142. At Brogne: the *Life of St. Gerard* (*Vita sancti Gerardi, BHL* 3422), MGH *Scriptores* 15: 655–73 (probably mid-eleventh century). Hammes: *Sanctae Eusebiae Hammaticensis translationes et miracula* (*BHL* 2738, twelfth century), *Acta sanctorum quotquot toto orbe coluntur, vel a Catholicis scriptoribus celebrantur*, March 2:457–61. (This series will be cited hereafter as *Acta sanctorum*.) Blangy: *Sanctae Bertae, Blangiaci abbatissae, translatio et miracula* (*BHL* 1267–70), *Acta sanctorum*, July, 2:54–60 (tenth century, miracles in eleventh century and later). Bergues: Drogo of Bergues, *Liber miraculorum S. Winnoci* (*BHL* 8956) in Mabillon, *Acta Sanctorum ordinis S. Benedicti*, 3/1: 315–27 (eleventh century); also *Historia translationis S. Lewinae* (*BHL* 4902), *Acta sanctorum*, July, 5:613–27 (between 1060 and 1070); and the life of S. Godeleva (*Vita sanctae Godelevae, BHL* 3592), M. Coens, ed., *Analecta Bollandiana* 44 (1926): 102–37. Waulsort: *Vita Forannani, abbati Walciodorensis monasterii* (*BHL* 3080), *Acta sanctorum*, April, 3:808–14 (between 1130 and 1145). Saint-Bavon: *Miracula et translationes S. Bavonis* (*BHL* 1054), *Acta sanctorum*, October, 1:293–303 (before 1010); *Sanctorum Livini et Briccii Gandavum translatio* (*BHL* 4962), in Mabillon, *Acta sanctorum ordinis S. Benedicti*, 6/1: 65–70 (composed around 1039); *Sancti Macharii vita*,

Acta sanctorum, April, 1:875–77 (*BHL* 5100, composed in 1014) and 877–92 (*BHL* 5101 [5101a, 5101c), composed in 1067). Maroilles (a biography of the founder, the *Vita prima Humberti Maricolensis, BHL* 4036, 4039–40): *Acta sanctorum*, March, 3: 561–67.

143. *Gesta pontificum Cameracensium, MGH Scriptores*, 14:186-248 (mid-eleventh century with continuations) and the *Gesta episcoporum Cameracensium, MGH Scriptores*, 7: 402–504 (first quarter of the eleventh century, with later continuations); *Gesta pontificum abbreviata per canonicum Cameracensium, Recueil des historiens des Gaules et de la France*, 13: 534–42. On the *Gesta pontificum*, see G. Duby, *The Three Orders: Feudal Society Imagined*, trans. A. Goldhammer (Chicago, 1980), 21–27.

144. Lambert of Wattrelos, *Annales Cameracenses, MGH Scriptores*, 16: 509–54 (composed from 1152 on). *Chronicon sancti Andreae castri Cameracensis, MGH Scriptores*, 7: 526–50 (only the third, original book).

145. Heriger of Lobbes and Anselm of Liège, *Gesta episcoporum Tungrensium, Traiectensium, et Leodiensium* in *MGH Scriptores*, 7: 134–234 (Heriger wrote sometime between 972 and 1007 — scholars vary; Anselm, 1052–56). Rainer of Saint-Laurent in Liège wrote many biographies of abbots and saints and histories in his lifetime (c. 1110/20–1188).

146. *Catalogus episcoporum Morinensis*, ed. A. Wauters in "Courte chronique des évêques de Thérouanne," *Commission d'histoire de Belgique, Compte rendu*, 4th series, 3 (1876): 90–91. The chronicle runs to 1133.

147. *Genealogiae comitum Flandriae*, ed. L. C. Bethmann, *MGH Scriptores* 9:302–4.

148. *Genealogiae Flandriae*, 304; see above, n. 36.

149. *Genealogiae Flandriae*, 305–8; on Lideric, see Lambert, 2.

150. *Genealogiae Flandriae*, 308.

151. *Genealogiae Flandriae*, 308–13; also A. Derolez, *Lamberti s. Audomari canonici Liber floridus* (Ghent, 1968).

152. *Flandria generosa* in *Genealogiae comitum Flandrensium*, 313–34 (with various continuations and interpolations).

153. *Genealogia comitum Buloniensium, MGH Scriptores* 9: 299–301; also L. Genicot, *Etudes sur les principautés lotharingiennes* (Louvain, 1975), 242–68.

154. *Genealogiae Namurcensium et Boloniensium comitum origo, Recueil des historiens des Gaules et de la France*, 11:205; 13:585 (eleventh century).

155. On this text, see Duby, *The Chivalrous Society*, 135ff.

156. See, for example, the comments of Philip of Harvengt, in J. Thompson, *The Literacy of the Laity in the Middle Ages* (New York, 1960), 139–41; 143–44. On libraries (including Baldwin's), see Stirnemann, "Quelques bibliothèques princières," 7- 38. Stirnemann notes what she calls a slow laicization of book production which undermined the clerical dominance of this field in the twelfth century. For Baldwin's library, see Lambert, 81.

157. Lambert, 96. Two of these, the anonymous *Chanson des chétifs* (an account of those taken captive at Ramla in 1101 and Richard le Pélerin's *Chanson d'Antioch*, survive in versions reworked by Graindor of Douai. Ambrose d'Evreux composed the *Estoire de la guerre sainte* (on the third Crusade) for Richard I of England. There were other verse crusade narratives as well.

158. For the French, see Robert de Clari, *La Conquête de Constantinople*, 2 vols,

ed. P. Lauer (Paris, 1924); translated as *The Conquest of Constantinople*, trans. E. H. McNeal (reprint ed. Toronto & Buffalo, 1996). Geoffroi de Villehardouin, *La Conquête de Constantinople*, 2 vols. in 1, ed. E. Faral (Paris, 1938–9); trans. by M. R. B. Shaw, *Chronicles of the Crusades* (Harmondsworth, 1963).

159. De la Gorgue-Rosny, *Recherches généalogiques*, 1:368, notes that Anselm of Cayeux, who lived in the mid-twelfth century, had three sons named William, Stephen, and Arnold/Arnulf; William seems to have inherited, and become the father of the patron of history. William of Cayeux, the patron, was married to Elizabeth of Béthune. On the lords of Cayeux, see R. Fossier, *La Terre et les hommes en Picardie jusqu'a la fin du XIIIe siècle* (Paris and Louvain, 1968), 517 n. 208. On Arnold/Arnulf of Cayeux, see Lambert, 34.

160. On these texts see Spiegel, *Romancing the Past*, 53–54.

161. J. R. Kenyon and M. Thompson, "The Origin of the Word 'Keep'," *Medieval Archaeology* 38 (1994): 175–76 suggest that the pattern of alternating light and dark stonework in the castle inspired the English holders of the castle to call it the "kipe" or basket, thereby creating the word "keep." The records of Ardres in the public archives (Ardres replaced Guines as the regional center in the fifteenth century) date from the fifteenth century at the earliest. See P. Bréemersch, *Ardres: Repertoire numérique détaillé des archives communales déposées E dépôt 38* (Ardres, 1989).

162. See Espinas, *Le Droit économique*, for the text of the *Customs*, which is accompanied by a study. The text of the surviving manuscript dates from the second half of the fifteenth century (p. 2), and it is composed in French. Little of the material is dated. For the earliest dated custom, see pp. 85–88.

163. On Robert and the Anonymous, see Spiegel, *Romancing the Past*, 225ff.; for editions see Anonymous of Béthune, *Chronique des rois de France et ducs de Normandie* in *Recueil des historiens des Gaules et de la France*, vol. 24, pt. 2 (1904; reprint ed. Westmead, 1967): 750–75 (only part of the text); *Histoire des ducs de Normandie*, see n. 125.

164. Flemish scholars working in this period have had more to say about the Flemish heartland; the major exception is J. Dhondt, *Les Origines de la Flandre et de l'Artois* (Arras, 1944). French scholars generally stop at Picardy.

165. See A. Duchesne Tourangeau, *Histoire généalogique des maisons de Guines, d'Ardres, de Gand, et de Coucy, et de quelques autres familles illustres, qui y ont esté alliées. Le tout illustré par chartes de diverses églises, tiltres, histoires anciennes et autres bonnes preuves* (Paris, 1631). Subsequent studies are of varying worth, in part depending on how much their narratives depend on Lambert alone. De la Gorgue-Rosny, *Recherches généalogiques*, draws on a wide variety of sources. P.-J.-M. Collet, *Notice historique sur l'état ancien et modern du Calaisis, de l'Ardresis, et des pays de Bredenarde et de Langle* (1833; reprint ed. Paris 1993) depends largely on Lambert for the early history of Guines, but usefully lists what materials have survived from the county and describes the geography of some of its seigneuries and hamlets. E. Ranson, *Histoire d'Ardres depuis son origine jusqu'en 1891* (1891; reprint ed. Lille, 1988) is less helpful. In 1936 Mme Chanteux-Vasseur wrote a dissertation on Guines for the École des Chartes (see Dhondt, *Origines*, 98), but this was never published, and I have been unable to consult it.

166. See Flodoard, *Annales de Flodoard*, ed. Ph. Lauer (Paris, 1905), 69 and n. 6.

Guines is mentioned in charters dated 807 and 877 in the cartulary of Saint-Bertin and a list of holdings in the villa from the period in between (Folcuin, *Chartularium* in *PL* 136: 1218, 1248–49, 1236), but Folcuin composed his cartulary in the eleventh century. The creation of a narrative monastic cartulary was often an opportunity to correct the omissions of the past by "recreating" "lost" documents, in some cases by reconstruction, in other cases by outright forgery (on this point, see Geary, *Phantoms of Remembrance*, 100–7). The papal confirmation of the possession of Guines dates only from 1093. Still, the cartulary situates Guines in Boulogne, to which territory it seems originally to have belonged; Guines is described in the cartulary as a "villa."

167. Nicholas, *Medieval Flanders*, 42.

168. Dhondt, *Origines*, 24–25; Nicholas, *Medieval Flanders*, 16.

169. Nicholas, *Medieval Flanders*, 16–17; Dhondt, *Origines*, 25–27.

170. Nicholas, *Medieval Flanders*, 18; Dhondt, *Origines*, 33–37.

171. Dhondt, *Origines*, 50. Although he had ambitions south of the Boulonnais, Arnulf did not succeed in establishing any permanent foothold there (Dhondt, *Origines*, 40–42).

172. Dhondt, *Origines*, 50–51 suggests that this occurred after Arnulf I's death, but Nicholas, *Medieval Flanders*, 42–43 suggests that difficulties were already beginning at the end of Arnulf's life, and were then exacerbated by the succession of a minor.

173. Dhondt, *Origines*, 54–56.

174. Dhondt, *Origines*, 53.

175. Lambert, 7.

176. On this story, see Duby, *Chivalrous Society*, 144–45.

177. The chronicler Flodoard, *Annales*, 32–33, mentions Viking activity in the region around Arras in 925–26, and further reports that when King Ralph made a pact with these Vikings, he allowed them to raid Flanders. He also says (32) that Hugh the Great, the duke of France, made a pact with a group of Vikings settled in Flanders in 925.

178. See, for example, Dhondt, *Origines*, 53.

179. Warlop, *Flemish Nobility*, 1/1:30–33.

180. Warlop, *Flemish Nobility*, 1/1:52.

181. Duby, *Chivalrous Society*, 144–45, puts forth that argument. Although it seems odd to us, the nobility of the eleventh century often traced their origins to legendary founders, even when modern historians have been able to establish the family's descent from members of the Carolingian elite; see Geary, *Phantoms of Remembrance*, 50–51.

182. See Warlop, *Flemish Nobility*, 1/1: 45, 112.

183. Lambert, 4. J. Dunbabin, *France in the Making, 843–1180* (Oxford, 1985), 73, without citation, reports that the first count of Guines was the advocate of Saint-Bertin.

184. Nicholas, *Medieval Flanders*, 80; for the castellanies, see 47, which is based on Warlop, *Medieval Nobility*, 1/1:106–8.

185. Lambert suggests, incorrectly, that the counts of Guines were on Robert's side, as he paints Richilde as a villain and a witch (chapter 27). However, the *Flandria generosa* (see n. 152 above) quite clearly places Guines on Richilde's side (*Genealo-*

giae, 322), along with the castellan of Saint-Omer and the counts of Boulogne, Hesdin, and Saint-Pol, in other words, all the southern lordships. This source also places the Ostrevant (the area north of Ghent) on Richilde's side, but notes that Ghent itself supported Robert. However, Nicholas, *Medieval Flanders*, 52 points out that Richilde had some support in Ghent as well.

186. William of Andres, *Chronicon*, 785. Baldwin's son, however, was generally known by the name of Manasses, rather than Robert; see Lambert, 25, 33. The marriage of Adelaide of Guines, as I note above, also seems to be tied to the reconciliation.

187. Lambert, 30.

188. On Castellan Winemar II, Manasses's nephew, see Warlop, *Flemish Nobility*, 1/1:216–18. On Castellan Henry of Bourbourg, see Warlop, *Flemish Nobility*, 1/1:224–25. Arnold of Ghent, the brother of Winemar II, married the daughter of Castellan William of Saint-Omer, another opponent of Thierry (Warlop, *Flemish Nobility*, 1/1:225).

189. Instead of permitting Arnold to succeed, Thierry appointed Roger of Courtrai to the castellany of Ghent in 1151. However, Arnold entered into an alliance with Roger; Roger married Arnold's daughter (Warlop, *Flemish Nobility*, 1/1:219). Roger was succeeded in Ghent by Siger III, the son of Arnold's niece Alice, so that Thierry was ultimately unsuccessful in replacing Winemar's descendants. Nevertheless, good relations seem to have been established between Ghent and Courtrai, for Siger III married Petronilla, Roger's daughter by his first marriage (ibid., 1/1:220–23). Thierry had also punished Henry of Bourbourg, who had married Beatrice, the heiress of Aalst, as his second wife. Thierry permitted her uncle Ivan to usurp her inheritance, and thus prevented Henry from adding a substantial domain to his holding. Ivan was later murdered by Roger of Courtrai, and Warlop (1/1:227–28) suggests that the murder was actually at the instigation of Arnold of Guines to benefit the castellans of Bourbourg. Thus, after the civil war, there seems to have been a conscious attempt to repair broken alliances among the houses of Ghent, Guines, and Bourbourg.

190. On Arnold's appointment, see Lambert, 119. All the evidence for the existence of the peers comes from the twelfth century, but it refers to the later eleventh century. Galbert of Bruges, writing in 1127, mentions five peers, while Lambert mentions twelve. R. Monier, *Les Institutions centrales du comté de Flandre de la fin du IXe siècle à 1384* (Paris, 1943), 52–33, suggests that the number of peers may have fluctuated. However, Warlop argues that there were twelve peers, although this number may only have been settled on in the later twelfth century. On the peers generally, see Warlop, *Flemish Nobility*, 1/1:136–56.

191. Lambert, 126.

192. Arnold II of Ardres had inherited the holding of Ardres, while his brother, Gonfrid, had inherited their mother's holding of Marquise (Lambert, 110).

193. Lambert, 53–54.

194. Lambert, 60–61.

195. Lambert, 67.

196. Lambert, 93–95. Success here would have made Arnold a much more important figure, as indeed, it made Reynold of Dammartin.

197. Lambert, 96, 149.

198. Lambert, 149; Warlop, *Flemish Nobility*, 2/1:704. Beatrice's mother was Bea-

trice of Aalst, whose uncle had usurped her inheritance (see n. 189 above). Ivan's son, Thierry, died without heirs in 1166, and Philip of Alsace took over the county.

199. Spiegel, *Romancing the Past*, 31–32.

200. For a fuller account of the Vermandois and Flemish inheritances and the outcome, see Nicholas, *Medieval Flanders*, 73–74; and J. W. Baldwin, *The Government of Philip Augustus: Foundations of French Royal Power in the Middle Ages* (Berkeley, 1986), 80–82, 203–4, 207–8, and 119–25.

201. The Anonymous of Béthune specifically mentions that Baldwin received the homage of the count of Guines in this pact (*Chronique des rois de France*, 760).

202. Warlop, *Flemish Nobility*, 1/1:154–55. These lands were later were called the "estate of Ghisen" (Guines) because they were the possessions of that family.

203. Baldwin was elected emperor of Constantinople, but died a prisoner of the Bulgarians. On the final stage of Baldwin's career, see Villehardouin, *The Conquest of Constantinople* in *Chronicles of the Crusades*, 94–97, 121–22, 143. Countess Mary left Flanders to join him on crusade, but died before being reunited with him.

204. Warlop, *Flemish Nobility*, 1/1:264. On the lives of Joan, Margaret, and their mother Marie, see K. Nicholas, "Countesses as Rulers in Flanders," in *Aristocratic Women in Medieval France*, ed. T. Evergates (Philadelphia, 1999), 127–35.

205. On the Flemish succession, see Nicholas, *Medieval Flanders*, 150–53; on Philip II's maneuvers, see E. Hallam, *Capetian France, 987–1328* (London and New York, 1980), 131ff., and Baldwin, *Philip Augustus*.

206. See Lambert, 153; Warlop, *Flemish Nobility*, 1/1:262.

207. On his career, see Spiegel, *Romancing the Past*, 39–40, 48, 305–6; Baldwin, *Philip Augustus*, 200–202, 207–8.

208. See Map 1.

209. William of Andres, *Chronicon*, 833.

210. William of Andres, *Chronicon*, 840.

211. William of Andres, *Chronicon*, 847.

212. William of Andres, *Chronicon*, 848. This may be hindsight on William's part, however, for he knew the unhappy ending of the story.

213. Anonymous of Béthune, *Histoire des ducs de Normandie*, 141.

214. William of Andres, *Chronicon*, 853. The Anonymous of Béthune mentions Arnold's participation in the battle as well (*Chronique des rois de France*, 768–69). William of Saint-Omer was on the French side after 1180 (Spiegel, *Romancing the Past*, 39); Lambert, 150, notes that William defended his town as King Philip's provost during the siege of 1198. Siger III, the castellan of Ghent, fell from Ferrand's grace in 1212, and fled to France; he also fought the French side at Bouvines (Warlop, *Flemish Nobility*, 1/1:265).

215. William of Andres, *Chronicon*, 853–54. Desmarchelier, "Guînes et Cîteaux," 222, says that Beatrice was a prisoner of Countess Joan in Flanders; however, William of Andres, *Chronicle*, 834, says that "she preferred to remain in Flanders in exile, as many said, than to be kept shut up in Guines against her will." The Anonymous of Béthune says that Robert of Béthune rescued her and took her with him to Flanders (*Chronique des ducs*, 141) and that it was her husband Arnold who had imprisoned her (*Chronique des rois de France*, 767).

216. On these penalties, see Spiegel, *Romancing the Past*, 48ff.

217. Arnold III, the grandson of Arnold II, agreed to do homage to its count (Warlop, *Flemish Nobility*, 1/1:152).

218. Espinas, *Droit économique*, 85–88 contains the charter by which Arnold III and his son Baldwin IV in 1272 renounced various rights in the county in repayment for financial assistance in dealing with their debts. On the sale of the county in 1282, see Collet, *Notice historique*, 147; Duchesne Tourangeau, *Histoire généalogique*, 174 (and *Preuves*, 294). On the recovery, see Duchense, *Histoire généalogique*, 179–80; *Preuves*, 302–4.

219. Warlop, *Flemish Nobility*, 1/1:152–55.

220. Nicholas, *Medieval Flanders*, 92.

221. Nicholas, *Medieval Flanders*, 92, argues that the nobility were probably functionally bilingual in French and Flemish.

222. William of Andres, *Chronicon*, 837. William reports that legal proceedings were commonly held in the Flemish vernacular (*Flandrensi idiomate*). He uses this as an argument against accepting an abbot from Charroux (where Occitan would have been spoken).

223. Denise Poulet, *Au Contact du picard et du flamand: Parlers du Calaisis et de l'Audomarois* (Lille, 1987), 33–34.

224. Nicholas, *Medieval Flanders*, 32.

225. See Map 1; on canals, Nicholas, *Medieval Flanders*, 100.

226. Lambert, 111 attributes this to Arnold I, but it may have come later.

227. Lambert, 83. The incursion Lambert discusses here was probably the Dunkirk III incursion of the tenth/eleventh centuries. On the coast of Flanders generally, see N. Pounds, *An Historical Geography of Europe* (Cambridge, 1973), 10–11, 279–81, fig. 5.4 (p. 235).

228. Nicholas, *Medieval Flanders*, 7–8, 21–22, 97–98; see also 443, for a map of the soils of Flanders, although it stops at the border of Guines. On Picardy, see Fossier, *Picardie*, 163. Collet, *Notice historique*, enumerates a number of settlements on the edge of marshes, such as Andres (105), Balinghem (109), Bonnais (112), and Nielles (174), or on raised ground, such as Boningues (111), Coquelles (115), Coulogne/Colvida (118).

229. Lambert, 15. However, Pounds, *Historical Geography*, 280 suggests that in this region of Flanders, as drainage systems became better, crops replaced animals.

230. Lambert, 77, 104. On pisciculture in the Middle Ages generally, see R. C. Hoffman, "Economic Development and Aquatic Ecosystems in Medieval Europe," *American Historical Review* 101 (1995): 631–69, particularly 640–42 on mills and ponds, and 652–53. for noble domination of fishing rights.

231. Bourdat, "La Chronique de Lambert," 41–43. Godefroy de Menilglaise dated the Vatican manuscript to the fourteenth century (Godefroy, xvi–vii), but Bourdat proposes a fifteenth-century date. For Godefroy de Menilglaise's discussion of the manuscripts (he knew of nine), see ibid. xvi–xxi.

232. A seventeenth-century copy of the translation is also extant. Godefroy de Menilglaise and Bourdat again differ on the date of the original; Godefroy de Menilglaise (Godefroy, xxii) argues for the fifteenth century, while Bourdat suggests the sixteenth. On the second French manuscript, see Bourdat, "La Chronique de Lambert," 42.

233. *Reliquiae manuscriptorum omnis aevi diplomatum* (Frankfort and Leipzig, 1727), 8: 369–613. This edition was based on Wolfenbuttel, Herzog-August 502, composed in 1586. On earlier editions, see Godefroy, i–ii.

234. *Recueil des historiens des Gaules et de la France*, 11:295–307; 13:423–53; 18: 583–88.

235. *MGH Scriptores*, 24: 550–642.

236. Lambert, 137.

237. See Richter, "Kommunikationsprobleme," 43–45.

238. See above, n. 31.

239. Map, *De nugis*, l.

240. Lambert, 107.

241. M. Bloch, *Feudal Society*, trans. L. A. Manyon (Chicago, 1961), 1:141–42.

T E X T

1. The title "patrician" had ceased to have an exact meaning by Lambert's day, but it was still sometimes applied as a honorific title to more important territorial princes. See J. Niermeyer, *Mediae latinitatis lexicon minus* (Leiden, 1984), 775.

2. Lambert's description of his task as "arduous" (*arduum*) is probably an intentional play on words, since Lambert is telling the history of Arnold's holding of Ardres (*Ardea*).

3. Isidore of Seville, whose description of history was the one most generally known in the Middle Ages, writes in *Etymologies*, I:41, "Among the ancients no one wrote history unless he was there and saw the things to be described. For we understand better things that happen before our eyes than we can grasp by hearing. Those things which are seen can be related without a lie." Lambert, therefore, is going against Isidore's recommendations by including hearsay.

4. Charters—Lambert's term is *caedulis* (*schedulis*), which can mean leaves, as in leaves of a book or loose sheets of parchment (see Niermeyer, *Mediae latinitatis lexicon minus*, 945). However, since Lambert cites several charters later in his text, I have translated this term as charters.

5. Arnulf I of Flanders.

6. On Arnold, Walbert, and Siegfried, see Lambert, 2–11.

7. Lambert refers here to the conquests of England by Danish kings in 1013 (by Sven) and in 1017 (by Cnut) and possibly also the attempted conquest of England in 1066 by Harold Hardraada of Norway.

8. Lambert is clearly thinking of the Exodus, when he refers to "springing forth" and to Moses' ascents of Mount Sinai [see Ex. 19: 24, and 34] where Moses speaks to God, enters the cloud of divinity, and is given the tables of the law.

9. Ovid, *Metamorphoses*, I.5–7.

10. Ovid, *Metamorphoses*, I.2–4.

11. Ovid, *Metamorphoses*, I.1–2.

12. Heller, 558 n. 1, points out that a letter attributed to a Cornelius circulated with the text of Dares Phrygius; however, Lambert may also be thinking of Iulius Africanus, the third-century Greek author of a synchronic chronicle used by Eusebius in

composing his own universal chronicle. Dares Phrygius is mentioned in Homer as a priest of Hephaestus at Troy. However, the *De excidio Troiae historia* attributed to him, which was enormously popular in the Middle Ages, was actually written in late antiquity or the early Middle Ages. Pindar, a Greek poet who lived at the beginning of the fifth century b. c. e., was primarily known for his odes, although an epitome of Homer was attributed to him (Heller, 558 n. 2). Of these three, Lambert is likely to have seen only the text of "Dares Phrygius," if that.

13. Here Lambert is playing with medieval notions of truth and fiction. Isidore, in the *Etymologies*, I.40, argues that there are three types of narratives, histories, arguments, and fables. "Histories are things that happened; arguments are things which even if they have not happened could happen; fables, however, are things which neither have happened nor could happen because they are against nature." A truthful fable is therefore a natural contradiction.

14. The grammarian Priscian lived in the sixth century c. e., while Herodian lived in the second. The younger Appolonius of Alabanda was a rhetorician in Rhodes who came to Rome as an ambassador in the first century b. c. e. He treated the Homeric poems. Lambert would have known about him from Cicero's *De oratore*.

15. Lit. "fold wrinkles of derision."

16. On Sigebert, see p. 21. Lambert here seems to be thinking of Bede's *Chronicle*, a chronicle from creation to Bede's own time, part of a larger work, *De temporibus*.

17. To wrest away the club of Hercules is an idiom meaning to do the impossible (see also Macrobius, *Saturnalia*, 5.3).

18. There is an untranslatable passage here. Lambert says "*quod dentium rubiginem marcescat in eis*," which makes an allusion to a passage in Ovid, *Ars Amatoria*, I.515, which describes how the lover should be careful not to display himself to his prey with dirty teeth [*rubiginem* here being stains]. Lambert's usage is strained here—*marcescat* means to weaken, but how this would apply to stains on the teeth, I have no idea. Godefroy de Menilglaise (411 n. 15) simply comments that it is not good Latin. Rather than making any attempt to translate this literally, I have supplied what I think to be the sense of the passage.

19. Lambert's argument seems odd to the modern reader. He is addressing three possible cases: that he has quoted nonsense from old sources, that he has made things up, and that things he has been told by others are foolish. In the first instance, Lambert is saying that he has simply done what historians are supposed to do, that is, repeated what authoritative texts have said. In the second instance, Lambert is arguing that everyone includes material that is not quite true, and that his narrative is no different from anyone else's. In the third case, Lambert suggests that if the readers don't like what people have said, they need not pay attention to it, that is, they can stop reading. None of these responses is quite what a modern historian would say to accusations of inaccuracy. See pp. 4–6.

20. Horace, *Ars poetica*, l. 359.

21. Ovid, *Ars amatoria* 3.62, 64.

22. This idea was a twelfth-century commonplace, also expressed by Orderic Vitalis, *Ecclesiastical History*, 2:189, who also uses the metaphor of the river, and Wace, *Maistre Wace's Roman de Rou et des ducs de Normandie*, 2 vols, ed. H. Andreson (Heilbronn, 1877–79), 1:13.

23. The term *fossatum* (earthwork) is ambiguous and can mean a ditch, moat, earthen wall, causeway, or dike. I have generally translated it as earthwork, because many Flemish fortifications consisted of an earth wall surrounded by a ditch (Nicholas, *Medieval Flanders*, 18). Where it is clear that something else is meant, I have translated the term accordingly.

24. The term Lambert uses is *Colvekerli*, which is a Latinization of the Flemish vernacular term *colvekerl: kerl* = man (cognate with the English word "churl"); *colve* = club.

25. Lambert here calls Beatrice's husband Albericus, or Aubrey, but he more often calls him Albert. I have used Albert throughout.

26. These last two chapters are missing in all the manuscripts.

27. Lambert calls Adalulf "Ardulf" throughout the text. Arnold is Arnulf the Great, count of Flanders, c. 919–64. Baldwin the Bald is Baldwin II (879–918). On these counts, see pp. 25–26. Lambert drew the italicized passages here and immediately below, with some changes, from *Flandria generosa* in *Genealogiae comitum Flandrensium*, 318.

28. In fact, Adalulf left three sons, one murdered by Arnulf, one (also named Arnulf) who became count of Boulogne in 962, and an illegitimate son, Baldwin Baldzo, who became count of Courtrai (see Nicholas, *Medieval Flanders*, 40, 42–43).

29. Baldwin Ferrum (Iron) who came later to be known as Fierebras, or Bras de Fer (Ironarm), 863–c. 879.

30. On Lideric of Harlebeke, a legendary character, see F. L. Ganshof, *La Flandre sous les premiers comtes* (3rd. ed. Brussels, 1949), 11–12; Dhondt, *Origines*, 23–24. The title "count palatine" seems to have been honorific, to indicate the most important counts. Other texts of Lambert's period refer to the count of Flanders as a palatine (see Godefroy, 411 n. 17).

31. A Walbert was the third abbot of Luxueil (c. 625–665), but the Walbert who appears in Lambert's history and in the cartulary of Saint-Bertin was not the abbot of Luxueil. The two figures are already conflated in Folcard's *Vita Bertini* (*PL* 147:1095); Lambert's adoption of this conflation permitted him to give Guines a more illustrious origin. Some ambiguities in the biography of Abbot Walbert may have permitted this conflation; his first biography was only written two centuries after his death (see *AA SS*, May, 1:277–82), nor is it clear where in the Frankish realm he was from. In some sources, the abbot Walbert is said to be the brother of Faro and Fara (whom Lambert mentions below), but in these sources, he is said to be Burgundian as they were. See *Gallia christiana, in provincias ecclesiasticas distributa*, 16 vols. (2nd ed. Paris, 1856–1900), 15:149–50; hereafter cited as *Gallia christiana*.

32. The site of the monastery of Saint-Bertin.

33. St. Omer was a bishop of Thérouanne (638–c. 695). For an account of the donation, see Folcuin, *Chartularium*, *PL* 136: 1185–86. Lambert used the *Vita sancti Bertini* of Folcard (Heller, 564 n. 3). The donation of Arques (but not the other places) is mentioned Folcard's biography (*PL* 147:1095), while the cartulary mentions that other properties were donated, but does not name them. (*Chartularium*, 1192). All these are places near Saint-Omer except Escales, which was at one time on the maritime coast. A portion of the coastline there was reclaimed from the sea between 900 and 1100 (this includes the area around Sangatte, which Lambert describes in chap-

ter 83). Many of the earliest reclamation efforts were carried out by the great abbeys (Nicholas, *Medieval Flanders*, 98).

34. The mark was more a unit of measure than a coin, generally the equivalent of eight ounces.

35. *Terra censualis*, that is, land for which the holder had to make an annual payment.

36. The yoke and perch varied in size from place to place. The perch was a more consistent measurement, in that it was a unit of certain dimensions, the size of which varied from place to place. The yoke was the amount of land a team of oxen could plough in a day, and thus was even more variable.

37. The monks did indeed claim Guines, as Folcuin's cartulary contains a charter confirming the monks' possession of Guines, dating from 877, with a later confirmation (Heller, 564 n. 8; Folcuin, *Chartularium*, 1248–49). This charter mentions the office of provost, but that the holder, like other monastic officials, should be a monk.

38. Arnold I of Ardres. See chapters 112 and 119 for his office of advocate, his becoming a monk at Saint-Bertin, and his death.

39. The Vulgate reads differently from the Revised Standard; where the former reads "stultorum infinitus est numerus," the latter reads "what is lacking cannot be numbered."

40. "Light of the sheep" = *lux ovium*.

41. Faro was bishop of Meaux (627–72) and before that the royal chancellor. In the earliest biography of Faro, the *Vita Pharonis* of Hildegar, composed in the second half of the ninth century (*Acta sanctorum ordinis sancti Benedicti*, ed. J. Mabillon, 2: 607–25), Walbert is not Faro's brother. Heller, 566 n. 1, suggests that Lambert might have had another biography of Faro to hand. The *Vita Pharonis* included a fragment of a poem now known as the *Song of Saint Faro* (P. Zumthor, *Histoire littéraire de la France médiévale, VIe–XIVe siècles* [Paris, 1954]: 89–90); perhaps Lambert knew the original version.

42. *Wit* = white; *sant* = sand.

43. It is unknown what history of Meaux Lambert was referring to. The epic *Gormont et Isembard* survives in only fragmentary form, but the story was widely known in the Middle Ages. The surviving fragment was composed in the second half of the eleventh century (R. R. Bezzola, *Les Origines et la formation de la littérature courtoise en occident (550–1200)*, pt. 2 [reprint ed. Paris and Geneva, 1984], 491 n. 1). Although it refers to an historic event, the battle of Saucourt (881) in which King Louis III (d. 883) won a resounding victory over the Vikings, it is far removed from history. In the epic, Gormund is a pagan, Isembard a Frankish renegade who aids him to avenge a wrong done him by the Frankish king. Gormund and Isembard also appear in the *Chronicon Centulense* (the *Chronicle of Saint-Riquier*), composed in 1088 by Hariulf (Godefroy, 440 n. 163). Finally, Lambert's contemporary, the Anonymous of Béthune, used *Gormont et Isembard* in his *Chronicle of the Kings of France* (see Spiegel, *Romancing the Past*, 233).

44. Fara (Burgundefara) was the abbess of Farmoutiers near Meaux. For her biography, see *Acta sanctorum ordinis sancti Benedicti*, ed. J. Mabillon, 2:439–48.

45. The system of castellanies was not created until the late tenth century.

46. Stephen of Thérouanne, ruled c. 920–935. See *Gallia christiana*, 10:1536.

47. On Siegfried, see p. 26.

48. Lambert uses a variety of terms to describe Siegfried's relationship to the king: *nepos* (translated here as "nephew" but also meaning "grandson"), *cognatus germanus*, and *colateralis*. These terms seem to be general ways of saying that the two men were closely related; Lambert probably had no idea of the "actual" relationship of what probably was, after all, a mythical character!

49. Virgil, *Aeneid*, X.284.

50. See n. 48 above. While one can imagine, with some contortions, how it is possible for Siegfried to be the king's nephew and also the uncle of the king's brother (if, for instance, different kings were meant), it is more likely that Lambert is making up the relationship and means only to say that the two men were fairly close relatives.

51. Needless to say, Lambert is describing an idealized court of the late twelfth century, not a tenth-century court. He is also implicitly creating a kinship between the counts of Guines and Count Charles the Good (1119–27), whose father was Cnut IV of Denmark.

52. Lambert says "after the first," but the prince is the first citizen, the *princeps*.

53. Lambert's chronology is wrong here. Baldwin III (d. 962) actually predeceased his father Arnulf the Great. Arnulf I was succeeded by Baldwin's son, Arnulf II (d. 988), whom Lambert calls Arnold (see chapter 12).

54. There is no record of a daughter of Arnulf the Great named Elftrude.

55. Baldwin I Fierebras married Charles the Bald's daughter Judith. His son Baldwin II the Bald married Elftrude/Aethelfryth, daughter of Alfred the Great of England.

56. The reference here seems to be to Andreas Capellanus, the author of the *Art of Courtly Love*, who warns in book three that love can make people ill or crazy.

57. Baldwin IV (988–1035).

58. For the historically accurate account of this succession, see p. 26.

59. On the importance of spiritual kinship, see J. Lynch, *Godparents and Kinship in Early Medieval Europe* (Princeton, N. J., 1986).

60. Just as Lambert's courts belong to the later twelfth century, so do the rituals he describes. Some ritual seems always to have accompanied the moment a young man first took up arms in the Germanic tradition. However, the notion of knighthood as a order and the notion that knights were in some sense noble originates in the late eleventh or the early twelfth century. (On dubbing, see Keen, *Chivalry*, 66–69; on knighthood as a noble class, see Duby, *The Chivalrous Society*, 76–80, 178–80.)

61. Lambert's meaning here is utterly unclear. The two expressions he includes ("a re veris" or "the object for true men" [which can also be translated, "the Spring's object"] and "a rei vero") are unclear. (I have translated the latter as though it read "*a re vera*"). The French translator (Godefroy, 38) simply omitted the passage, a very tempting solution!

62. Bredenarde = *breite* [broad] *erde* [land].

63. Lambert says "nephew" (*nepos*) here.

64. Lambert seems to mean Count Arnulf of Boulogne (in the following chapter he indicates that he is aware that Erniculus was also called Arnulf). Arnulf was the son of Adalulf and the nephew of Arnulf of Flanders (see p. 26). Arnulf of Boulogne signed a charter in 972 (Heller, 569 n. 1).

65. The village of Silviacus, three miles from Boulogne, housed the church of Saint-Vulmar. It was founded in 688, destroyed by Vikings, refounded and then extensively restored after 1082 by Ida of Boulogne. (*Gallia christiana*, 10:1593–94) Samer seems to be a syncopated form of Saint-Vulmar.

66. Despite Lambert's denial, Arnulf of Boulogne did temporarily hold these territories. See p. 26.

67. See p. 26.

68. Greek historians thought their own myths arose in this way, through the errors and superstitions of simple people, and rather than simply rejecting these stories, they attempted to discover the kernel of truth in them (see P. Veyne, *Did the Greeks Believe in Their Myths?*, trans. Paula Wissing [Chicago, 1988], particularly 13–15, 59–60). Lambert similarly tries to purify his information. Here he accepts that the story itself was true, but argues that it was told about *someone other than* Erniculus.

69. Godefroy, 415 n. 34, says that William was count of Ponthieu in the mid-tenth century, but he makes Arnold of Boulogne and Herluin of Montreuil his sons, which is incorrect (see p. 26). Roger was count of Ponthieu until 957 (Flodoard, *Annales*, 144 n. 5), but Herluin of Montreuil was Roger's contemporary and not a kinsman. Nor was there a count of Ponthieu after 974, when Hugh Capet took over the county, until the eleventh century (Dhondt, *Etudes sur la naissance des principautées territoriales en France*, 73 n. 4; Heller, 569 n. 5). Lambert is the first source to mention this William (569 n. 4), who seems to be an invention.

70. On Saint-Pol, see p. 26.

71. The Flemish were seen in the Middle Ages as being particularly bellicose and uncouth (see Nicholas, *Medieval Flanders*, 59, 89).

72. The story of the swan knight (Lohengrin) first occurs in William of Tyre. As the legend goes, Beatrice of Bouillon was pursued by the duke of Saxony, but rescued from him by the swan knight. Beatrice and this knight were the parents of Countess Ida, the mother of Godfrey of Bouillon, the first Latin king of Jerusalem (see Godefroy, 415 n. 35). However, this chronology is impossible. Ida lived in the second half of the eleventh century and cannot be a forebear of Ralph, whom Lambert places earlier.

73. "fighting prowess" = *gladiatura*; "grandiose" = *pomposus*. Gladiatura is a more loaded term than *militia* (knighthood), for the term *gladiator* was, by the eleventh century, taking on the strongly negative connotations of "executioner" and "assassin." *Pomposus* can simply mean solemn, but also had a secondary meaning of overblown. Lambert chooses his vocabulary carefully here, to highlight his negative opinion of Ralph.

74. Cf. Council of Clermont, caput 9, *Detestabiles autem nundinas* (see p. 202 n. 101). The Church explicitly banned tournaments between 1130 and 1316; those who died in them were supposed to go to hell, while those who killed them were obligated to do penance for murder. France was seen as the home of knighthood and of the tournament, which is why Ralph is going there to fight. Lambert's story, however, is anachronistic, since the tournament first appears c. 1100. (On these points, see Keen, *Chivalry*, 83–84; 94–96.)

75. *Montfelon* is the hill (*mont* in OF, *mons* in Latin) of someone named Philo or of a rebel or evil man (*felun* or *felon* in OF) or of a fuller (*fullo* in Lat).

76. On this incident, see Fossier, *Picardie*, 564–68, 568 n. 322. Fossier sees this

sort of insurrection as part of a general rural unrest produced by the transformation of society in the late eleventh and early twelfth centuries, characterized by the decline of Carolingian modes of production, the rise of castles and the growing self-awareness of the nobility, and increasing economic burdens imposed on the rural population.

77. Virgil, *Aeneid*, VI.854.

78. "Romulus" = *Quirinus*. Romulus was called Quirinus after his deification. Quirinus could also be used generally of things Roman, so that Lambert may simply mean a "Roman spear." Lambert may be aware that classical writers thought the word Quirinus was derived from a Sabine word meaning spear (that etymology is given in Ovid's *Fasti*). This is typical of Lambert's fantastic wordplay, but it is particularly odd here, because his speakers are, ostensibly, simple shepherds!

79. In 1034.

80. Virgil, *Aeneid*, VI.854; see also chapter 18, where Lambert echoes this passage in prose.

81. To persevere in goodness is *stare in bono*. Lambert seems to know enough Greek to know that the *eu* prefix in that language means "good." Thus *Eu-stare* is to cling to the good. The past participle would give us *Eustatus*, a play on *Eustacius* or *Eustatius*.

82. Cf. Ovid, *Amores*, I.8.3.

83. Another pun on the name Eustace: "be" = *esto* and "your people" = *tuis*.

84. Ragnar Longneck, who was count of Hainaut around the turn of the tenth century, had a son named Rainier, who is mentioned by Flodoard (*Annales*, 929). There was also a Raganar, whose death is mentioned in the annals of Saint-Bertin in 875 (Nelson, *Annals of St-Bertin*, 197). Lambert may also have been thinking of Ralph, the lay abbot of Saint-Bertin and Saint-Vaast, and the count of the Ternois and Arras, a kinsman of king Carloman of France (d. 884), who appointed him to these positions (R. McKitterick, *The Frankish Kingdoms Under the Carolingians* [London and New York, 1983], 250. This Ralph died in 892, and Baldwin II claimed his holdings (Dhondt, *Origines*, 34). Lambert's Rainier is clearly none of these; his Rainier may figure in a local story or may be his own invention, intended to comment obliquely on Lambert's contemporary, Reynold of Boulogne.

85. Lambert's reference to the way Rainier understood scripture reflects Christian images of Jews that dated from at least the second century. The Christian accusation against the Jews was that they read scripture literally (and hence preserved Mosaic customs like circumcision) rather than spiritually. On these attitudes, see K. R. Stowe, *Alienated Minority: The Jews of Medieval Latin Europe* (Cambridge, Mass., 1992), 15ff.

86. Lambert is the only source for this story. However, members of the family of Ordres appear in other sources. A Humphrey of Ordres married Arnold I of Ardres's daughter, while an Arnold of Ordres went on the first Crusade, and a Gozelin of Ordres witnessed a charter of Eustace III of Boulogne (de la Gorgue-Rosny, *Recherches généalogiques*, 3:1096).

87. Godefroy, 416 n. 59 takes *marchisie* as the place name, Marquise.

88. The place name, *Gherminiis*, can be translated as either Grimmingen or Grammene. Godefroy de Menilglaise preferred Grimmingen (495), but Warlop (*Flemish Nobility*, 1/1:157) prefers Grammene. The family of Grammene were the chamberlains of Flanders in Lambert's day, but the office did not exist until the second half

of the twelfth century, and the family that held the office then cannot be traced back before 1100 (see Warlop, *Flemish Nobility*, 2/1:849ff.).

89. Before 1065. Eustace does not appear in any records prior to Lambert's (Heller, 573 n. 2).

90. Baldwin appears as a witness in a charter of Philip I in favor of the monastery of Hasnon in 1065 (Heller, 573 n. 3).

91. "Through education" = *disciplinaliter*. The term can mean behaving in an ascetic or penitential manner, but since Lambert has here emphasized Baldwin's literacy, he seems to mean that Baldwin has learned the nature of God through formal study rather than through more informal or verbal instruction.

92. Florentin has not been identified. There were no dukes of Lorraine named Florentin in the eleventh century. Godefroy de Menilglaise (417 n. 47) suggests that Lambert was thinking of Florence I of Holland (†1061), and Heller (573 n. 4) accepts that suggestion but notes that there is no record of any daughter named Adele or Christine.

93. G. Duby, *The Knight, the Lady, and the Priest*, 44–45, argues that this renaming occurred when women married and that the families into which they married renamed them to create a new identity linked to the marital house. While this may be the case, Lambert mentions at least two men commonly known by nicknames, Count Robert/Manasses of Guines (below) and Abraham/Pagan of Northout (see chapters 25, 106). Instead, the severe contraction of the name pool beginning toward the end of the tenth century may be partially responsible. (On this, see Geary, *Phantoms of Remembrance*, 73–76.) Baldwin's sister was also named Adele, so calling Baldwin's wife Christine may have avoided confusion.

94. Robert/Manasses's godfather was Robert the Frisian, who gave Manasses his own name, as was quite common (Godefroy, 417 n. 49). Manasses, Fulk, Guy, and Hugh first appear in a charter in favor of Andres from 1084 and later in other documents (Heller, 574 n. 1).

95. Although Godefroy found no connection between Guines and Forez (418 n. 50) and Heller (574 n. 2) suggested Forest in the Pas-de-Calais as an alternative, C. Frachette, "Guy de Guines, fut-il comte de Forez au XIIe siècle?" in *Les Princes et le pouvoir au Moyen Age* (Paris, 1993): 155–65 has argued that Guy may have for a few years claimed the title by marriage.

96. Geoffrey IV of Semur, not Geoffrey II, as Godefroy de Menilglaise thought (Frachette, "Guy de Guines," 164; Godefroy, 418 n. 53).

97. Reigned c. 1061–95 (Heller, 574 n. 3).

98. H. Platelle, "Le Problème du scandale: Les nouvelles modes masculines au XIe et XIIe siècles," *Revue belge de philologie et de l'histoire* 53 (1975): 1071–96, describes the several waves of fashion involving strikingly new styles of clothing and barbering that passed from southern France through France and England, which were duly denounced by the clergy.

99. Winemar I (c. 1074–c. 1120), although he is first called the castellan c. 1088 (Warlop, *Flemish Nobility*, 2/1:828).

100. On Ghent and its castellans, see Nicholas, *Medieval Flanders*, 32–34, 47.

101. The future Arnold I of Guines. Despite Lambert's remarks, Arnold seems not to have been the firstborn. See p. 28.

102. Siger I (d. 1122) and Winemar II (d. 1135) succeeded their father as castellan.

103. He seems to have joined the order of the Templars, rather than simply to have broken his monastic vows. See Warlop, *Flemish Nobility*, 2/1:829.

104. There was also a daughter named Alice, whose husband, Hugh of Encre, succeeded her brothers Winemar and Siger as castellan. Her son by her second marriage to Steppo of Viggezele became Siger II of Ghent (Warlop, *Flemish Nobility*, 2/1: 829–30).

105. Steppo appears in a diploma of Count Philip of Flanders in 1171 (Heller, 574 n. 8).

106. *Felicem*, literally "happy," but which has overtones of blessedness.

107. Richilde was the heiress of Hainaut and the widow of Herman of Mons; Baldwin VI of Flanders was her second husband (see Nicholas, *Medieval Flanders*, 51–52).

108. On these events, see p. 27. Lambert's comments obscure the fact that Baldwin supported Richilde.

109. This Arnold is Arnulf III. His burial place was disputed in the sources (see Heller, 575 n. 4).

110. February 22.

111. The chronicle of Watten says that Watten was originally a priory of Saint-Bertin, founded in 1072 by Odfrid, the first prior, who was assisted by Robert the Frisian's mother (Heller, 575 n. 5.).

112. Charroux in Poitou profited from its position on the pilgrimage route to the church of St. James in Galicia (Santiago de Compostela) and rebuilt its church with a grand rotunda, an ambulatory, and radiating chapels (to meet the needs of pilgrims) in the early twelfth century. On Charroux, see Conant, *Carolingian and Romanesque Architecture*, 157; for a general account of the pilgrimage route to Compostela and map, see ibid., xxxiii, 91–93.

113. Fulrad (d. 1088) was the abbot of Charroux when Baldwin arrived, not Peter II (Godefroy, 420 n. 63).

114. Gerald or Gerard (c. 1083–97).

115. Lambert's details differ from those provided by William of Andres in his chronicle.

116. Lucan, *Pharsalia*, I.281.

117. The foundation charter, given in William of Andres, *Chronicon*, 783, dates from 1084.

118. Abbot Gilbert appears in a charter benefiting the abbey dating from 1119 (William of Andres, *Chronicon*, 788); his successor was confirmed in his possessions by a charter of 1122 (ibid., 792–94).

119. William of Andres, *Chronicon*, 782, says that Bochard challenged the authenticity of the relics hoping to protect his own property.

120. Charles the Good (1119–27). Godefroy de Menilglaise (421–22 n. 70) points out that Baldwin died around 1091, while Charles didn't become count until 1119.

121. William of Andres, *Chronicon*, 794, reports that Paschal (1099–1118) granted the right of free burial.

122. Calixtus was pope between 1119 and 1124; Gregory VII (1073–85) was the pope in 1084.

123. Gerald was suspended, probably around 1096, because he could not prove himself innocent of the charge of simony (see *Gallia christiana*, 10:1542). Lambert is the only one to say that he was buried at Patras; Iperius says he retired to Mont-Saint-Eloi near Arras (Godefroy, 421 n. 69; Heller, 576 n. 10).

124. Milo II (1159–69); Peter II "Marmot" of Andres (1161–1195) (see *Gallia christiana*, 10:1605). Arnold I of Guines is Arnold of Ghent, who died in 1169. These events, therefore, occurred sometime in the 1160s. On the translation, see William of Andres, *Chronicon*, 811.

125. Rictrude (d. c. 668), the founder of Marchiennes, seems to have become conflated with Rotrud, the patron of Andres. Rictrude is well attested and several biographies and collections of miracles remain (see *AA SS*, May, 3:78–153), the earliest of which was composed by Hucbald of Saint-Amand around 907. She was a matron and the mother of many children. In contrast, little is known about Rotrud. It is conjectured that she is the daughter of Charlemagne mentioned in the Saint-Bertin Annals (see Nelson, *Annals of St-Bertin*, 138), although she also was not a virgin. The earliest surviving account of Rotrud is by William of Andres. William of Andres, *Chronicon*, 781–82, claimed that Rotrud had been translated furtively from Marchiennes, and the authenticity of the relics was proven by their miraculous resistence to fire. (On this confusion, see the discussion in *AA SS*, May, 3:80.)

126. Died 1113. She married Eustace in 1057.

127. The foundation charter is lost, but the foundation was confirmed in 1100 (Godefroy, 422 n. 77).

128. Godfrey II (1044–70).

129. Eustace II (†1093).

130. Eustace III of Boulogne.

131. On Godfrey's legend, which grew in the twelfth and thirteenth centuries, see Keen, *Chivalry*, 58–59; 122–23.

132. Baldwin, King of Jerusalem (1100–1118).

133. The Benedictine monastery of Hammes was founded in 1080 (Godefroy, 495).

134. That is, lay people who possessed ecclesiastical properties either gave them outright to Capella to absorb, or they stipulated that the properties should maintain some sort of autonomy under the control of Capella, which would offer the donors the prospect of maintaining some control themselves, but would allow some of the spiritual benefits of association with an important monastery to accrue to these properties; at the same time, it would mobilize the resources of Capella to protect these properties, should neighbors wish to absorb them.

135. See chapters 115–16 for the founding of Ardres.

136. If the church of Ardres were founded in 1069, it would have been founded before Cassel (1071) and Watten (1072). This date appears to be wrong; Ardres seems to have been founded around 1073. See the notes to chapter 115 on the dating.

137. William of Andres, *Chronicon*, 785 says that Baldwin died seven years after his wife; he places Christine/Adele's death after a charter of 1084, so perhaps she died in 1084 or 1085, thus Baldwin died around 1091.

138. "Tournaments" = *nundinas*; Lambert here again echoes his language in chapter 18.

139. Heremar was one of the early benefactors of Andres, and the lords of Balinghem appear a number of times in the record in association with the counts of Guines (de la Gorgue-Rosny, *Recherches généalogiques*, 1:93).

140. Adelaide became the heiress of Balinghem; she married Daniel by 1210 (de la Gorgue-Rosny, *Recherches généalogiques*, 1:94) and Arnold of Cayeux around 1196 (Heller, 579 n. 3).

141. Gregory was originally elected at too young an age and was refused by the bishop of Thérouanne on that account. He was reelected in 1158 and confirmed at Charroux, but was never consecrated and was then deposed. He was succeeded by Peter the Marmot (*Gallia christiana*, 10:1604, which draws on William of Andres, *Chronicon*, 805–7).

142. On the Tancarvilles, see D. Bates, *Normandy before 1066* (London, 1982), 155. The king is William II Rufus (1087–1100).

143. See Fossier, *Picardie*, 557–59, 559 n. 300 on this passage in Lambert's history.

144. These sorts of payments, the head tax, which was beginning to disappear in Picardy in the twelfth century (Fossier, *Picardie*, 698), *foremariage* and death taxes, were common markers of servile status.

145. Lambert calls her a *vavassorissa*, and thus clearly thinks of the rear-vassals as a social class. On the growth of the notion of knighthood as a class, see Duby, *Chivalrous Society*, particularly 105–7.

146. See William of Andres, *Chronicon*, 784–86.

147. See chapter 51.

148. On the subject of masculine fashion, see Platelle, "Les nouvelles modes masculines," particularly 1091–94 on beards. Despite a fashion in southern France and Normandy in the eleventh century for shaving beards, a custom denounced by the clergy as either effeminate or too imitative of clerical customs, beards were still seen as the norm into the twelfth century. The nickname, then, would seem to date from the later period, when shaving was the norm.

149. Milo I, bishop of Thérouanne (1131–58), was the first abbot of Domp-Martin (Domnus-Martinus), a Premonstratensian house in the diocese of Amiens. Milo belonged to the first generation of Premonstratensian abbots, those converted by St. Norbert himself; he was originally a hermit living at St. Josse in Ponthieu, who instituted the rule of St. Augustine as interpreted by Norbert around 1121. (See *Gallia christiana*, 10:1347 on Domp-Martin; 10:1546ff. on Milo's holding of episcopal office.)

150. The Premonstratensians wore white.

151. This charter of 1132 is extant; see *Gallia christiana*, 10, *instrumenta*, 400–1.

152. Henry, abbot of Licques (1132–50). He was a kinsman of Louis VI of France and served as royal chaplain for a time. (*Gallia christiana*, 10:1618).

153. On the relationship of the lords of Fiennes to those of Ardres, see chapter 102.

154. Tingry is in Boulogne. William Faramus married Beatrice of Guines but had no children (see chapter 48), so his sister Sybil became the heiress. Her husband Enguerrand eventually inherited Fiennes as well (de la Gorgue-Rosny, *Recherches généalogiques*, 3:1428–29).

155. Philip of Alsace (1167–91). Philip, like Enguerrand, died on the third Crusade.

156. Eustace married Adelaide around 1200, but was wounded in a tournament and died at Andres (de la Gorgue-Rosny, *Recherches généalogiques*, 1:362).

157. The family that ruled Campagne were also the lords of Hames (see de la Gorgue-Rosny, *Recherches généalogiques*, 1: 314f., 2:721f.)

158. Conteville is near Boulogne.

159. The brother of Henry of Campagne.

160. William ruled from 1153 to 1159. Since Manasses died in 1137, Lambert is showing his usual vagueness about dates.

161. Ruisseauville itself was relatively new at the time; it was founded around 1090 (*Gallia christiana*, 10:1607).

162. North of Boulogne.

163. *Sonting* = sinner; *veld* = field.

164. *Santing* = saint; *veld* = field.

165. Henry I (1127–68). He was not castellan at the time, however, although the hope clearly was that he would produce an heir who would unite the two territories. On Bourbourg and the castellans, see Nicholas, *Medieval Flanders*, 47; Warlop, *Flemish Nobility*, 2/1: 699–704.

166. In classical Aristotelian thought, the man provided the seed, the woman the material substance when a baby was created. Therefore, Manasses's sisters' children would be of another man's seed. Of course, his granddaughter Beatrice, under this system, would also be of another man's seed! It might be best to see this as a display of Lambert's learning, without taking the actual content too seriously.

167. Albert the Boar remains unidentified.

168. See also chapter 25.

169. This quotation is ironic, for in the Biblical passage, it is love that endures all things.

170. See also chapters 25, 63.

171. William II (1126–c. 1143). On the castellans of Saint-Omer, see Warlop, *Flemish Nobility*, 2/2:1106–16.

172. Carolingian descent was particularly significant at the time Lambert was writing; many lords claimed Carolingian descent, among them the king of France, Philip Augustus, and the counts of Flanders. The return of the French throne to the lineage of Charlemagne was a theme of the writing of Andrew of Marchiennes (Werner, "Andreas von Marchiennes," 409ff.).

173. William III (1132–c. 1170).

174. Godefroy de Menilglaise says he was later the castellan of Saint-Omer (426 n. 109), but he seems to have conflated this Hosto with his uncle, also named Hosto, the brother of William II, who also appears in one record as castellan (Warlop, *Flemish Nobility*, 2/2:1112). This may be why Heller, 584 n. 4, says that Hosto was older than William. William III's brother Hosto was a Templar.

175. Walter († c. 1173) went to the Middle East in 1152/3, returned to Europe in 1157, but then went back and married Eschiva, the lady of Tiberias. He also carried the title of castellan of Saint-Omer (Warlop, *Flemish Nobility*, 2/2:1113).

176. Baldwin I of Bailleul (his dates are very uncertain but he lived until at least 1123). This was probably his second marriage. See Warlop, *Flemish Nobility*, 2/1:638.

177. In Hampshire.

178. Near Arras.

179. This marriage must have taken place in 1136 at the latest, for Manasses, who stood godfather for the first child, died in 1137. It may well have been earlier (see p. 200 n. 77).

180. Robert of Boves, the count of Amiens, married Beatrice, the daughter of Hugh Candavène. Their daughter married William of Guines (Godefroy, 426 n. 97).

181. She appears in charters until 1215 and died in 1222 (Heller, 585 n. 3).

182. Eustace III of Fiennes.

183. Roger I of Courtrai (d. 1190). On this marriage, see also chapter 62.

184. Hugh of Lille (d. c. 1169) became castellan of Lille on the death of his brother Reynold II (Warlop, *Flemish Nobility*, 2/1:941). Godefroy de Menilglaise (426 n. 98) argues that Adelaide actually married Reynold, rather than Hugh, but Warlop (ibid.) presents other evidence that Reynold married a daughter of Roger III of Wavrin.

185. Adelaide's marriage to Robert "the Uncle" of Wavrin brought him the lordship of Sainghain-en-Weppes (Warlop, *Flemish Nobility*, 2/2:1197). Robert died on the third Crusade (Heller, 585 n. 7).

186. On Baldwin Morannus of Hondschote (†1205), see Warlop, *Flemish Nobility*, 2/1:894.

187. Pollaer is near Aalst; Walter was dead by 1191, as Giselle appears in that year as his widow (Heller, 585 n. 13).

188. See also chapter 46.

189. In 1137.

190. William of Andres, *Chronicon*, 805 says that Manasses became a monk at Andres on his deathbed.

191. On the memorial function of the strong links between monasteries and the families of their patrons, see P. Geary, *Phantoms of Remembrance*, 77–80.

192. The text reads "King William," but Stephen was king in 1137.

193. Thierry of Alsace, count of Flanders (1128–64).

194. Undoubtedly lands that came from Beatrice's grandmother, Emma of Tancarville.

195. I. e., Beatrice was afraid to have sex with Albert. It seems likely, from the events Lambert narrates in chapter 60, that Albert and Beatrice never consummated their marriage (or at least that they claimed this during the proceedings by which their marriage was annulled).

196. The Vulgate reads slightly differently at the end: "[to God, who is to be feared], and to the terrible one who carries off the spirits of princes." Lambert has adapted the biblical phrase to his own purpose, substituting *offert* (offers) for *aufert* (carries off) and adds *votivum* (offering). While this may be a trick of oral memory, the play on words is most likely intentional.

197. Lambert is clearly mistaken about this. The foundation charter of St. Leonard's was dated 1117, twenty years before Manasses's death, and he confirmed other gifts later. (Godefroy, 427 n. 103).

198. See also chapter 25.

199. This date also seems mistaken. Possibly the copyist read MCII (1102) for

MCXX (1120), which is closer to the date given in the foundation charter, but Lambert may be working from memory.

200. Near Dunkirk.

201. Another play on words. *Eu* = good, *femia* = *femina* = woman.

202. Arnold may be a relative of the comital family; one of Manasses's illegitimate sons, Hugh, married Matilda, the daughter of Laurette of Hames.

203. Arnold of Merck was married to the sister of Arnold and Baldwin of Ardres, and eventually became the lord of Ardres himself. See chapters 65, 132.

204. Because of his landlessness, Baldwin would not have done homage to Albert the Boar, and therefore was not acting treasonably (although, as Lambert makes clear, he was acting wrongly) in supporting Arnold's claim to Guines. In contrast other lords, who had presumably done homage to Albert, were committing treason, while Arnold of Merck fulfilled his obligations according to the letter rather than the spirit.

205. "*Alderwicus*" from the Flemish *alder* = elder, *wick* = place.

206. See also chapter 135.

207. Lit, "given to death."

208. Statius, *Thebais*, 3.348.

209. "*Almari-vallum vel -aggerem*." The name of the place, as Lambert explains below, derives from a man's name, Amaury, and the word for an earthwork; I have rendered the name Amaurival in translation.

210. A fief near Audruick (Godefroy, 494).

211. *Ad Florem*, literally "at the Flower." I have followed the sixteenth-century French translation in calling this castle "The Flower."

212. Gosso of Northout is unidentified. He may have been related to Pagan (Abraham) of Northout, who was married to Arnold of Merck's sister (see chapter 133). Arnold of Merck himself was Baldwin of Ardres's brother-in-law.

213. Lambert takes up this narrative again in chapter 137.

214. Thierry reigned c. 1141–49.

215. *Neptem suam*. This seems to be a slip of the pen on Lambert's part, since Beatrice was Henry's daughter, not his granddaughter.

216. The reference to Eustace is obscure. Godefroy de Menilglaise (428 n. 107) suggests that Lambert is using the name adjectivally, that is "a Eustace-like" son, and is referring to the etymology of the name he offers in chapter 19.

217. Once again, the text says "his granddaughter."

218. Lambert has already suggested in chapter 50 that the marriage had never been consummated.

219. The psalm reads *curam* (care) not *cogitatum* (thought).

220. See also chapter 25.

221. Lambert has here adapted the words of the psalm to the needs of his story.

222. Horace, *Epistles*, I.4.14.

223. This notion of how the truth became distorted by oral transmission and thus gave rise to myth also appeared among the Greek antiquarians; the point is discussed in Veyne, *Did the Greeks Believe in Their Myths?*

224. On the substitution of monks for canons at Ardres, see chapter 137.

225. Matilda was Beatrice's half-sister, the daughter of Henry of Bourbourg and Beatrice of Aalst (see chapter 122).

226. As Arnold first appears as the count of Guines in a charter of Thierry in 1142, Manasses must have died in 1137 (Heller, 592 n. 1).

227. Roger became castellan around 1150 (Warlop, *Flemish Nobility*, 1/1:219). Winemar I (1074/88–1120) was not directly succeeded by Roger of Courtrai. His sons Siger I (d. 1122) and Winemar II (d. 1135) appear in the records as castellans after his death, as does the husband of his granddaughter Alice, Hugh of Encre, as well as a Henry and Vivian of Munte, who do not seem to be related to the family (Warlop, *Flemish Nobility*, 2/1:828). Since Manasses died in 1137 and Beatrice died in 1142, Lambert seems to have telescoped events, skipping over Arnold's brothers and other intervening castellans.

228. On Geoffrey's parentage, see chapter 25.

229. In one of his labors, Hercules held the world on his shoulders, while Atlas, whose task this normally was, procured the golden apples of the Hesperides for him.

230. Ascra was Hesiod's birthplace; to have a dream there was to make things up. Lambert is therefore defending himself against accusations that he is lying.

231. The law concerning the succession of sisters was only developing at this time. Generally, proximity came to be a deciding factor in France, in which case Giselle as the most proximate survivor had the best claim (and her son through her). See also chapter 144, for a case decided along similar lines. However, the legalities may have been less important in deciding this case than the politics. Arnold had an extensive kinship in Flanders, both through his father's family at Ghent and his wife's family at Saint-Omer. Moreover, Arnold had succeeded de facto in winning the county with Thierry's assent. From the point of view of the count of Flanders, therefore, to reject Arnold at this late stage would have been impolitic.

232. Louis VII (1137–80) of France; this was the second Crusade. Louis actually left in 1147.

233. Arnold appears in various charters of the period. Goël or Gohel appears to be a family surname, as others bear it as well (de la Gorgue-Rosny, *Recherches généalogiques*, 3:1400–1401).

234. See also chapter 142.

235. This Stephen appears in a charter c. 1160 (de la Gorgue-Rosny, *Recherches généalogiques*, 3:1381).

236. "Young woman" = *Iuvenculam*.

237. Lambert provides both a vernacular etymology (*Col* = coal) and a Latin one (*cultura sive colore forme* = the cultivation or color of the ground). Collet (*Notice historique*, 117) suggests that the name meant wild cabbage, *cole* = cabbage, *wide* = wild. The modern name is Coulogne.

238. The separation of the sexes in leprosaria was customary to prevent intercourse among them, since lepers were characterized as sexually insatiable and leprosy was believed to be transmitted by sexual contact. On the western European view of leprosy, see Moore, *Persecuting Society*, 63–64.

239. Theseus and Pirithous began as enemies, when Pirithous stole Theseus's cattle. When he saw Theseus, however, he was so filled with admiration that he surrendered and the two became blood brothers. Theseus went to the underworld with Pirithous (who wanted to carry off Persephone), but they were caught. Hercules rescued Theseus but left Pirithous behind.

240. His father was John I of Petegem and Cysoing (died before 1154); his mother was Petronilla of Avesnes, and was the sister of the bishop of Tournai. Mabel and John II (†1220) had four children (Warlop, *Flemish Nobility*, 2/2:1055–56).

241. Manasses appears in the record as late as 1222 (Heller, 595 n. 2).

242. Baldwin's generosity to Manasses suggests that although the second-born son, he may have been the favorite. Lambert later shows Manasses acting very independently of his brother, although he did Arnold homage for Rorichove on the death of their father.

243. Died c. 1229 (Heller, 595 n. 4).

244. The parson had the right to appoint someone to fill a specified ecclesiastical office and enjoyed a portion of the revenues of the office. As far as the reference to Nestor is concerned, "Nestor was the son of Neleus, a name which through its sound is related to Neleii, the Latin name of Nielles-lez-Ardre, the parish whose church was dedicated to St. Peter" (Godefroy, 430 n. 118).

245. Stevington is in the counties of Essex and Cambridge, Stisted in Essex, Town-Malling in Kent (Heller, 595 nn. 8–10). Bactons and Beigtons are common in central England (see Godefroy, 430 n. 119); Heller, 595 n. 11, suggests Baicton in Oxfordshire.

246. Newington is near Folkestone (Heller, 595 n. 12), so may have come to Emma from her first husband.

247. Lambert here may be referring to minstrels or other people who might popularize his name. For Lambert's attitudes about expenditures to minstrels, see chapter 130.

248. William of Andres, angry that his house, the traditional burial place of the counts of Guines, had been slighted, comments spitefully in his history that the winds blew against the ship and so the body came to Saint-Ingelvert in such a state as to make the bearers ill (*Chronicon*, 811–12).

249. Mary of Boulogne inherited Boulogne through her mother, Matilda of Boulogne. Mary was a nun, but after the death of her last surviving brother William, she was carried off from the convent where she was abbess and married to Matthew of Alsace, who claimed Boulogne through her. She and Matthew had two children, Ida and Matilda (see chapter 93). As a nun, Mary was barred by canon law from marrying, hence the interdict. While Lambert says she retired to Messine, another tradition says she went to Saint-Austreberte of Montreuil. On Mary, see Godefroy, 431 n. 121; also A. L. Poole, *From the Domesday Book to Magna Carta (1087–1216)* (Second ed. Oxford, 1958), 440 n. 2.

250. These virgins and the translation Lambert refers to have not been identified.

251. If Arnold died in 1169, Baldwin cannot have done homage to Thierry, who died in 1168.

252. This alliteration is also found in the Latin. Lambert uses alliteration in many places in the text, most of which do not survive translation.

253. Thomas à Becket was archbishop of Canterbury from 1163 to his murder at Canterbury in 1170. Between 1164 and 1170 he was in exile in France as the result of a dispute with King Henry II (1154–89). (Louis VII of France took Becket's side.) For Becket, see also chapter 87.

254. Between 1157 and 1163, according to William of Andres (Heller, 602 n. 1).

255. The nature of Michael's charge is unclear. He may have been the school-master, although "master" may be a more general title. Lambert bore this title as well.

256. What Lambert means here is not entirely clear; either the roof jutted out considerably over the house, so that when one looked from above one could not see the house, or the house had a cantilevered design, so that when one was looking up, one couldn't see the roof. It also seems possible to me that by *equatam*, which I have translated as "even," Lambert may mean squared off, so that the top part of the frame, above the round part of the building, was squared off to take a regular roof, but that this couldn't be seen.

257. i.e. the Temple.

258. St. Nicholas was the patron of merchants, among many others.

259. *Decet et docet*; Lambert's use of *docet* in this context is unclear.

260. Killing the Hydra was one of the twelve labors of Hercules. Lambert's reference to this particular labor may be because the hydra lived in a swamp, but it may also be that the killing the hydra (with its watery associations) was an apt metaphor for draining a swamp, since containing one of the contributing rivulets might well cause it simply to flow into another course.

261. The word Lambert uses to describe Giles is *literatum*, or "literate man." Literacy was so closely associated with clerical status that a person who could read Latin was often assumed to be a member of the clergy. This does not mean, however, that Giles actually took higher clerical orders that would have required him to take an oath of celibacy. (On the association between literacy and clerical status, see Grundmann, "Literatus-Illiteratus." Giles appears in the record until 1227 (Heller, 597 n. 4).

262. Eustace and Philip of Montgardin signed a charter favoring Clairmarais in 1174 (de la Gorgue-Rosny, *Recherches généalogiques*, 2:1020); presumably Eustace was a son or brother.

263. As far as the Celtic tower is concerned, some manuscripts read *Memerim*, some *turrim Celtim* and some leave the place blank. Godefroy de Menilglaise believes that the latter makes more sense and suggests Celtunium as the original version of Zeltun (433 n. 130).

264. Baldwin of Engoudsent is mentioned as in various charters from 1145 to 1174 (de la Gorgue-Rosny, *Recherches généalogiques*, 2: 514). It is unclear what connection he had with Cayeux. His father was Baldwin the Old of Marquise (de la Gorgue-Rosny, *Recherches généalogiques*, 2:955). Lambert (chapter 110) says that Adeline married the son of Baldwin the Old. Godefroy renders *Caiochum* as "Caieu" and argues that it cannot be Cayeux, because the narrative in chapter 22 makes it appear that Ordres and *Caiochum* are close to each other, and Cayeux is 60 km. from Boulogne (492). I have rendered it Cayeux, wherever it appears, because Lambert does seem to be thinking of the Cayeux family.

265. Godefroy de Menilglaise (501) suggests that *Rumis* (as his text reads) is an error for *Hamis* (Hames) or *Busnis* (Busnes). Radbod has not been identified.

266. Thiembronne is in the Boulonnais. William and Matilda never had children, but William's sister Adeline married Manasses of Guines, who became the lord of Thiembronne (de la Gorgue-Rosny, *Recherches généalogiques*, 3:1414–15).

267. Minerva was the goddess of wisdom.

268. Although the text reads *avertebat*, the context clearly calls for *advertebat*.

269. For this text, see *Histoire littéraire de la France*, 41 vols. (Paris, 1733–), 15:502.

270. See *Histoire littéraire*, 13:114 on this translation. St. Anthony (c. 250–356) was considered to be the "Father of Monks."

271. This would be the *Physics* of Aristotle.

272. This author is unidentified.

273. Solinus was a third-century author of a natural history that was widely read during the Middle Ages.

274. This Simon of Boulogne (Simon li clerc) was probably the Simon who collaborated on the *Roman d'Alexandre*. See *Histoire littéraire*, 7:80; 9:150; 15:501; on the *Roman d'Alexandre*, see also Spiegel, *Romancing the Past*, 100.

275. Perhaps Lambert here means books about music, rather than musical instruments themselves; otherwise, it is difficult to see the connection between this sentence and the previous one.

276. Thales was a philosopher; Lambert probably means Aristides of Miletus, to whom popular poems were attributed. Lambert would have known about them from Ovid (Godefroy, 435 n. 138).

277. Walter is only mentioned by Lambert, and the entries in *Histoire littéraire*, 10:562 and 15:502, refer back to this text. As Stirnemann, "Quelques bibliothèques princières," 37, points out, Baldwin seems to have built his library using largely local talent.

278. Philip of Alsace, count of Flanders (1168–91).

279. See chapter 95.

280. Godefroy de Menilglaise (435 n. 139) and Heller (599 n. 2) think Lambert means Henry of Brabant (lower Lorraine), who married Matilda of Boulogne in 1180. However, Lambert may have conflated Henry in his mind with Baldwin of Hainaut, the brother-in-law of Count Philip of Flanders and the uncle of the heiresses of Boulogne, Ida and Matilda. See also chapters 95 and 154.

281. Ovid, *Met.* 4.428.

282. See chapter 5.

283. Cape Blanc-Nez.

284. The two editors give different readings here. Godefroy de Menilglaise gives, *Ubi cum inter dunas et fluxae soliditatis oras* (Godefroy, 179); Heller's text reads *Ubi cum inter dunas et Sliviace soliditatis oras*. (Heller, 599) There was a church called Saint-Martin of Sclive near Sangatte; the term *sclive* was applied to a place where streams discharge through dunes into the sea.

285. "Waters" = *Thetios*, i.e., the sea; Thetis was a sea-nymph, the mother of Achilles.

286. Sangatte = Sand gate. On the fluctuations of the coastline, see p. 33.

287. "Its affairs" = *negoticii*.

288. These events are presented out of chronological sequence, for Reynold did not become the count of Boulogne until 1192 (see chapter 94).

289. Godefroy (436 n. 143) prefers *drasticis remediis* (drastic remedies); Heller, 600, suggests *chalasticis remediis* (purgative remedies), which is in the Vatican ms.

290. Godeschalk of Saint-Bertin (1163–77); Alger of Capella (after 1166–before 1190); Peter II of Andres (1161–95); Robert of Licques (1163–84).

291. Virgil, *Aeneid*, 5.228.

292. William of la Podenie is otherwise unidentified. La Podenie paid its rents to the castle of Tornehem. William of Colvida appears twice more in the history; he seems to be one of Baldwin's knights, since he leads the forces that repel the people of Merck (chapter 154). He may have been a relative, since Christine's father, Arnold of Merck, built the fortress at Colvida (chapter 68).

293. William of Reims (1176–1202). On his career, see Bur, *La Formation du comté de Champagne*, 408–15; *Gallia christiana*, 9:95–101. William was the son of Thibaud II of Chartres and Champagne (†1152), the brother of Henry the Liberal and Thibaud III of Chartres. Henry and Thibaud married Marie and Eleanor, the daughters of Louis VII of France by Eleanor of Aquitaine, while Louis married their sister Adele of Champagne.

294. St. Thomas was martyred in 1170, but his cult sprang up with astonishing rapidity. This pilgrimage took place in 1178 (Heller, 601).

295. The process of memorizing material was often likened to eating in the Middle Ages, and the stomach was often spoken of as the seat of memory. The person then ruminated upon what had been learned, chewing it over like a cow chewing cud, which, of course, had to be belched up (M. Carruthers, *The Book of Memory* [Cambridge, 1990], 161; 164–65). Since the archbishop is actually eating and physically belching, Lambert is here making a joke.

296. It is possible that I have mistranslated this phrase, but if not, I have no idea what Lambert means. The extant lives of Becket all stress that his parents were respectable people of at least worthy life (the lives single out his mother as particularly pious). Perhaps this represents a tradition that didn't survive or the manuscript tradition is garbled, or it is vaguely possible that the author meant something like *natato* for *nato* (born), that is, "tossed about by reprobates in scandal" referring to Becket's earlier secular career.

297. On Baldwin's knighting, see chapter 75. Another play with words here–the accolade is the blow that cannot be returned, but Baldwin "returns" it with gifts.

298. An untranslatable play on words: "*ut gratiam sancto viro pro gratia non gratis, sed meritorie.*"

299. On December 29, 1170.

300. The great Flemish lords generally pursued a pro-English policy, and many possessed lands and money fiefs in England. On these connections, see Spiegel, *Romancing the Past*, 37–38.

301. The connection here between hunting and sex is not gratuitous. The confluence of the medieval Latin term for hunting (*veneris*) and the Latin goddess of love (Venus), both declined the same way–giving rise to the English term "venery" to mean either hunting or sexual pleasure—and the images of the chase proper to both occupations, as well as the fact that in the Middle Ages hunting and sex were both (in theory) secular pursuits, meant that these two things fell quite naturally together in the mind.

302. I must thank David Townsend, who suggested to me that Lambert is here referring obliquely to Jupiter's well-known taste for boys as well as girls.

303. William of Andres, *Chronicon*, 833, says that 33 of Baldwin's children were present at his funeral, of whom Christine bore nine (one of her ten children died in adolescence).

304. Bohorts (or behourds) were a kind of tournament. In the thirteenth century they were less violent than regular tournaments, since the combatants wore leather armor and did not use metal weapons (Keen, *Chivalry*, 86).

305. Philip of Alsace, count of Flanders (1168–91).

306. On the accolade, *collée*, or *paumé* (the blow that cannot be given back), see Keen, *Chivalry*, 7, 65.

307. The count of Guines is imitating on a small scale the lavish dubbing ceremonies that were becoming common at the end of the twelfth century. At these ceremonies scores of young men might be knighted together. See Keen, *Chivalry*, 69–70.

308. Heller, 604 n. 1, suggests that this is Porphyry's, *De abstinentia*, which Lambert might have known of through Boethius.

309. Both Philip of Montgardin and Eustace of Montgardin appear in a charter of Baldwin II of Guines in 1174 (de la Gorgue-Rosny, *Recherches généalogiques*, 2:1020).

310. This seems to have happened sometime after 1177.

311. "On duty" = *stationarius*, a word with many possible meanings, both classical and medieval (policeman, sacristan), but all of them implying that one was posted to one place.

312. Henry, the young king, the eldest son of Henry II, crowned in 1170, who died in 1183. As Lambert does not name Arnold's nephew, he cannot be identified. The family, however, was numerous and active. See de la Gorgue-Rosny, *Recherches généalogiques*, 1:368–67.

313. Hugh also appears in a charter of 1170 in favor of the abbey of Licques (de la Gorgue-Rosny, *Recherches généalogiques*, 2:1046).

314. On Henry of Campagne, see chapter 40. Henry and Arnold were also loosely related, as Ralph of Fiennes married Adele of Campagne, while his sister married Baldwin of Hames.

315. Matthew of Alsace, the count of Boulogne (†1173). See also chapter 73.

316. Ida married Gerard III of Ghelria (now part of the crown lands of the Netherlands) in 1180 and was widowed in 1183 (Heller, 605 n. 2).

317. Bertulf died in 1186 (Heller, 605 n. 3). The lords of Zeringhen were the counts of Brisgau, an important family (Godefroy, 501).

318. Lambert seems to think that neither union went beyond betrothal; however, he may also be casting Ida in the negative role of the "naughty widow." I am indebted to Katherine Clark for her comments on medieval thinking about widows.

319. Mary, Reynold's first wife, later married John of Vendôme (Godefroy, 439 n. 159).

320. Walter of Châtillon married Hugh's daughter Elizabeth; the later counts of Saint-Pol were descended from him.

321. Philip II Augustus (1180–1223). The cause of dissension was the Vermandois inheritance. See p. 30.

322. *Mercham sive Mercuricium.*

323. The elopement took place in 1191; the marriage was confirmed by Philip Augustus in 1192 (Baldwin, *Philip Augustus*, 201).

324. The lords of Brunembert were linked to the lords of Ardres (see chapter 110). However, how Enguerrand is related to them is unclear. For connections with the counts of Guines, see de la Gorgue-Rosny, *Recherches généalogiques*, 1:277.

325. On these events, see Godefroy, 439 n. 160. The *primicerius* of Metz was named Hugh.

326. Albert of Hirgis was elected in 1186, but confirmed only in 1189 (Heller, 606 n. 4).

327. Philip Augustus; Louis VII.

328. This was the third Crusade. Philip Augustus took the cross in 1188, and went on the crusade in 1190, but abandoned it after the conquest of Acre in 1191. Philip of Alsace died on the crusade. Arnold's captivity, therefore, comes after the crusaders had left, so in 1190 or later.

329. It is not clear who this archbishop of Trier is.

330. Lambert perhaps means Henry of Brabant. See also chapters 82 and 154, where he makes the same error.

331. On translations of classical history into the French vernacular, see Introduction above.

332. The earliest surviving French version of the *Song of Roland* was composed at the beginning of the twelfth century. Roland was Charlemagne's nephew; Oliver was Roland's best friend. Other twelfth-century works further developed the Charlemagne mythology, such as the *Pilgrimage of Charlemagne* and the *Coronation of Louis*.

333. With the publication of Geoffrey of Monmouth's Latin *History of the Kings of Britain*, King Arthur became an enormously popular hero. Geoffrey's work was translated into French by Wace (*Brut*), while Chrétien de Troyes (second half of the twelfth century) set his vernacular romances at Arthur's court. To the Arthurian material also belong the poems about the search for the Grail.

334. On the crusade texts, see p. 206 n. 157.

335. See also chapter 6.

336. The story of Tristan was extant in a number of versions by the end of the twelfth century; both Thomas and Béroul composed French verse narratives.

337. Robert de Boron wrote a *Merlin* in French verse as part of his Grail cycle around the turn of the thirteenth century; it is unlikely that Lambert knew Geoffrey of Monmouth's Latin *Vita Merlini*. On these texts, see W. P. Gerritson and A. G. van Melle, *A Dictionary of Medieval Heroes*, trans. T. Guest (Woodbridge, 1998), 180–81.

338. The text says *Merculfus*, but the only possibility I've been able to find for this character is Morolf/Marculf. This character figures in a German vernacular text, *Salman und Morolf*, probably circulating by the late twelfth century. There was also a Latin satiric dialogue between Solomon and a peasant of that name. See D. Beecher, *The Dialogue of Solomon and Marcolphus* (Ottawa, 1995): 59–73, 86–90 for the history of the various Solomon and Marculf texts and, for a synopsis of the epic, Gerritson, *A Dictionary of Medieval Heroes*, 243–44.

339. *Candentis-vel Campestris-Avene*. Hugh Candavène (†1205); while the name implies white-blond hair, Candavène is also a place name. On this engagement, see also chapter 149.

340. From this point to the end of chapter 146, Walter of Le Clud is the putative narrator. The narrative thus returns to the mid-eleventh century.

341. Frameric (c. 975–1004). Although Lambert places the beginnings of Ardres in the late tenth century by naming Frameric as the bishop, other elements of the story suggest the mid-eleventh century. Lambert says that the count of Guines at the time this story takes place was Eustace, who ruled in the mid-eleventh century.

342. On allodial property, see p. 19.

343. Cf. Mt. 25:2–13.

344. The specifics of this story are unlikely to be true. Warlop points out that female vassalage was unusual in Flanders in the eleventh century. However, the donation of allodial property to the church was typical of this period, when many individuals, not all of them noble, but many of them women, donated their lands in free alms to religious institutions. The purpose of such donations, quite apart from any religious benefits the donors might expect, was, as Lambert suggests, to shield these possessions from more powerful individuals by bringing them under the protection of the church. On this issue, see Warlop, *Flemish Nobility*, 1/1:37–39.

345. *Belinghem iuxta Witsandum*: this may also be Hervelinghem (Godefroy, 490).

346. As Walter is still narrating, "us" means the people of Ardres.

347. From *Krom* (backwards) and *rok* (tunic) in Flemish (Godefroy, 441 n. 168).

348. Arnold II of Guines, whose mother was Christine of Ardres.

349. Helbeodeshen; may also be Beussent (Godefroy, 496). Eilbod was Adele's second husband (see chapter 103).

350. Other sources do not mention episcopal "peers."

351. *Deferret*, which means to bring or bear, but here seems to mean something like wear.

352. Lambert here refutes a tale that suggests that Herred was not really noble, because peasants insist on wearing their clothing out and turn garments inside out to get more wear out of them. Nobles were expected to "live nobly," which meant spending their money freely. As an alternative to this tale of miserliness, Lambert presents a tale that shows Herred's noble credentials (his participation in the noble sport of hunting).

353. Godefroy de Menilglaise (475) defines *cheolare*, which I have translated as loitering, as playing with a ball and Heller (609 n. 6) follows him in this. However, Poulet, *Au Contact du picard et flamand*, 425, notes that *chòler* is a dialect word from the region meaning variously, to do dirty work, to strike, to heckle, or to loiter, that is to hang about doing something disreputable, and that meaning seems more in line with the other expressions Lambert uses here.

354. What Lambert has in mind is not clear. He may be referring to the vernacular *erde* (earth), in which case the people are simply saying that they should go to that piece of land. The French translator of the sixteenth century seems to understand the text this way (Godefroy, 228).

355. *Ardea* = heron. Ovid mentions the legend that the heron was born from the ashes of Ardea in *Metamorphoses*, 14.573; Virgil mentions the city in *Aeneid*, 7.411.

356. See chapter 153 for the Blauwvoets.

357. Lambert's contemporaries were full of derogatory remarks about the lies

of the poets. The commonplace was an old one by the beginning of the thirteenth century, but it was enjoying a new life among vernacular writers (see Spiegel, *Romancing the Past*, 55–69).

358. Eustace II (1049–93). However, Heller, 610, n. 2, suggests that the donor may actually have been Eustace III, Ida's son.

359. Le Waast was founded in 1098.

360. A variant of the earlier story, except that it emphasizes Herred's peasant origins by making him plough his fields himself.

361. The edited text reads, *haud immerito blasphemantes* (although all the manuscripts read *aut immerito blasphemantes*; see Heller, 610, apparatus). However, clearly Lambert cannot have meant *haud*, "not at all."

362. Fiennes is in the Boulonnais. Since Eustace I of Fiennes went on the first Crusade, this confirms that the events Lambert is narrating belong to the second half of the eleventh century, not the late tenth. Eustace's son Conon appears in the record as the lord of Fiennes between 1099 and 1112. Eustace II "the Old" appears to be the son of Conon, not of Eustace I. On the house of Fiennes, see de la Gorgue-Rosny, *Recherches généalogiques*, 2:561.

363. Alembon is in Guines. *Putepelisse* = stinking pelt.

364. Lambert is our only source for Eilbod.

365. Folcuin was archbishop of Thérouanne between 817 and 855.

366. In other words, Eilbod created a polder. On such early poldering, see Nicholas, *Medieval Flanders*, 8.

367. For Philip, see chapter 113.

368. Saint-Valery in Vimeu. A Reynold of Saint-Valery went on the first Crusade (de la Gorgue-Rosny, *Recherches généalogiques*, 3:1350).

369. Lambert (chapter 147) mentions a young man named Raulin, who was one of Arnold II of Guines's companions. It is possible that this is the same man, who would be a contemporary of Walter of Le Clud.

370. Walter was thus doubly related to the family. Arnold I of Ardres was his great-great-grandfather on his mother's side, and his great-grandfather on his father's side. (Walter's father was Baldwin of Ardres; see chapter 134.)

371. Perhaps after visiting his sons in England? See chapter 114.

372. Cappelhove no longer exists. However, a church of St. Quentin existed on the road between Nortkerque and Ardres in the nineteenth century (Godefroy, 492). Place names beginning with "Kapelle" represent villages reclaimed by monastic poldering (Nicholas, *Medieval Flanders*, 98), while the *hove* suffix meant a great estate (*Medieval Flanders*, 10).

373. Norhout or Northout, now a farm called Nortou (Godefroy, 499); "parents'" is literally "fathers'" (*patrum*).

374. *Dicke* = thick; *buch* = wood.

375. That is, the husbands and/or children of Adele's daughters by Herred. See chapter 102.

376. Statius, *Thebais*, 3.348.

377. Eustace II.

378. On Eustace, Godfrey, and Baldwin, see chapter 31.

379. The Carolingian office of seneschal was one of the offices which, in the

eleventh and twelfth centuries, was normally held by an important noble (see Fossier, *Picardie*, 536, 49). The office of bailiff appeared in the second half of the twelfth century (so Lambert is here being anachronistic). Philip of Alsace and Baldwin VIII of Flanders appointed bailiffs to handle certain legal matters as well as other functions in lieu of the count. Unlike noble officials, bailiffs were salaried and served at the count's pleasure (Nicholas, *Medieval Flanders*, 87–88). Bailiffs eventually became the most important comital officials (ibid., 84).

380. See chapter 128 for the story of the oven dues and the bear.

381. Marquise is in the Boulonnais.

382. In chapter 79 Lambert says that Adeline married Baldwin the Old's son, Baldwin of Engoudsent.

383. These places are in the Boulonnais.

384. That is, Baldwin I of Guines.

385. Saint-Omer was generally the model for free towns in southern Flanders. On Saint-Omer's organization, see Nicholas, *Medieval Flanders*, 36–37; 47; 117–18. However, since Lambert narrates these events before he tells of the founding of the church of Ardres in 1069, and since the charter of Saint-Omer was issued in 1127, Lambert is probably being anachronistic here about the rights that might have been granted to the settlement; he is very likely wrong about when Ardres first became a chartered town. The charter of Saint-Omer has been translated in D. Herlihy, *Medieval Culture and Society* (New York, 1968), 180–84.

386. Heller, 614 n. 9, notes that no privileges are still extant in which Arnold bears the name advocate. On the advocacy of Saint-Bertin, also see chapter 4.

387. Eustace of Boulogne was among the important nobles in the army of William the Conqueror in 1066; lesser nobles like Arnold would have fought as part of his entourage.

388. Domesday Book records Arnold as holding Duxford and Trumpington of Eustace of Boulogne and Adalulf of Merck as holding Holland, Ilford and Tollehaut (Heller, 615 n. 1.). However, by the late twelfth century, these holdings may well have been held directly of the king. The houses of Merck, Ardres, and Guines had fused by the time Lambert was writing, which may explain the discrepancy between his narrative and the other evidence. Or Lambert, who didn't care that much about facts, might have made a mistake.

389. Lit. "places overseas." I have translated this as "Outremer," because Anselm probably went on the first Crusade.

390. See chapter 105, for an earlier mention of Philip.

391. Nestor and Ulysses were the classical types of wise advice and wiliness. Arnold, unlike Ulysses, has no Penelope, because his wife has died.

392. In comparing Arnold to Paris (Alexander in the Latin) Lambert is referring to the judgment of Paris, in which Paris awarded the prize for beauty to Venus and received Helen of Troy in return, starting the Trojan War.

393. On Absalom's beauty, see 2 Sam. 14:25.

394. Triptolemus was the king of Eleusis and the inventor of agriculture, while Achilles was the most warlike of the Greek heroes; in other words, Arnold is a man of war and not of peace.

395. See 1 Kg. 3 for Solomon's wisdom.

396. Perhaps around 1070. The counts of Saint-Pol did homage to the counts of Boulogne (Nicholas, *Medieval Flanders*, 42), so Clemence would have required her lord's permission to marry.

397. Geoffrey, count of Aumale, died in 1190 (Heller, 615 n. 7.) Baldwin (†1211), the son of Robert V of Béthune (†1191), married Avice, the heiress of Aumale (Warlop, *Flemish Nobility*, 2/1:665–66). The Anonymous of Béthune, *Histoire des ducs de Normandie*, 88 reports this marriage, as well as Avice's previous two marriages, without, however, putting in the detail that she was impregnated before the marriage. Although I have rearranged the syntax of this sentence, in the original Latin the pregnancy is mentioned before the marriage.

398. In the Vulgate. In the Revised Standard version, this line appears in Sir. 3:18.

399. Honor in this case could be either his personal honor or his "honor," that is, the office entrusted to him, more likely the latter in this case.

400. Lambert's meaning in this sentence is not entirely clear to me. He may intend to imply that Arnold behaved in a way that would not embarrass him later in church, although a different conclusion might be drawn, which is that Arnold feels driven to make amends in church for his conduct elsewhere.

401. Drogo, bishop of Thérouanne (c. 1030–78).

402. See chapter 105.

403. Blessed Mary of Saint-Omer, founded in 820, by a schism within the monastery of Saint-Bertin (*Atlas de la France de l'an mil*, ed. M. Parisse [Paris, 1994], 18).

404. "Figures around the hall" = *subsilles*. The meaning of this word is unclear. Lewis and Short, *A Latin Lexicon*, 1782 cites Paul the Deacon's commentary on Festus, which defines these as metal plates necessary for sacrifices. Du Cange, who mentions only this passage of Lambert, suggests that these are sheets with figures on them used in religious ceremonies (Godefroy, 486). Godefroy proposes that these are figures around the cemetery at Hondschote, but he thinks it more likely that the copyist made an error. I wonder whether these aren't wall shrines; the church would then be entitled to collect the offerings.

405. This whole passage, beginning with "So then Arnold rejoiced richly in the Lord," is all one sentence in the Latin, and mostly uses the language of charters.

406. On the replacement of the canons by monks at Ardres, see chapter 137.

407. Sainte-Colombe in Blendecques, near Saint-Omer, founded 1182 (Godefroy, 445 n. 190).

408. On the mill, see chapters 104 and 109.

409. Lambert has made an error, since Robert of Frisia did not become count of Flanders until 1071; in the charter below, Lambert makes 1069 the second indiction, rather than the 7th/8th indiction. Godefroy de Menilglaise suggests 1073 as the date of foundation, and that the copyist read "ii" for "ix" (Godefroy, 445–46 n. 191). The king of France is Philip I (1060–1108).

410. Presumably wax offered instead of money, as a votive offering, or in penance.

411. Gerald, the dean, appears in other charters between the years 1065 and 1075 (*Gallia christiana*, 10:1578). A. Miraeus, *Opera diplomatica*, ed. J. F. Foppens, 4 vols.

(Louvain-Brussels, 1723–48), 1:158, prints this charter drawn from Lambert's history. The dating error raises questions about the authenticity of the charter.

412. Walter may not only be commenting on the difficulty of translation here, but also advancing a contemporary notion that material aimed at the clergy needed to be simplified for lay consumption. Peter of Blois makes a similar comment about the relationship between a vernacular sermon he wrote and the Latin translation of it he was requested to provide. See Richter, "Socio-linguistic Approach," 76. For similar comments by Walter, see chapter 137.

413. These privileges are not extant (Heller, 618 n. 3).

414. Herbert (1065–81).

415. Pancras, Nereus, and Achilleus shared a saint's day, May 12. On these saints, see D. H. Farmer, *The Oxford Dictionary of the Saints* (corrected ed., Oxford, 1983), 290, 311.

416. Saint-Paul at Saint-Pol. There is just a hint in this passage that Arnold, in his capacity as the husband of the countess of Saint-Pol, removed materials from the church there against the will of the clergy.

417. In 1078.

418. Count Robert II (1093–1111). This must have happened in 1093 or early 1094, as Arnold died in 1094.

419. Godefroy de Menilglaise (446–47 n. 195) points out that this privilege was a significant one in Flanders, where the legislation severely punished the harboring of outlaws. It also represents the granting of a quasi-comital right to the lords of Ardres.

420. Abbot John I of Ypres (1081–95).

421. Although Lambert assumes that all the land naturally went to Arnold II, it was still common in the late eleventh century to dole out discrete properties among the children of the family, as had happened in England when William the Conqueror died.

422. Baldwin II of Aalst (1082–97), who died on the first Crusade (Warlop, *Flemish Nobility*, 2/1:591).

423. Lambert says his wife was named Matilda, but other sources say Reinewif. Baldwin and Ivan were probably her sons, not Matilda's. See Warlop, *Flemish Nobility*, 2/1:591.

424. Warlop, *Flemish Nobility*, 2/1:592, suggests that Ingelbert of Petegem was Baldwin's brother-in-law, rather than his brother.

425. Arnold may have been called the Old to distinguish him from his son, and he does appear in the record as "Arnoldus Senior" (Heller, 620 n. 1), but if Lambert is correct that he participated in the Norman Conquest in 1066 and died in 1139, he must have been in his nineties at the time of his death and was thus strikingly old as well.

426. Baldwin III of Aalst (1097–1127) and Ivan of Aalst (1127–45). On Ivan's usurpation of Aalst, see Introduction above.

427. Theinard of Bourbourg (1091–1127).

428. Weert-Saint-Georges = Wercia; the identification is tentative (Godefroy, 504); Meinthia/Meninthia is unidentified.

429. See chapter 42.

430. Galbert of Bruges (*De multro Caroli*, ed. Rider, 37ff.; *Murder of Charles*, 120ff.) makes it clear that Theinard did not help the count because he was being attacked himself. Galbert adds that two of Theinard's sons, Henry's brothers Walter and Gilbert, were also killed at Bruges.

431. Henry died in 1168.

432. Torthonium (Corthonium?—see Godefroy, 502) = Kortenhoek. In 1166, Ivan's son Thierry (1144–66) had died without heirs, and Count Philip reclaimed Aalst.

433. Duras is a castle near Saint-Trond; Juliana came from the family of the Counts of Loon (Warlop, *Flemish Nobility*, 2/1:703). It is not clear, however, that Juliana ever bore the title of countess. As her mother had the same name, Godefroy de Menilglaise (448–49 n. 283) suggests that perhaps Baldwin married the widowed mother.

434. Elizabeth of Béthune (also called Clemence) died after 1178. Her father was Robert V of Béthune (1145–91). See Warlop, *Flemish Nobility*, 2/1:666–67.

435. In 1164, before his brother Baldwin.

436. Ralph died before he could be consecrated, in 1174.

437. Walter of Bourbourg (died c. 1190) married Matilda of Béthune, who after his death may have married Baldwin III of Comines (see Warlop, *Flemish Nobility*, 2/1:668, 670, 702).

438. Henry II (†1194).

439. On the castellans of Bourbourg, see Warlop, *Flemish Nobility*, 2/1:699–704.

440. Baldwin III of Bailleul (1176–1201), castellan of Ypres and Bailleul (see Warlop, *Flemish Nobility*, 2/1:639).

441. Another one of Lambert's untranslatable plays on words. The Latin reads "rapta et illecta, pocius electa." *Rapta* can mean both "raped" and "seized," hence the play on *illecta/electa*, "seduced"/"elected."

442. Lambert actually says "abbot" rather than "abbess."

443. This place has not been identified.

444. Stephen II of Seninghem (c. 1146/7–c. 1191). They had five children, Elenard, John, Stephen III, Gilbert, and Beatrice (Warlop, *Flemish Nobility*, 2/2:1133).

445. Concerning Beatrice's property, see also chapter 154.

446. The Latin uses the first-person singular here.

447. Gertrude of Aalst (d. 1138). On this marriage, see Introduction above.

448. Vulendica = Vulendick. Vulendick does not currently exist. Godefroy speculates that it was reclaimed by the sea, as was part of Gaternesse (503).

449. This story depends on an untranslatable pun. The peasant has asked for a horse, *equus*, and has been hung on a gibbet, *equuleus*. (*Equuleus* can also mean a colt or young horse.) This story probably comes from a French vernacular oral tradition, for the word *cheval* means both a horse and a gibbet (but also a torture rack). Lambert is able to approximate the French pun, but not to reproduce it fully in Latin. It is unclear from the Latin whether the rogue is actually killed or just tortured, but the French translator (Godefroy, 288) thought he had been executed.

450. For their earlier demands, see chapter 107.

451. Another play on words: *ardentes Ardenses*.

452. War hedgehogs were great beams studded with spikes, which would impale an attacker who fell into the ditch.

453. The confirmation of this grant, dated 1117, is still extant in the cartulary of Saint-Bertin (Heller, 623 n. 1).

454. Just as every great house in Lambert's narrative is likened to the labyrinth of Knossos, so the skillful architect is likened to Daedalus, the builder of the labyrinth.

455. A play on words: "solium solio longe a solo."

456. The French translator says this alcove was for the children after they had been nursed (Godefroy, 298), but it seems more likely to have been the place where toddlers and other very young children, weaned (*ablactatos*) but not independent, slept; their elder siblings slept on the next floor.

457. *Confricate*, which literally can mean rubbed or ground up.

458. "Solariorum," which can also mean terraces or galleries; related to the archaic English term "sollar."

459. Heller (625 n. 3) suggests "violated" as one reading for *apostata* (which I have translated "repudiated"). My sense of the meaning of this passage is that the man had promised to marry Eremberg and had sex with her; therefore other men were uninterested in marrying her.

460. The syntax of the single long sentence here presented as a paragraph is unusually tortured, and I have taken more than the usual liberties with it. To note only one of the difficulties, Gertrude's name appears at the beginning of the sentence, but her actions only appear in the clause at the end, the rest of the material being enclosed in that clause.

461. In all likelihood, these peasants paid to have themselves donated to the church, which was a step toward fuller freedom for them. On this strategy, see Warlop, *Flemish Nobility*, 1/1:248–52.

Lambert's narrative also shines a light on regional differences of custom and practice. While it is clear from Lambert's narrative that serfdom was in decline in Guines, as it was generally in adjacent Picardy and maritime Flanders, in the part of Flanders the counts held of the emperor and the lands that bordered on it, serfdom was still common. Serfdom was so entrenched in Aalst, Gertrude's home, that at the end of the Middle Ages, all the peasants were still technically considered serfs (Nicholas, *Medieval Flanders*, 106). While Lambert sees Gertrude's behavior as abusive (and also manages to blame the "foreigner" for the existence of serfdom in Ardres), from Gertrude's perspective it must have seemed simply that she was exercising her rights over her serfs.

462. The Council of Clermont, at which the first Crusade was preached, actually took place in 1095; however, the chronicler Alberic of Trois-Fontaines also gives the same date (Heller, 626, n. 1).

463. Lambert is incorrect about Philip I's participation. Philip was excommunicated at the time and was not permitted to go.

464. This information is most like that contained in the *Chanson d'Antioch* (Heller, 626 n. 4), perhaps Lambert's source.

465. Lambert is probably thinking of Ademar of Montueil, the bishop of Puy, but Ademar died before the capture of Jerusalem, and no source shows any relation-

ship between Ademar and Arnold (Heller, 626 n. 5). However, by the help he mentions here, he may mean that Ademar helped Arnold get his relic of the Holy Lance, mentioned slightly below.

466. The Holy Lance was "discovered" during the siege of Antioch. Not all the crusaders accepted its authenticity.

467. Although the patron saint of England, St. George, whose cult was very old, was widely venerated. As a warrior-saint, he was particularly popular with the military class.

468. On crusade epics, see p. 206 n. 157. The extant versions of the *Song of Antioch*, in fact, do not mention Arnold of Ardres (Godefroy, 451 n. 231 *bis*).

469. Godefroy (503) suggests the Varneselia (Voormezele, near Ypres) should be read Veineselia (Vinnezeele), as the text specifies that the site is near Harselia (Herzele) (495) and there is no Franco in the family of Voormezele. Vinnezeele and Herzele are not too far from Aalst, so Gertrude's connections may have played a role.

470. Elembert of Coulogne/Colvida and his family participated in the foundation of Andres in 1084. He became the viscount of Merck by marriage (de la Gorgue-Rosny, *Recherches généalogiques*, 2:947–48).

471. Pagan was a nickname for Elembert II, who succeeded his father (de la Gorgue-Rosny, *Recherches généalogiques*, 2:948); see also Heller, 628 n. 1.

472. The text says "count."

473. The term Lambert uses to describe Baldwin is *hascarus*. *Hascarium* or *harmiscarium* meant a humiliating punishment in medieval Latin. The term, however, seems to have been obscure to the French translator, who translated it as a name, Baldwin Hascard (Godefroy, 316).

474. Around 1137.

475. Petronilla's identity is mysterious, as is her relationship to Thierry. All of Thierry's known legitimate offspring and their children can be accounted for. However, the name Petronilla does appear among the children of Thierry's siblings, and Godefroy de Menilglaise (452–53) thought that this Petronilla may have come from one of these families. Likewise, her place of origin has not been identified, although there are also several possibilities in the regions where Thierry's siblings married. Warlop, *Flemish Nobility*, 2/1:781–82 identifies the place as Bouchain, near Valenciennes, which was ruled by the lords of Ribemont-Bouchain, who were the castellans of Valenciennes and the counts of Ostrevent.

476. See also chapter 105.

477. That is, a youth because he was not married.

478. That is, the brother of Baldwin II of Guines. William later married Flandrine, the daughter of Robert I, count of Amiens.

479. Herchem no longer exists, but was probably near Nielles-lez-Ardre.

480. This Master Lambert seems to be our author.

481. Duby, *The Knight, the Lady, and the Priest*, 274 suggests that Petronilla had not yet reached puberty based on this part of Lambert's description. However, the rest of the story makes no sense if she is not yet nubile. Lambert, instead, presents her as simple-minded.

482. This is the same story that is told very briefly in chapter 54.

483. The play on words here is untranslatable. The daggers are called *misericor-*

diis in Latin, or mercies, because they were used to finish off the mortally wounded quickly.

484. Jacob, "Le Meurtre du seigneur," points out several features of this narrative that are formulaic: that Arnold's vices are the cause of his death (251), that the murder occurs as the result of a conspiracy (253), that Arnold's throat is cut like a sacrificial victim (255) and thus that the murder has a magical and ritual aspect. It also takes place on the feast of the Holy Innocents, when Herod's men slaughtered children in an attempt to kill Jesus.

485. See also chapter 54.

486. See also chapter 58.

487. Lambert's insistence on the free nature of the gift may be particularly marked because there were questions later on about whether it truly was a gift. See chapter 139.

488. In the Middle Ages, people were less likely to memorize word for word than to memorize the gist of what they read, although both types of memory were known. On this question, see Carruthers, *The Book of Memory*, 86–89. However, Walter here reverses the process; he recollects the words themselves to get at their meaning.

489. The text reads, "*B.*"

490. Heller, 631 n. 2 suggests that the expression "my brother-in-law" (the text actually reads "our") has been inserted by Walter into an otherwise authentic document.

491. Lambert's version of this charter has been published in Duchesne, *Preuves*, 175; *Gallia christiana*, 10, *instrumenta*, 403; Miraeus, *Opera diplomatica*, 1:179; and *Annales Praemonstratensiana*, 1:187, but to my knowledge, the original charter does not exist. Given the elaborate game that Lambert plays in Walter's comments following the charter, in which Walter purports to have given the contents of the charter in the vernacular and apologizes for the inaccuracies involved, the historical status of this charter is unclear.

492. For similar comments, see chapter 116.

493. Archbishop Samson (1140–61).

494. Philip and Matthew were Thierry's sons, the future counts of Flanders and Boulogne, respectively.

495. See chapters 60 and 61.

496. The tax paid when a noble man or woman received inheritance of a dependent tenure.

497. This state of indebtedness was increasingly common for members of the nobility in the second half of the twelfth century. See Spiegel, *Romancing the Past*, 26–27 for the Flemish nobility; Georges Duby, *Rural Economy and Country Life in the Medieval West*, trans. Cynthia Postan (Columbia, S.C.: University of South Carolina, 1968), 233–36 for the general picture.

498. Caradoc succeeded Thierry in 1149 and died before 1166, when Alger appears in a charter of Milo of Thérouanne as the abbot of Capella (*Gallia christiana*, 10:1585).

499. See chapters 135 and 135; Arnold died excommunicate.

500. Baldwin Wallameth appears as a witness to the charter Lambert records in chapter 137. Heller, 633 gives the name as Wallaviectus, as it appears in some mss.

501. Louis left in 1147.

502. See also chapter 65.

503. In the next century, impersonation of this type was tried on a larger scale in Flanders, when Bertrand de Rains appeared impersonating Baldwin IX of Flanders (who had died a prisoner of the Bulgarians) and became the tool of those wishing to oust Countess Joan, his daughter. Bertrand similarly appeared as a pilgrim and initially denied being Baldwin. However, none of the people who had known Baldwin IX accepted Bertrand (see Nicholas, *Medieval Flanders*, 155). For several later cases of this type of impersonation see N. Davis, *The Return of Martin Guerre* (Cambridge, Mass., 1983), 40–41.

504. *Sibilam, Cibelem, sive Cebiliam.*

505. Thierry returned to Flanders in 1149.

506. "Pay the relief" = *relevare*, that is, to pay the relief or inheritance tax that an heir had to pay upon taking possession of a dependent tenure.

507. Baldwin's mother, Agnes of Ardres, was Adeline's older sister. See chapter 132 for Agnes's marriage to Franco of Vinnezeele and Harzeele.

508. A similar rationale was used in deciding the case between Arnold of Ghent and Geoffrey of Semur (see chapter 63).

509. When knighthood became a mark of nobility, many nobles of the later twelfth century and afterward referred to themselves and were referred to from time to time simply as knights. See Duby, *Chivalrous Society*, 76–78.

510. This happened in 1149 (see *Gallia christiana*, 10:1584–85).

511. The manuscripts call the prior of Ardres Baldwin, but clearly Boldekin is meant.

512. Lucan, *Pharsalia*, I.281 See also chapter 29.

513. Since Baldwin of Hondschote was married to Matilda of Guines, the sister of Count Baldwin II of Guines, Arnold of Colvida may have forced this deal to benefit an ally.

514. Walter's narrative ends here.

515. Melibœus is the name of a shepherd in Virgil's *Eclogues*. Ganshof, "Lambert d'Ardres," 230–31, suggests that Lambert describes his work in this way because in the seventh Eclogue, Melibœus is the narrator who describes a poetic battle between two others, and includes their poems in his own text. Ganshof argues that Lambert is here describing the manner in which he has inserted Walter of le Clud's narrative in his own.

516. Lambert tells this story in ambiguous terms, so that it is not entirely clear whether Mark's death was accident or murder. Lambert does not follow this matter up or say what happened to William Pragot. One possibility was that the arrow was actually aimed at Manasses, who invaded the marsh of Ardres and angered many of the local inhabitants, although this seems to have happened later on (see chapter 151).

517. These popes are Alexander III (1159–81), Lucius III (1181–85), and Clement III (1188–91). The case therefore was under consideration for at least ten years.

518. Hugh IV, dean of Cambrai, appears in acts as late as 1189. Adam, his successor, first appears in 1192. John II was the dean of Arras, and appears in acts around 1190 (Godefroy, 455–56 n. 233).

519. See chapter 96.

520. Beatrice's mother was the sister of William of Béthune and the others; thus her maternal uncles gave their consent to this alliance.

521. Henry of Bailleul was another relative by marriage. Beatrice's aunt Mabel had married Henry's brother Baldwin III, castellan of Ypres (see Warlop, *Flemish Nobility*, 2/1:639–40). Henry was perhaps the "justiciar" of Ypres, so perhaps in this case he represented his brother.

522. Lambert was bishop of Thérouanne between 1191 and 1207. The ecclesiastical consent which Lambert so carefully mentions was necessary because Arnold had been excommunicated (see below).

523. Once again, the above paragraph is one long sentence in the Latin.

524. Contemporary liturgical books do have liturgies for blessing a marriage bed, but they differ from each other and from the formulae used here (Godefroy, 457 n. 240).

525. Lambert puns on Beatrice's name by calling her blessed, *beata Beatrix*.

526. Baldwin IX of Flanders (1195–1206).

527. William V (1191–1246).

528. William of Saint-Omer was one of the few Flemish lords who had joined Philip (Nicholas, *Medieval Flanders*, 75; Spiegel, *Romancing the Past*, 39–40).

529. Reynold of Boulogne was in this period briefly on the Flemish side.

530. Baldwin IX had entered a treaty in 1196 with John of England, who was acting on his brother Richard's behalf.

531. In 1191.

532. For the connection between Bourbourg and Aalst, see chapter 122.

533. Another play on words: "*domina inter* beata beat*issima* Beat*rix*."

534. The identification of Mentque is uncertain (Godefroy, 458 n. 252).

535. Eustace of Fiennes was Manasses's uncle, having married Manasses's aunt Margaret, and Ralph was therefore his first cousin.

536. This remark seems to date these events to 1196–97, when there was a severe famine in Flanders. The 1195 and 1196 harvests were inadequate and the price of wheat rose to ten times the normal amount. The famine ended with the good harvest of 1197 (Nicholas, *Medieval Flanders*, 102, 108). If this is correct, Lambert has the events out of order here.

537. "Clearers" = *deuperarii*, which may be a variant spelling for *deoperarii*. Niermeyer, 320 gives "uncover" as a meaning for *deoperire*. Many of the terms in this passage are technical terms whose meanings are not known exactly. See Godefroy, 459–60 n. 255.

538. Matilda/Theresia married Philip in 1183 and died in 1218. Count Ferrand of Flanders (1212–33) was her nephew.

539. The Blauwvoets were a clan, descendants of Blauwvoet, opposed by the Ingrekins, who took their name from Sigebert Ingheryck. Walter of Hondschote belonged to the Blauwvoet party, which sided against Matilda of Portugal, while the Ingrekins and the castellan of Saint-Omer supported her (see Nicholas, *Medieval Flanders*, 74). Traditionally this struggle has been viewed as a class struggle between farmers and nobles, but both parties had noble adherents. The Blauwvoets challenged comital authority in general, not only Matilda's, and continued to be active until 1227 (see Warlop, *Flemish Nobility*, 1/1:261–63).

540. June 24th.

541. Eustace the Monk later became the hero of an outlaw romance; on this subject and on Eustace's factual history, see M. Keen, "The Romance of Eustace the Monk" in *Outlaws of Medieval Legend* (revised paperback ed. London and New York, 1987): 53–63; for a translation of the romance, see *Two Medieval Outlaws: The Romance of Eustace the Monk and Fouke Fitz Waryn*, trans. G. S. Burgess (Rochester, N.Y., 1997). These events probably took place early in 1203, when Eustace became Reynold's seneschal, but before Countess Mary of Flanders left to follow her husband on crusade.

542. The Latin is ambiguous here; it is possible that Lambert means that Mary had already gone to the Holy Land; however, if that had been the case, Arnold would not have been acting on Mary's behalf, but on that of Philip of Nemours and the other regents.

543. Probably Henry, duke of Brabant. Lambert similarly confuses matters in chapters 82 and 95.

544. Beatrice, the beguine and lay director of St. Mary at Bourbourg. See chapter 122.

545. Daniel of Ghent was a cousin of Baldwin of Guines, since Arnold of Ghent, Baldwin's grandfather, was Daniel's great-great-uncle. He married Adelaide, the heiress of Balinghem, who was the descendent of an illegitimate child of Manasses of Guines (see Godefroy, 463 n. 264).

546. Another play on words: "Arden*ses vero* arden*ti animo.*"

547. The surviving text ends here.

Bibliography

PRIMARY SOURCES

Acta sanctorum ordinis sancti Benedicti. Edited by Jean Mabillon. 6 vols. 1668–1701.
Acta sanctorum quotquot toto orbe coluntur, vel a Catholicis scriptoribus celebrantur. 50 vols. Paris and Rome, 1866–1940. (Hereafter cited as *Acta sanctorum.*)
Andrew of Marchiennes. *Annales Marchianenses.* Edited by Ludwig Conrad Bethmann. In *MGH Scriptores,* 16: 609–17.
———. *Chronicon Marchianense.* Partial edition. Edited by Ernst Sackur in "Reise nach Nordfrankreich." *Neues Archiv* 15 (1890), 455–61.
———. *Continuatio Aquicinctina Sigeberti Gemblacensis.* Edited by Ludwig Conrad Bethmann. In *MGH Scriptores,* 6: 406–38.
———. *Genealogiae Aquicinctinae.* Edited by Oswald Holder-Egger. In *MGH Scriptores,* 14: 619–22.
———. *Historia monasterii Aquicintctini.* Edited by Georg Waitz. In *MGH Scriptores,* 14: 584–92.
———. *Historia succincta de gestis et successione regum Francorum.* Extract. Edited by Georg Waitz. *Monumenta Germaniae historica, Scriptores,* 26: 205–12.
Annales Blandinienses. Edited by Ludwig Conrad Bethmann. In *MGH Scriptores,* 5:20–34.
Les Annales de Saint-Bertin. Edited by Félix Grat, Jeanne Vieillard, and Suzanne Vitte Clémencet. Paris, 1964.
Les Annales de Saint-Bertin et de Saint-Vaast. Edited by Chrétien César Auguste Deshaines. Paris, 1871.
Annales Elnonenses. Edited by Georg Heinrich Pertz. *MGH Scriptores,* 5:11–20.
Annales Floreffienses. Edited by Ludwig Conrad Bethmann. In *MGH Scriptores,* 16: 618–31.
Annales Laubienses, Leodienses et Fossenses. Edited by Georg Heinrich Pertz. In *MGH Scriptores,* 4:9–35.
The Annals of St-Bertin. Translated by Janet Nelson. Manchester, 1991.
"Appendice" (to the *Cartulaire de l'abbaye de Saint-Bertin*). Edited by François Morand. Paris, 1867.
Beecher, Donald, ed. and trans. *The Dialogue of Solomon and Marcolphus.* Ottawa, 1995.
Brunel, Ghislain and Élizabeth Lalou. *Sources d'histoire médiévale IXe-milieu du XIVe siècle: Textes essentiels.* Paris, 1992.
Béthune, Anonymous of. *Chronique des rois de France et ducs de Normandie,* 750–75. In *Recueil des Historiens des Gaules et de la France,* vol. 24, pt. 2. 1904. Reprint ed. Westmead, 1967.

———. *Histoire des ducs de Normandie et des rois d'Angleterre*. Edited by Francisque Michel. Société de l'histoire de France, Publications in octavo, 18. Paris, 1840.

Burgess, Glyn S., trans. *Two Medieval Outlaws: The Romance of Eustace the Monk and Fouke Fitz Waryn*. Rochester, 1997.

Cartulaire de l'abbaye de Saint-Bertin. Edited by Benjamin Edme Charles Guérard. Paris, 1841.

Catalogus episcoporum Morinensis. Edited by A. Wauters in "Courte chronique des évêques de Thérouanne." *Commission d'histoire de Belgique, Compte rendu*, 4th ser., 3 (1876): 90–91.

Chrétien de Troyes. *Arthurian Romances*. Translated by William W. Kibler and Carleton W. Carroll. Harmondsworth, 1991.

———. *Le chevalier au Lion (Yvain)*. Edited by Mario Roques. Paris 1971.

———. *Cligés*. Edited by Wendelin Foerster. Halle, 1921.

Chronica monasterii Watinensis. Edited by Oswald Holder-Egger. In *MGH Scriptores*, 14:161–63.

Chronicon Affligemense. Edited by Ludwig Conrad Bethmann. In *MGH Scriptores*, 9:407–17.

Chronicon Laetiense. Edited by Johann Heller. In *MGH Scriptores*, 14:487–502.

Chronicon sancti Andreae castri Cameracensis (third book only). Edited by Ludwig Conrad Bethmann. In *MGH Scriptores*, 7:526–50.

de Clari, Robert. *The Conquest of Constantinople*. Translated by Edgar Holmes McNeal. Reprint ed. Toronto and Buffalo, 1996.

———. *La Conquête de Constantinople*. 2 vols. Edited by Philippe Lauer. Paris, 1924.

Catalogus episcoporum Morinensis. Edited by Alphonse Wauters in "Courte chronique des évêques de Thérouanne." *Commission d'histoire de Belgique, Comptes rendus* 4th series, 3 (1876): 90–91.

Derolez, Albert, ed. *Lamberti s. Audomari canonici Liber floridus*. Ghent, 1968.

Drogo of Bergues. *Historia translationis sanctae Lewinae, Acta sanctorum*, July, 5:613–17.

———. *Liber miraculorum sancti Winnoci*. Edited by Jean Mabillon. In *Acta sanctorum ordinis sancti Benedicti*, 3/1: 315–27.

———. *Vita sanctae Godelevae*. Edited by Maurice Coens. *Analecta Bollandiana* 44 (1926): 102–37.

Erembald of Saint-Bertin. *Libellus de miraculis sancti Bertini*. (The first book of the miracles with some continuations). Edited by Oswald Holder-Egger. *MGH Scriptores*, 15/1:509–16.

Espinas, Georges. *Le Droit économique et social d'une petite ville artésienne a la fin du moyen-age: Guines*. Volume 4 of *Les origines du capitalism*. Lille and Paris, 1949.

Flodoard. *Annales de Flodoard*. Edited by Philippe Lauer. Paris, 1905.

Folcard. *Miracula s. Bertini*. In *PL* 147: 1097–1140.

———. *Vita sancti Bertini*. In *PL* 147: 1083–98.

Folcuin of Lobbes. *Chartularium*. In *PL* 136: 1183–1278.

———. *Gesta abbatum Lobiensium*. Edited by Georg Heinrich Pertz. *MGH Scriptores*, 4: 52–74.

Fundatio monasterii Aquicinctini. Edited by Georg Waitz. In *MGH Scriptores*, 14: 579–84.

Galbert of Bruges. *De multro, traditione et occisione gloriosi Karoli comitis Flandri- arum*. Edited by Jeffrey Rider. Corpus christianorum, continuatio medievalis, 131. Turnhout, 1994.

———. *The Murder of Charles the Good, Count of Flanders*. Translated by James Bruce Ross. New York, 1967.

Genealogia comitum Buloniensium. Edited by Ludwig Conrad Bethmann. In *MGH Scriptores*, 9: 299–301.

Genealogiae comitum Flandriae, Edited by Ludwig Conrad Bethmann. In *MGH Scriptores*, 9:302–36.

Gesta abbatum Lobiensium (continuatio). Edited by Wilhelm Arndt. In *MGH Scriptores*, 21:307–33.

Gesta episcoporum Cameracensium. Edited by Ludwig Conrad Bethmann. In *MGH Scriptores*, 7: 393–504.

Gesta pontificum abbreviata per canonicum Cameracensium. In *Recueil des historiens des Gaules et de la France*, 13: 534–42.

Gesta pontificum Cameracensium. Edited by Georg Waitz. In *MGH Scriptores*, 7: 393– 504.

Giselbert of Saint-Amand. *Carmen de incendio S. Amandi Elnonensis*. Edited by Ludwig Conrad Bethmann. In *MGH Scriptores*, 11:409–32.

———. *Historia miraculorum S. Amandi, corpore per Galliam deportato*. In *PL* 150: 1435–48.

Gislebert of Mons. *La Chronique de Gislebert de Mons*. Edited by Léon Vanderkindere. 1904. Reprint ed. Brussels, 1950.

Guibert of Nogent. *Autobiographie*. Edited and translated by Edmond-René Labande. Paris, 1981.

———. *Self and Society in Medieval France*. Translated by John F. Benton. Reprint ed. Toronto, 1984.

Herimannus of Tournai. *Liber de restauratione S. Martini Tornacensis*. In *PL* 180: 39– 106.

———. *The Restoration of the Monastery of Saint Martin of Tournai*. Translated by Lynn H. Nelson. Washington, D.C. 1996.

Heriger of Lobbes and Anselm of Liège. *Gesta episcoporum Tungrensium, Traiectensium, et Leodiensium*. Edited by R. Köpke. In *MGH Scriptores*, 7: 134–234.

Herlihy, David. *Medieval Culture and Society*. New York, 1968.

Hildegar. *Vita Pharonis*. Edited by Jean Mabillon. In *Acta sanctorum ordinis sancti Bertini*, 2: 607–25.

Historia monasterii Viconiensis. Edited by Johann Heller. In *MGH Scriptores*, 24:291– 313.

Historiae Tornacenses. Edited by Georg Waitz. In *MGH Scriptores*, 14:327–52.

Historiae Tornacenses. Edited by J.-J. de Smet (as *Chronica Tornacenses*). In *Corpus chronicorum Flandriae/ Recueil des chroniques de Flandre*, 2: 479–563. Brussels, 1841.

Isidore of Seville. *Isidori Hispalensis episcopi Etymologiarum sive originum libri XX*. Edited by Wallace Martin Lindsay. Oxford, 1911.

John of Hauville. *Architrenius*. Edited and translated by Winthrop Wetherbee. Cambridge, 1994.

John of Salisbury. *Entheticus Maior and Minor*. 2 vols. Edited and translated by Jan van Laarhoven. Leiden, 1987.

Lambert of Ardres, *Chronique de Guines et d'Ardre*. Edited by Denis Charles Godefroy de Menilglaise. Paris, 1855.

———. *Lamberti Ardensis historia comitum Ghisnensium*. Edited by Johann Heller. In *MGH Scriptores*, 24: 550–642.

Lambert of Wattrelos. *Annales Cameracenses*. Edited by Georg Heinrich Pertz. In *MGH Scriptores*, 16: 509–54 (Hannover, 1859).

Ludewig, Johann Peter von, ed. *Reliquiae manuscriptorum omnis aevi diplomatum diplomatum ac monvmentorum, ineditorum adhuc*. 12 vols. Frankfort and Leipzig, 1727–43.

Mansi, J. *Sacrorum conciliarum nova et amplissima collectio*, vol. 21. 2nd edition. Venice, 1776.

Map, Walter. *De Nugis curialium*. Edited and translated by Montague Rhodes James, revised by Christopher Nugent Lawrence Brooke and Roger Aubrey Baskerville Mynors. Oxford, 1983.

MGH Scriptores, see *Monumenta Germaniae historica*.

Miracula et translationes S. Bavonis. In *Acta sanctorum*, October, 1:293–303.

Monumenta Germaniae historica inde ab anno Christi quingentesimo usque ad annum millesimum et quingentesimum. Scriptorum. 32 vols. Hannover and Leipzig, 1826–1934. (Cited as *MGH Scriptores*.)

Orderic Vitalis. *The Ecclesiastical History of Orderic Vitalis*. 6 vols. Edited and translated by Margery Chibnall. Oxford, 1969–80.

Patrologiae cursus completus, series Latina. Edited by Jacques-Paul Migne. 221 vols. Paris, 1844–64. Cited as *PL*.

PL, see *Patrologie cursus completus*.

Poncelet, A. "Un Manuscrit hagiographique provenant de l'abbaye d'Hautmont," in *Analecta Bollandiana* 15 (1896): 283–84.

Radulph Glaber. *Rodulfus Glaber Opera*. Edited and translated by John France, Neithard Bulst, and Paul Reynolds. Oxford, 1989.

Recueil des historiens des Gaules et de la France. 24 vols. Paris, 1840–1904.

Sanctae Bertae, Blangiaci abbatissae, translatio et miracula. In *Acta sanctorum*, July, 2:54–60.

Sanctae Eusebiae Hammaticensis translationes et miracula. In *Acta sanctorum*, March, 2:457–61.

Sancti Macharii vita. In *Acta sanctorum*, April, 1:875–77.

Sanctorum Livini et Briccii Gandavum translatio. Edited by Jean Mabillon. In *Acta sanctorum ordinis sancti Benedicti*, 6/1: 65–70.

Scholz, Bernhard Walter, trans. *Carolingian Chronicles: Royal Frankish Annals and Nithard's Histories*. Ann Arbor, 1972.

Sigebert of Gembloux. *Catalogus Sigeberti Gemblacensis monachi de Viris illustribus*. Edited by Robert Witte. Bern and Frankfort, 1974.

Tomellus of Hasnon. *Deeds of the Abbots of Gembloux*. *MGH Scriptores* 8:523–557.**

———. *Historia monasterii Hasnoniensis*. Edited by Oswald Holder-Egger. In *MGH Scriptores*, 14: 149–58.

Versus de abbatibus S. Martini Tornacensis. Edited by Georg Waitz. In *MGH Scriptores*, 13: 384–87.

Villehardouin, Geoffroi de. *La Conquête de Constantinople.* 2 vols. in 1. Edited by Edmond Faral. Paris, 1938–39.

———. *The Conquest of Constantinople.* In *Chronicles of the Crusades.* Translated by trans. by Margaret Renée Bryars Shaw. Harmondsworth, 1963.

Vita Farae. Edited by Jean Mabillon. In *Acta sanctorum ordinis sancti Benedicti*, 2:439–48.

Vita Forananni, abbati Walciodorensis monasterii. In *Acta sanctorum*, April, 3:808–14.

Vita prima Humberti Maricolensis. In *Acta sanctorum*, March 3: 561–7.

Vita sancti Gerardi. Edited by Lothar von Heinemann. In *MGH Scriptores*, 15: 655–73.

Wace. *Maistre Wace's Roman de Rou et des ducs de Normandie.* 2 vols. Edited by Hugh Andreson. Heilbronn, 1877–79.

Walter of Châtillon. *The Alexandreis of Walter of Châtillon: A Twelfth-Century Epic.* Translated by David Townsend. Philadelphia, 1996.

Walter of Thérouanne. *Vita Karoli comitis.* Edited by B. Köpke. In *MGH Scriptores*, 12: 537–61.

———. *Vita domni Iohannis Morinensis episcopi.* Edited by Oswald Holder-Egger. In *MGH Scriptores*, 15/2:1138–50.

William of Andres. *Chronicon Andrensis monasterii.* Edited by Luc d'Achery. In *Spicilegium*, 2: 780–874. Paris, 1723.

SECONDARY SOURCES

Baldwin, John W. *The Government of Philip Augustus: Foundations of French Royal Power in the Middle Ages.* Berkeley, 1986.

Bates, David. *Normandy before 1066.* London, 1982.

Beck, Patrice. See Brunel, Ghislain and Lalou, Elizabeth.

Bezzola, Reto R. *Les Origines et la formation de la littérature courtoise en occident (550–1200).* 3 vols. in 5. Paris, 1958–1967.

Bliese, John R. E. "Rhetoric and Morale: A Study of Battle Orations from the Central Middle Ages." *Journal of Medieval History* 15 (1989): 201–226.

Bloch, Marc. *Feudal Society.* 2 vols. Translated by L. A. Manyon. Chicago, 1961).

Bourdat, Marie-Françoise. "La Chronique de Lambert d'Ardres: Edition critique." In *Positions des thèses soutenues par les élèves de la promotion de 1970 pour obtenir le diplome d'archiviste paleographe*, 41–43. Paris, 1970.

Bréemersch, Pascale. *Ardres: Repertoire numérique détaillé des archives communales déposées E dépôt 38.* Ardres, 1989.

Carruthers, Mary. *The Book of Memory: A Study of Memory in Medieval Culture.* Cambridge, 1990.

Clanchy, M. T. *From Memory to Written Record: England, 1066–1307.* Second ed. Cambridge, Mass., 1992.

Collet, P.-J.-M. *Notice historique sur l'état ancien et modern du Calaisis, de l'Ardresis, et des pays de Bredenarde et de Langle.* 1833. Reprint ed. Paris, 1993.

Conant, Kenneth John. *Carolingian and Romanesque Architecture: 800–1200*. Third ed. Harmondsworth, 1973.

Davis, Natalie. *The Return of Martin Guerre*. Cambridge, Mass., 1983.

Desmarchelier, Michel. "La Maison de Guînes et l'ordre de Citeaux." *Cîteaux* 13 (1961): 217–32.

Dhondt, Jan. *Etudes sur la naissance des principautées territoriales en France (IXe–Xe siècle)*. Bruges, 1948.

———. *Les Origines de la Flandre et de l'Artois*. Arras, 1944.

Duby, Georges. *The Chivalrous Society*. Translated by Cynthia Postan. Berkeley and Los Angeles, 1980.

———. *The Knight, the Lady, and the Priest: The Making of Modern Marriage in Medieval France*. Translated by Barbara Bray. New York, 1983.

———. *Medieval Marriage: Two Models from Twelfth-Century France*. Translated by Elborg Forster. Baltimore and London, 1978.

———. *Remembering the Dead*, vol. 2 of *Women of the Twelfth Century*. Translated by Jean Birrell. Chicago, 1997.

———. *Rural Economy and Country Life in the Medieval West*. Translated by Cynthia Postan. Columbia, S.C., 1968.

———. *The Three Orders: Feudal Society Imagined*. Translated by Arthur Goldhammer. Chicago, 1980.

Duchesne Tourangeau, André. *Histoire genealogique des maisons de Guines, d'Ardres, de Gand, et de Coucy, et de quelques autres familles illustres, qui y ont esté alliées. Le tout illustré par chartes de diverses églises, tiltres, histoires anciennes et autres bonnes preuves*. Paris, 1631.

Dunbabin, Jean. *France in the Making: 843–1180*. Oxford, 1985.

Echard, Siân. "Map's Metafiction: Author, Narrator and Reader in *De nugis curialium*." *Exemplaria* 8 (1996): 287–314.

Elias, Norbert. *The Civilizing Process*, vol. 2: *Power and Civility*. Translated by. Edmund Jephcott. New York, 1982.

Erben, Wilhelm. "Zur Zeitbestimmung Lamberts von Ardre." *Neues Archiv* 44 (1922): 314–40.

Espinas, see Primary Sources.

Evergates, Theodore. "The Feudal Imaginary of Georges Duby." *Journal of Medieval & Early Modern Studies* 27 (1997): 641–61.

Farmer, David Hugh. *The Oxford Dictionary of the Saints*. Corrected edition. Oxford, 1983.

Fossier, Robert. *La Terre et les hommes en Picardie jusqu'a la fin du XIIIe siècle*. Paris and Louvain, 1968.

Frachette, Christian. "Guy de Guines fut-il comte de Forez au XIIe siècle?" 153–65. In *Les Princes et le pouvoir au moyen âge: XXIIIe congrès de la S.H.M.E.S.*, May 1992. Paris, 1993.

Freeman, Edward Augustus. "The Lords of Ardres." *British Quarterly Review* 71 (1880): 1–31.

Gallia christiana, in provincias ecclesiasticas distributa. 16 vols. 2nd ed. Paris, 1856–1900.

Ganshof, François Louis. *La Flandre sous les premiers comtes*. Third ed. Brussels, 1949.

————."A Propos de la chronique de Lambert d'Ardres." In *Mélanges d'histoire du moyen age offerts à M. Ferdinand Lot*, 205–34. 1925. Reprint, Geneva, 1976.

Geary, Patrick J. *Phantoms of Remembrance: Memory and Oblivion at the end of the First Millenium*. Princeton, N.J., 1994.

Genet, Jean-Philippe. "Cartulaires, registres et histoire: L'exemple anglais." In *Le Métier d'historien au moyen age: études sur l'histoiographie médiévale*, 95–129. Edited by Bernard Guenée. Paris, 1977.

Genicot, Léopold. *Etudes sur les principautés lotharingiennes*. Louvain, 1975.

Genicot, Léopold and Paul Tombeur. *Index scriptorum operumque latino-Belgicorum medii aevi: Nouveau repertoire des oeuvres mediolatines belges*. Three parts in four vols. Brussels, 1977.

Gerritson, Willem P. and Anthony G. van Melle. *A Dictionary of Medieval Heroes*. Translated by Tanis Guest. Woodbridge, 1998.

de la Gorgue-Rosny, Louis-Eugène. *Recherches généalogiques sur les comtés de Ponthieu, de Boulogne, de Guines, et pays circonvoisins*. 4 vols. 1874–77. Reprint ed. Paris, 1974.

Grundmann, Herbert. "Literatus-illiteratus: Der Wandel einer Bildunsnorm vom Altertum zum Mittelalter." In *Ausgewälte Aufsätze*, 3: 1–66. Stuttgart, 1978.

Hallam, Elizabeth. *Capetian France, 987–1328*. London and New York, 1980.

Histoire littéraire de la France. 41 vols. Paris, 1733– .

Hoffman, Richard C. "Economic Development and Aquatic Ecosystems in Medieval Europe." *American Historical Review* 101 (1995): 631–669.

Jacob, Robert. "Le Meurtre du seigneur dans la société féodale. La mémoire, le rite, la fonction," *Annales ESC* 45 (1990): 249–63.

Jaeger, C. Stephen. *The Origins of Courtliness: Civilizing Trends and the Formation of Courtly Ideals, 923–1210*. Philadelphia, 1985.

Keen, Maurice. *Chivalry*. Corrected edition. New Haven, Conn. 1984.

————. *Outlaws of Medieval Legend*. Revised paperback ed. London and New York, 1987.

Kenyon, John R. and Michael Thompson. "The Origin of the Word 'Keep'." *Medieval Archaeology* 38 (1994): 175–76.

Lawrence, Clifford Hugh. *Medieval Monasticism: Forms of Religious Life in Western Europe in the Middle Ages*. Second ed. London, 1989.

Lynch, Joseph. *Godparents and Kinship in Early Medieval Europe*. Princeton, N. J., 1986.

Janet Martin. "John of Salisbury as Classical Scholar." In *The World of John of Salisbury*, 179–201. Edited by Michael Wilks. Oxford, 1984.

McKitterick, Rosamond. *The Frankish Kingdoms under the Carolingians*. London and New York, 1983.

Merrilees, Brian S. "Anglo-Norman Literature." In *Dictionary of the Middle Ages*, 1: 259–72. New York, 1982.

Milis, Ludovicus. "La Frontière linguistique dans le comté de Guînes: un problème historique et méthodologique." *Actes du 101ᵉ congrès national des sociétés savantes*, 1: 249–62. Lille, 1976.

Molinier, Auguste. *Les Sources de l'histoire de France, des origines aux guerres d'Italie*. 6 vols. Paris, 1901–6.

Monier, Raymond. *Les Institutions centrales du comté de Flandre de la fin du IXe siècle à 1384*. Paris, 1943.

Moore, John S. "The Anglo-Norman Family: Size and Structure." *Anglo-Norman Studies* 14 (1991): 153–96.

Moore, R. I. *Formation of a Persecuting Society: Power and Deviance in Western Europe, 950–1250*. Oxford, 1987.

Morse, Ruth. *Truth and Convention in the Middle Ages*. Cambridge, 1991.

Narrative Sources of the Southern Low Countries. 1999. University of Ghent. Accessed December 21, 1999. <http://www.lib.rug.ac.be/n-exec.html>; choose "secondaire bronnen" and then "Narrative Sources."

Nicholas, David. *Medieval Flanders*. London and New York, 1992.

Nicholas, Karen S. "Countesses as Rulers in Flanders." In *Aristocratic Women in Medieval France*, 127–35. Edited by Theodore Evergates. Philadelphia, 1999.

Niermeyer, Jan Frederik. *Mediae latinitatis lexicon minus*. Leiden, 1984.

Parisse, Michel, ed. *Atlas de la France de l'an mil*. Paris, 1994.

Partner, Nancy. "The New Cornificius: Medieval History and the Artifice of Words." In *Classical Rhetoric and Medieval History*, 5–59. Edited by Ernst Breisach. Kalamazoo, Mich., 1985.

Platelle, Henri. "Le Problème du scandale: Les nouvelles modes masculines au XIe et XIIe siècles." *Revue belge de philologie et de l'histoire* 53 (1975): 1071–96.

Poole, Austin Lane. *From the Domesday Book to Magna Carta (1087–1216)*. Second edition. Oxford, 1958.

Pounds, Norman John. *An Historical Geography of Europe*. Cambridge, 1973.

Poulet, Denise. *Au Contact du picard et du flamand: Parlers du Calaisis et de l'Audomarois*. Lille, 1987.

Ranson, Ernest. *Histoire d'Ardres depuis son origine jusqu'en 1891*. 1891. Reprint ed. Lille, 1988.

Richter, Michael. "A Socio-Linguistic Approach to the Latin Middle Ages." In *The Materials Sources and Methods of Ecclesiastical History*, 69–82. Edited by Derek Baker. Oxford, 1975.

———. "Kommunikationsprobleme im Lateinischen Mittelalter," *Historische Zeitschrift* 222 (1976):43–80.

Russell, Josiah Cox. *The Control of Late Ancient and Medieval Population*. Philadelphia, 1985.

Shopkow, Leah. *History and Community: Norman Historical Writing in the Eleventh and Twelfth Centuries*. Washington, D. C., 1997.

Southern, Richard W. *Western Society and the Church in the Middle Ages*. Harmondsworth, 1970.

Spiegel, Gabrielle M. *Romancing the Past: The Rise of Vernacular Prose Historiography in Thirteenth-Century France*. Berkeley, 1993.

Stevens, Martin. "The Performing Self in Twelfth-Century Culture." *Viator* 9 (1978): 193–212.

Stirnemann, Patricia Danz. "Quelques bibliothèques princières et la production hors scriptorium au XIIe siècle." *Bulletin archéologique*, n. s. 17–18A (1981–82): 7–38.

Stowe, Kenneth R. *Alienated Minority: The Jews of Medieval Latin Europe*. Cambridge, Mass., 1992.

Thompson, James Westfall. *The Literacy of the Laity in the Middle Ages*. New York, 1960.

Townsend, David "'Michi Barbaries Incognita Linguae': Other Voices and Other Visions in Walter of Châtillon's *Alexandreis*." *Allegorica* 13 (1992): 21–37.

Turner, Ralph. "The *Miles Literatus* in Twelfth- and Thirteenth-Century England: How Rare a Phenomenon?" *American Historical Review* 83 (1978): 928–45.

———. "Old Men, New Men, and Government Service." In *Men Raised from the Dust: Administrative Service and Upward Mobility in Angevin England*, 1–19. Philadelphia, 1988.

Typologie des sources du moyen âge occidental, 80 vols. Turnhout, 1972-

Verhulst, Adriaan. "Les Franchises rurales dans le comté de Flandre aux XIe et XIIe siècles." In *Femmes: Mariages-lignages XIIe–XIVe siècles: Mélanges offerts á Georges Duby*, 419–30. Brussels, 1992.

Veyne, Paul. *Did the Greeks Believe in Their Myths?* Translated by Paula Wissing. Chicago, 1988.

Warlop, Ernest A. *The Flemish Nobility before 1300*. 2 parts in 4 vols. Translated by James Bruce Ross and H Vandermoere. Courtrai, 1975.

Werner, Karl Ferdinand. "Andreas von Marchiennes und die Geschichtsschreibung von Anchin und Marchiennes in der zweiten Hälfte des 12. Jahrhundert." *Deutsches Archiv* 9 (1951–52):402–63.

Zumthor, Paul. *Histoire littéraire de la France médiévale, VIe–XIVe siècles*. Paris, 1954.

Index

Modern scholars are listed only when their names are mentioned in the text. Place names are not listed when they appear only as part of a toponym. Saints' names are not listed when the saints appear only as patrons of churches. Entries in boldface refer to the text of the translation.